To Gena

Happy Birthday 2007

You are just choice!
Thanks for everything!

Love,

Mom · Dad

RISE TO THE
Divinity
WITHIN YOU

RISE TO THE Divinity WITHIN YOU

TALKS FROM THE
2006 BYU WOMEN'S CONFERENCE

DESERET
BOOK

SALT LAKE CITY, UTAH

Library of Congress Cataloging-in-Publication Data

Women's Conference (2007 : Brigham Young University)
  Rise to the divinity within you : talks from the 2006 BYU Women's Conference.
    p. cm.
  Includes bibliographical references and index.
  ISBN-10: 1-59038-712-0 (hardbound : alk. paper)
  ISBN-13: 978-1-59038-712-2 (hardbound : alk. paper)
  1. Mormon women—Religious life—Congresses. 2. Church of Jesus Christ of Latter-day Saints—Congresses. 3. Mormon Church—Congresses. I. Title.
  BX8641.W73 2007
  289.3'32082—dc22   2006031928

Printed in the United States of America
Worzalla Publishing Co., Stevens Point, WI

10   9   8   7   6   5   4   3   2   1

CONTENTS

COMMUNION WITH THE DIVINE

THE DIVINITY OF THE FAMILY

DIVINE TRUTHS OF THE GOSPEL

DIVINE QUALITIES OF THE HEART

CHILDREN OF GOD

Boyd K. Packer

Beloved sisters, the influence you have is overpowering.

The Twelve Apostles are called to "set in order" (D&C 107:58) and "regulate all the affairs of the [Church] in all nations" (D&C 107:33) under the direction of the First Presidency. That is not always easy to do.

I feel much as King Benjamin must have felt when he saw dangers among the people and said, "[I came not] to trifle with . . . words" (Mosiah 2:9). It can be very uncomfortable when we see thickening clouds and feel responsible to protect our families.

Nephi said, "I must speak concerning the doctrine of Christ; wherefore, I shall speak unto you plainly, . . . for my soul delighteth in plainness" (2 Nephi 31:2–3).

And Jacob said, "Wherefore I, Jacob, gave unto them these words as I taught them in the temple, having first obtained mine errand from the Lord" (Jacob 1:17). I too made that same preparation, as best I could, and obtained my direction from the same source.

Jacob and Joseph "had been consecrated priests and teachers of [the] people" (Jacob 1:18; see also 2 Nephi 5:26). They expressed concern for "the hearts of [the] tender wives" (Jacob 2:35) and for the children.

Whenever we speak of home and family and motherhood, we fear we might wound the tender hearts of those who may never marry or those

---

President Boyd K. Packer is currently the Acting President of the Quorum of the Twelve Apostles.

1

whose marriages have failed. There are those who are greatly disappointed with their children. There are heartbreaking gender problems, untimely deaths, abortion, abuse, pornography, and, in addition, an endless list of things which almost dissuade us from speaking with the plainness that the scripture commands us to do.

I return, as I have on countless occasions, to the inspired words of a Relief Society president. I will ever be grateful to Sister Alberta Baker. A convert of the Church, she was the mission Relief Society president when I was the mission president in New England. She was a very small woman and walked with a very pronounced limp from childhood polio.

We had sixty Relief Societies scattered across the mission. Some of them were off course and some of them were little more than sewing circles and a few had lost their way entirely. Sister Belle Spafford, president of the general Relief Society, provided some simple guidelines that could be followed.

We called the Relief Society leaders together in the chapel at the Joseph Smith Birthplace Memorial in Vermont. I asked Sister Baker to explain the changes we were asking them to make. She gently invited the sisters to conform more closely to the patterns set for the Relief Society.

One sister stood and said defiantly, "That doesn't fit us. We're an exception!" She repeated with more emphasis, "We are an exception!"

It was a very tense moment, something of a crisis. Sister Baker turned to me for help. I was not interested in facing a fierce woman, so I motioned for her to proceed. Then came the revelation!

With gentle firmness, she said: "Dear sister, we'd like not to take care of the exception first. We will take care of the rule first, and then we will see to the exception." She continued to explain what a Relief Society should be.

Later I told her I would be quoting her all over the world. And so I have. In many challenging moments, some very tense, I have quoted the revelation that came to that sweet, little Relief Society president.

Today I will speak of the rules first and later consider the exceptions.

I see in the tender hearts of women transcendent power. Listen to these words written by William Ross Wallace more than 125 years ago. They speak of you, and I agree with what they say:

Blessing on the hand of women!
Angels guard its strength and grace,
In the palace, cottage, hovel,
Oh, no matter where the place;
Would that never storms assailed it,
Rainbows ever gently curled;
For the hand that rocks the cradle
Is the hand that rules the world.

Infancy's the tender fountain,
Power may with beauty flow,
Mother's first to guide the streamlets,
From the souls unresting grow—
Grow on for the good or evil,
Sunshine streamed or evil hurled;
For the hand that rocks the cradle
Is the hand that rules the world.

Woman, how divine your mission
Here upon our natal sod!
Keep, oh, keep the young heart open
Always to the breath of God!
All true trophies of the ages
Are from mother-love impearled;
For the hand that rocks the cradle
Is the hand that rules the world.

Blessings on the hand of women!
Fathers, sons, and daughters cry,
And the sacred song is mingled
With the worship in the sky—
Mingles where no tempest darkens,
Rainbows evermore are hurled;
For the hand that rocks the cradle
Is the hand that rules the world.[1]

That is far more than just a poetic compliment. Later I will speak of
an uncertain future in which mothers will be our protection.

President J. Reuben Clark Jr. described a pioneer family. Always last into camp at night, the wife was about to be a mother, the husband taking such care as he could to ease the jolting of the wagon. Then the baby came:

"Morning came when from out that last wagon floated the la-la of the newborn babe, and mother love made a shrine, and Father bowed in reverence before it. But the train must move on. So out into the dust and dirt the last wagon moved again, swaying and jolting, while Mother eased as best she could each pain-giving jolt so no harm might be done her, that she might be strong to feed the little one, bone of her bone, flesh of her flesh. Who will dare to say that angels did not cluster round and guard her and ease her rude bed, for she had given another choice spirit its mortal body that it might work out its God-given destiny?"[2]

The rules and principles are in the scriptures. The revelations make it very clear that mankind is the offspring of Heavenly Parents. We have in God our Father and a Heavenly Mother the pattern of our parentage.

After being away four years, I came home from World War II and wanted, even yearned, to be married. In the years during the war, I became mature enough to realize that rather than making a list of specifications by which to measure a future companion, I should concentrate on what I myself must do. How could I be worthy of and able to fulfill the dreams of one with enduring values centered in home and family who would want to be my companion?

After more than fifty years, I am still trying to be worthy of her and good to her.

We were in school and had little material things to offer one another. We had our love and our faith and a determination to live the principles of the gospel—all of them, the difficult ones as well as the easy ones. We planned our life together and determined that we would accept each child born to us.

I remember clearly this incident: We had three small children. I had a very modest income. The bishop's wife, who was close to Donna's family (Donna's father was a counselor to the bishop), came to see her mother and said, "I've cried all morning. I heard that Donna is expecting again." We would not trade the child that came (it was our first girl), or the six that followed after, for anything you can imagine.

Once we said: "Perhaps if we plant a tree each time a child is born and pass that tradition to the coming generations, we may live in a small forest."

Now fifty-eight years later, it has come to pass in our children and grandchildren and great-grandchildren, who now number one short of 100. We live in a house that the real estate agents describe as old, sheltered under the trees at the end of a lane that reminds you of a forest.

I pay tribute to my wife. Now, I am bound to tell the truth. (I am on Church property!) I have without hesitation described her as being perfect. And so she is! She has borne each of our ten children; each is a child of God. And now they and their partners to whom they are sealed, and the children, grandchildren, and great-grandchildren that have come, all honor her.

We got by during difficult years because my wife, in matters of food and clothing and shelter, was able to make something good and usable out of very little—sometimes out of almost nothing at all.

We are all children of God. It is just as simple as that! We are, in fact, children of God.

Some years ago, I returned home to find our little children were waiting in the driveway. They had discovered a newly hatched batch of chicks under the manger in the barn. When they reached for them, the mother hen, as mothers do, protected her brood. So they had come for reinforcements.

I soon gathered a handful of little chicks for them to see and to touch. There were black ones and yellow ones and brown ones and gray ones.

As our little girl held one of them, I said in a teasing way, "That little chick will make a nice watchdog when it grows up, won't it?" She looked at me quizzically, as if I didn't know much. So I changed my approach: "It won't be a watchdog, will it?"

She shook her head. "No, Daddy."

Then I added, "It will be a nice riding horse."

She wrinkled up her nose and gave me that "Oh, Dad!" look, for even a four-year-old knows that a chick will not be a dog or a horse or even a turkey; it will be a chicken. It will follow the pattern of its parentage. She knew that without having had a lesson or a lecture or a course in genetics.

No lesson is more manifest in nature than that all living things do as the Lord commanded them in the Creation. They reproduce after their own kind (see Moses 2:12, 24–25). They follow the pattern of their parentage. Everyone knows that. Every four-year-old knows that! A bird will not become an animal nor a fish. A mammal will not beget a reptile, nor "do men gather . . . figs of thistles" (Matthew 7:16).

In all that you do as women, do not forget that we are all children of God. If you get that doctrine in place, with that rule established, it will serve you well in times when you are confronted with those who equate humankind with animals.

I had another lesson from a child. Two of our little boys were wrestling on the rug. They had reached that pitch—you know the one—where laughter turns to tears and play becomes strife. (I see you do know!) I worked a foot gently between them and lifted the older boy (then just four years of age) to a sitting position on the rug, saying, "Hey there, you monkey! You had better settle down."

He folded his little arms and looked at me with surprising seriousness. His little-boy feelings had been hurt, and he protested, "I not a monkey, Daddy. I a person!"

It is just that simple! I thought how deeply I loved him, how much I wanted him to be "a person," one of eternal worth, for "children are an heritage of the Lord" (Psalm 127:3). Each is a child of God. He is not a monkey; neither were his ancestors.

I have often thought that much of what I know that is most worth knowing I have learned from our children.

In the very beginning, God created both man and woman. He said, "It is not good that the man should be alone" (Genesis 2:18; Moses 3:18; Abraham 5:14) and "they twain shall be one flesh" (Matthew 19:5; Mark 10:8; D&C 49:16).

Our destiny is so established that man can only find complete fulfillment and fill the divine purpose for his creation with a woman to whom he is legally and lawfully married. The union of man and woman begets babies that are conceived and cross that frail footpath into mortality.

This divine pattern was planned and the gospel designed from "before the world was" (D&C 49:17). The plan provides for us to come to the world into a mortal body. It is "the great plan of happiness" (Alma 42:8). We did not design it. If we follow the pattern, happiness and joy will follow. The gospel and the moral standards are set to prevent us from straying into unworthy or unnatural behavior that will result in disappointment and unhappiness.

The virtue of tolerance has been distorted and elevated to a position of such prominence as to be thought equal to and even valued more than morality. It is one thing to be tolerant, even forgiving of individual conduct. It is quite another to collectively legislate and legalize to protect immoral conduct that can weaken, even destroy the family.

There is a dangerous trap when tolerance is exaggerated to protect the rights of those whose conduct endangers the family and injures the rights of the more part of the people. We are getting dangerously close to the condition described by the prophet Mosiah, who warned:

"Now it is not common that the voice of the people desireth anything contrary to that which is right; but it is common for the lesser part of the people to desire that which is not right; therefore this shall ye observe and make it your law—to do your business by the voice of the people.

"And if the time comes that the voice of the people doth choose iniquity, then is the time that the judgments of God will come upon you; yea, then is the time he will visit you with great destruction even as he has hitherto visited this land" (Mosiah 29:26–27).

Tolerance can be a dangerous trap.

The Prophet Joseph Smith said to the first Relief Society, "There must be decision of character, aside from sympathy."[3]

It suits the purpose of the Almighty to let it be that some will not have a marriage or find it broken through death or mischief. Some have great difficulty having any children, and some will not have children of their own—that is, it will not happen in mortal life. But in the eternal scheme of things, it will happen as surely as the commandments are kept. Those yearnings unfulfilled in mortality will be filled to overflowing in the life beyond where there is eternal love and eternal increase.

The Lord has spoken to His servants, and they have framed "The Family: A Proclamation to the World":

"The first commandment that God gave to Adam and Eve pertained to their potential for parenthood as husband and wife. We declare that God's commandment for His children to multiply and replenish the earth remains in force. We further declare that God has commanded that the sacred powers of procreation are to be employed only between man and woman, lawfully wedded as husband and wife.

"We declare the means by which mortal life is created to be divinely appointed [not to be redefined or rearranged]. We affirm the sanctity of life and of its importance in God's eternal plan.

"Husband and wife have a solemn responsibility to love and care for each other and for their children. 'Children are an heritage of the Lord' (Psalm 127:3). Parents have a sacred duty to rear their children in love and righteousness, to provide for their physical and spiritual needs, to teach them to love and serve one another, to observe the commandments of God and to be law-abiding citizens wherever they live. Husbands and wives—mothers and fathers—will be held accountable before God for the discharge of these obligations.

"The family is ordained of God. Marriage between man and woman is essential to His eternal plan. Children are entitled to birth within the bonds of matrimony, and to be reared by a father and a mother who honor marital vows with complete fidelity."[4]

These lines from "The Family: A Proclamation to the World" to me have taken on the stature of scripture.

There is another dangerous trend as mothers, sometimes beyond their control, are being drawn out of the home. What could a mother possibly bring into the home that can equal her being at home with the children while they grow and mature?

We may learn from events of the future that "the hand that rocks the cradle is the hand that rules the world."

Recently there was printed in an international publication an article under the strange title of "Babies Win Wars."[5] It chronicled several centuries of the history of countries that lost population. When they had difficulty in sustaining their population and themselves, they became vulnerable to invasion and occupation.

Now the birthrate is declining in every country in the world. In order for a nation's population to remain stable, the birthrate must be just over two children per woman of childbearing years.

In more than thirty countries in Europe, the birthrate is below the replacement rate. In several, it is hovering barely above half that replacement rate. The population of some countries is declining at an alarming rate.

The United States is barely above the replacement rate. Only because of immigration and the higher birthrate among the Hispanic people do we maintain our population.

All East Asian countries are currently below the replacement rate.

Latin America has witnessed a dramatic decline in birthrate in the past thirty years.

Virtually every social security and medical system in the developed world is facing bankruptcy. An aging population can neither work to sustain the people nor fight to protect them.

That trend is seen in the Church. Worldwide, the birthrate among members married in the temple is notably higher than in the world, but this rate too has been declining. In one European country with a sizeable population of Church members, for example, the birthrate among temple-married members, although higher than the national average, is below the replacement rate. Worldwide, the birthrate of Church members is only slightly higher than the world at large.

Like the rest of the population, members of the Church must suffer the consequences of these trends. We face a particular set of issues because the pool from which missionaries are drawn is in steady decline.

The First Presidency has written, "Marriage is ordained of God, and the paramount purpose of this sacred principle is to bring into the world immortal spirits to be reared in health and nobility of character, to fill the measure of their mortal existence."[6]

Mankind has gotten into an almost impossible predicament. In the ordinary home and the ordinary family, in almost every conceivable way, the destroyer leads humanity carefully away from the source of all happiness. The prophecy is now being fulfilled of wars and rumors of wars and plagues and pestilence (see Matthew 24:3–8).

Teach the children the plan of salvation, the sacredness of the body, the supernal nature of the power to give life. Mothers, in your gentle way, guide them, warn them against misusing those sacred powers. The future of the family depends on how those powers are protected.

The devil has no body. He and his angels try to possess the bodies of mankind.

When the sacred power to give life is used immorally, unnaturally, or in perversion, one stands in jeopardy of failing the test of mortality. Even then, through true repentance, the mercy of the Holy One has power to reclaim and to heal.

"The hand that rocks the cradle [does rule] the world."

"The plan of redemption, which was prepared from the foundation of the world, through Christ" (Alma 22:13), was unfolded in the Creation. In the very beginning, man was created, and because "it is not good that the man should be alone," the Lord created a wife, "an help meet for him" (Genesis 2:18). In the scriptures, the word *meet* means "equal." Man and woman are separate but equal, complementary to one another. Both the equal and the separate natures are essential to the onrolling of the great plan of happiness.

Do not envy a man his manhood or his priesthood. Foster and encourage, in every way you can, his role and the role of your sons in the destiny ordained for them.

To women is given a most supernal part of the plan of redemption. "And Adam called his wife's name Eve, because she was the mother of all living; for thus have I, the Lord God, called the first of all women" (Moses 4:26). Foster in yourself and in your daughters the exalted role of the woman, the incomparable gift of creation that attends motherhood.

The man was given to provide and protect; the woman was given to make it all worthwhile.

The ultimate end of all activity in the Church is that a man and his wife and their children can be happy at home, sealed together so that the family can continue throughout eternity.

I invoke the blessings of the Lord upon you, dear sisters, and all who are across the world. The future of the Church depends upon you and upon the spiritual power that you by nature have.

This is the Church of Jesus Christ. He presides over it. His doctrines will lead us safely through all the difficulty and shadows that are ahead.

I bless you and your families—your companions in life, your children, grandchildren, and great-grandchildren—that you will understand the doctrines of the Church and be determined to live them, all of them. I promise you that you will be blessed, that you will be rewarded, and that you will be redeemed.

Those who are limited in this life have a greater joy beyond the veil to find that all will be added upon you in that existence.

I bear this witness and invoke this blessing upon you as a servant of the Lord and in the name of Jesus Christ, amen.

NOTES

1. William Ross Wallace, "The Hand That Rocks the Cradle Is the Hand That Rules the World," in *Poems That Live Forever,* sel. Hazel Felleman (New York: Doubleday & Company, Inc., 1965), 149–50.
2. J. Reuben Clark Jr., "They of the Last Wagon," *Improvement Era,* November 1947, 705.
3. Joseph Smith, *History of The Church of Jesus Christ of Latter-day Saints,* ed. B. H. Roberts, 2d ed. rev. 7 vols. (Salt Lake City: The Church of Jesus Christ of Latter-day Saints, 1932–51), 4:570.
4. "The Family: A Proclamation to the World," *Ensign,* November 1995, 102.
5. See Gunnar Heinsohn, "Babies Win Wars," *Wall Street Journal,* March 6, 2006.
6. First Presidency letterpress copybooks, May 1, 1939, Archives of The Church of Jesus Christ of Latter-day Saints.

RISE TO THE DIVINITY WITHIN YOU

Sandra Rogers

I had only been home from Africa for about a year when a dear friend from Nigeria came to visit. In addition to her observations about how few African-Americans live in Utah and how bland our food is (despite my efforts to give her the spiciest meals I could make or buy), she continued to be amazed at the vast number of choices we had—including choices about food (our warehouse-sized grocery stores with so many brands of the same item nearly paralyzed her). She asked incredulously, "How do you white women manage all these choices?"

I suppose we do have more choices than any other women in history. While there isn't much danger in being mixed up about which of four brands of canned soup to buy, confusion about the merits and significance of other choices can be perilous. Choosing between different brands of soup means subtle differences in the soup's taste or texture. Confusion about who we are as women and what our eternal roles and possibilities are leaves us adrift, buffeted by doubt, spending our time in things that are not important and our labor for things that do not satisfy (2 Nephi 9:51).

While women in our era have achieved much in terms of opportunities for education and contribution to society, they also can struggle with

Sandra Rogers is the international vice president at Brigham Young University. A Gospel Doctrine teacher and a former welfare missionary, she served as chair of the 2006 BYU Women's Conference.

what is real, eternal, and important. Elder Richard G. Scott has said: "So many of our sisters are disheartened, even discouraged, and disillusioned. Others are in serious trouble because of the choices they make. Satan has unleashed a seductive campaign to undermine the sanctity of womanhood, to deceive the daughters of God and divert them from their divine destiny. He well knows women are the compassionate, self-sacrificing, loving power that binds together the human family."[1]

Satan has turned up the intensity and enmity of his attacks on the divine roles and contributions of women, hoping that we, who have critical responsibilities for and influence over God's children, will fail to successfully choose our way through his tempting but deceitful alternatives. In response, we "sisters in Zion"[2] have been given countless reassurances by prophets of God of the essentiality of our roles in the Lord's plan. There is no confusion for us. We have been given prophetic revelation with certitude and clarity. We aren't chattel. We aren't toys. We are not ornamental spear-carriers in the opera of life. We are center stage, singing major, crucial, difficult, and demanding roles. What a debt of gratitude we women owe the prophets of God.

The Prophet Joseph Smith told the members of the Relief Society that if they lived up to their privileges, the angels could not be restrained from being their associates. He said, "If this Society will listen to the counsel of the Almighty, through the heads of the Church, they shall have power to command queens in their midst."[3]

Almost 100 years later, President Heber J. Grant reaffirmed these truths when he said, "The true spirit of the Church of Jesus Christ of Latter-day Saints gives to woman the highest place of honor in human life."[4]

President James E. Faust added, "One of humankind's greatest blessings is for righteous women to hold 'the highest place of honor in human life' and to be 'the perfect workmanship of God.'"[5]

The prophets understand the nature and the magnitude of Satan's latter-day attack on women. No wonder President Gordon B. Hinckley has spoken on the divine nature of women on numerous occasions. I firmly believe he isn't doing it just to make us feel good. He is doing it so that we might rise to our inherent potential, overcome the adversary, and

become a mighty force for good in our families, in the Church, and in
society.

In the October 2002 general conference, President Gordon B.
Hinckley closed his Sunday message to the entire membership of the
Church by saying, "I challenge every one of you who can hear me to rise
to the divinity within you." He went on to say, "I believe with all my heart
that the Latter-day Saints, generally speaking, are good people. If we live
by the principles of the gospel, we must be good people, for we will be gen-
erous and kind, thoughtful and tolerant, helpful and outreaching to those
in distress. We can either subdue the divine nature and hide it so that it
finds no expression in our lives, or we can bring it to the front and let it
shine through all that we do."[6]

There are two truths that can help us bring our divine natures "to the
front and let [them] shine through all that we do." The first is that we are
the spiritual offspring of God, the Father. President Hinckley has said to
the women of the Church, "Know that you are daughters of God, children
with a divine birthright."[7] If we truly understand this inheritance of capacity and worth, we would never succumb to the enticements of the world.

We easily understand this concept of inheritance where physical traits
are concerned. When a new baby arrives, everyone is eager to make
connections between the baby's features and maternal or paternal relatives. When looking at photographs of my mother and me, both at age
seventeen, no one could doubt we are related. When your hemlines and
your shoes match your great-grandmother's over an interval of seventy
years, you know some serious genetic activity is going on. My tight-stitch
knitting and crocheting (when I knit or crochet at all) comes from my
great-grandmother Hunt. My facial expressions often reflect those of
my aunt, Twila Blau. People claim my closets are organized just like my
grandmother Rogers's closets were. In short, my gene pool is obvious.
Yours is probably likewise.

I wonder, then, why do I struggle sometimes to accept, embrace, and
celebrate the fact that I also have inherited divine attributes from my
heavenly parents?

As important and fundamental as our inherited divine nature is, we
have a second source of divine strength and character. This enabling
power comes to us through our acceptance of the atonement of Jesus

Christ. King Benjamin taught: "And now, because of the covenant which ye have made ye shall be called the children of Christ . . . for behold, this day he hath spiritually begotten you; for ye say that your hearts are changed through faith on his name; therefore, ye are born of him and have become his sons and daughters. . . . There is no other name given whereby salvation cometh; therefore, I would that ye should take upon you the name of Christ, all you that have entered into the covenant with God that ye should be obedient unto the end of your lives" (Mosiah 5:7–8).

This incredible gift of being born of Christ and becoming His daughters is available to us because Christ paid a terrible and awesome price for us in the Garden of Gethsemane and on the cross of Calvary. Abinadi, one of my favorite prophets, quoted from Isaiah 53 and then elaborated: "And now I say unto you, who shall declare his generation? Behold, I say unto you, that when his soul has been made an offering for sin he shall see his seed. . . . Behold I say unto you, that whosoever has heard the words of the prophets, yea, all the holy prophets who have prophesied concerning the coming of the Lord—I say unto you, that all those who have hearkened unto their words and believed that the Lord would redeem his people, and have looked forward to that day for a remission of their sins, I say unto you, that these are his seed, or they are the heirs of the kingdom of God. For these are they whose sins he has borne; these are they for whom he has died, to redeem them from their transgressions" (Mosiah 15:10–12).

Mormon understood this truth when he taught, "Wherefore, I beseech of you, [sisters], that ye should search diligently in the light of Christ that ye may know good from evil; and if ye will lay hold upon every good thing, and condemn it not, ye certainly will be a child of Christ" (Moroni 7:19).

We have been blessed with hope twice over because of the truths of the restored gospel of Jesus Christ. We know that we are children of God with inherited divine qualities. We also know that through the travails and tests of mortality we can sometimes behave in less than divine ways. We can, through our choices, subdue that divine nature. But because of the grace and mercy of our Father and His beloved Son, our Savior and Redeemer, we are able to repent, change, and become new. By coming to

Christ we can "lay hold upon every good gift" and be "perfected in him." And if we will love Him with all our "might, mind and strength," then "his grace [shall be] sufficient" (Moroni 10:30, 32). Through Christ's mediation, mercy, grace, and love for us, we can be sustained as we work in mortality to learn, acquire, develop, and nurture divine Christlike qualities.

I offer the following analogy. Our divine inheritance, a legacy from our Father in Heaven, is part of us, regardless of the circumstances of our mortal birth or our choices here on earth. It is part of who we truly are, just as the curve and grain of the wood, the angle of the neck of the instrument, and the finishing varnish become a particular violin. It is a wondrous instrument, capable of producing music from classical to bluegrass. The violin may be scratched or dented during its lifetime, but that doesn't take away the fact that it is still a violin. We also may be scratched, dented, or scuffed from our journey through mortality, but we will always be children of a divine parent.

Have you tried to learn to play the violin? Or have you had children who have tried to learn to play the violin? I know from experience what a violin sounds like in the hands of an untrained, awkward student, especially one more interested in hitting a softball or shooting baskets than practicing. We know the instrument has the capacity, but something is definitely lacking. But what happens to the capacity of the violin when it is placed in the hands of an Itzhak Perlman or a Jenny Oaks Baker? The music is beautiful, resonant, and moving.

If we were fortunate to own one of the few violins made by Stradivari, I doubt we would put it in the hands of a careless, naive performer. No, we would put such an instrument into the hands of a virtuoso, whose talent would magnify and enrich the inherent qualities of the violin. Likewise, when we willingly and completely put our divinely inherited legacy from our Father in Heaven into the masterful hands of His Son, the very best of our instrumentation, as it were, is developed and enhanced.

I can think of no better hands in which we might place ourselves. He knows who we are and what we can become. He knows what we face and how we feel. Remember, He took upon Himself every condition that meets us in mortality so that He could understand how to succor us in our weakness and our distress (Alma 7:11–12). It is through the atonement of Christ, the Lord, that we can, if we yield to the sweet enticings of the Holy Spirit, put off the natural man and become a Saint (Mosiah 3:19).

Alma likened himself to an instrument in the Lord's hands after he turned his life to the Master, saying: "I myself was caught in a snare, and did many things which were abominable in the sight of the Lord, which caused me sore repentance; nevertheless, after much tribulation the Lord did hear my cries, and did answer my prayers, and has made me an instrument in his hands in bringing so many of you to a knowledge of his truth. Nevertheless, in this I do not glory, for I am unworthy to glory of myself" (Mosiah 23:9–11).

One of the reasons we are counseled to rise to the divinity within us is so that others will understand the source of that divinity and "glorify [our] Father which is in Heaven" (Matthew 5:16) and seek His Son Jesus Christ. Rising to the divinity within is not making a strategic career move. It is being born again to Christ, to His purposes, to His will, and to His glory—not our own. No violin, regardless of how magnificent the construction, makes music on its own. We are given spiritual gifts, opportunities to make our weaknesses strengths, chances to serve and to bless, not to reflect our own goodness, but the glory of our God, whom we love, worship, and serve.

Christ began each of His great ministries of which we have record by laying out the blueprint for rising to the divinity within. On the shores of Galilee and in the land Bountiful, He taught the hallmarks of divine nature. They include being poor in spirit (or poor in pride, or humble); being meek (or gentle, forgiving, or benevolent); hungering and thirsting after righteousness; being merciful; being pure in heart (or clean in thought and motivation); being peacemakers; and enduring persecution for Christ's sake (Matthew 5:3–12; 3 Nephi 12:3–11). The blessings of rising to these divine traits are the Lord's comfort and peace, being filled with His spirit, obtaining mercy, seeing God, being called the children of God, and inheriting the earth and the kingdom of heaven.

I bear my witness of the spiritual power of the principles taught in the Beatitudes. On one occasion I felt alone, misunderstood, and unable to defend myself. I had made mistakes, but I was also hurt. I arrived home late one evening hoping for some insight, some respite from the alternating waves of guilt over my failures and resentment that my hard work wasn't appreciated. That night, in an almost defiant way, I decided to just let the scriptures fall open and see what the Lord wanted to tell me. I've always wondered what might have happened if my scriptures had opened to the maps. Instead, they opened to Matthew 5. As I read the familiar verses of the Sermon on the Mount, I realized I had two choices. I could feel picked on, vulnerable, and justified in being bitter, or I could choose to be like Job and "not remove [my] integrity from me" and hold fast to righteousness (Job 27:5–6). The power of the Beatitudes set my feet in the right direction, and I will be forever grateful.

I am an oldest child. A great portion of my early self-esteem came from being right—or as my younger brothers would say, thinking I was right. However, the Lord has carefully crafted assignments for me that have given me numerous opportunities for imperfection. There have been times when I felt I had to repent and ask forgiveness so often that I was like Maria von Trapp in *The Sound of Music*, kissing the floor in penitence whenever a particular sister appeared, just to save time. I have learned that being right can be a good thing—especially when it is about something eternal. And I have also come to learn that it takes strength and courage to apologize and work to restore the pledge (Ezekiel 33:13–16). Without the assurances of my Savior that being meek and poor in spirit are better things, that being teachable and taking counsel does help one develop and improve, I might still have been always insisting on being right, or at least excusable. I am still very much a work in progress, but I do know there is power in the Beatitudes.

It is the Atonement that makes the principles in the Beatitudes work. Christ did conquer death and the devil. Charity, the pure love of Christ, will never fail. Faith, virtue, temperance, patience, kindness, long-suffering, humility, and mercy are desirable traits, far better than the pettiness, pride, arrogance, smugness, and self-righteousness that make up the natural man (or woman). In the hands of the Master, we will seek to lift one another up and steadily experience the fruits of His Spirit, which are "love, joy, peace, longsuffering, gentleness, goodness, faith, meekness, temperance" (Galatians 5:22–23). We won't be translated in one day, but we can begin, and we will make steady progress.

Is it any wonder, then, that President Hinckley continues to encourage us with words like these: "You have such tremendous potential. . . . Every one of you was endowed by your Father in Heaven with a tremendous capacity to do good in the world. Train your minds and your hands that you may be equipped to serve well in the society of which you are a part. Cultivate the art of being kind, of being thoughtful, of being helpful. Refine within you the quality of mercy which comes as part of the divine attributes you have inherited. . . . In summary, try a little harder to measure up to the divine within each of you."[8]

The paradox in rising to the divinity within us is that we are especially asked to do it when situations around us are not divine at all. When we face what might be the signature temptations, challenges, and tests of our lives, we have the agency to decide whether we are going to put our divine heritage into the hands of the Master, the Savior and Redeemer of the world, or subdue it and put ourselves in the hands of the evil one, who persuadeth none to do good (Moroni 7:12–17).

With permission, I would like to share with you the story of M'lissa Griffith. M'lissa did not wake up one morning two years ago thinking, "Today my life is going to be permanently changed; today my faith is going to face its greatest test." She was going about her regular, normal routine of being a wife and mother when the news came that her husband had been fatally shot by an angry coworker, who then attempted suicide. M'lissa was left a widow with a young family of four children ranging in age from eleven years to seventeen months. Blessed with a loving and supportive extended family and an extraordinary faith in Christ's promises, M'lissa stayed the course and put herself in the hands of the Master. She and her children chose to forgive the poor man who had taken the life of their husband and father. Their statements of that forgiveness at the sentencing hearing moved both the judge and the defense attorney to say that in their forty-four combined years on the bench or in court hearing or defending such cases, they had never witnessed such an outpouring of forgiveness by the victim's family.

M'lissa's ability to rise to the divinity within her did not end with that public statement of authentic forgiveness. She learned that the man had no health insurance and the costs of his hospitalization after the suicide attempt were immense, an added stress to a family already dealing with the stigma and burden of what their husband and father had done. The costs of legal counsel added to the family's financial obligations. Following the trial, M'lissa and the man's wife befriended each other. M'lissa is now sharing this sister's burden by finding ways to help alleviate the crushing weight of hospital and legal debts to this family. If this isn't rising to the divinity within, I don't know a better example.

M'lissa is a humble example of a truth described by Dennis Rasmussen, who wrote: "Evil multiplies by the response it seeks to provoke, and when I return evil for evil, I engender corruption myself. The chain of evil is broken for good when a pure and loving heart absorbs a hurt and forbears to hurt in return. . . . Deep within every child of God the Light of Christ resides, guiding, comforting, [and] purifying the heart that turns to him."[9]

Elder Matthew Cowley taught that "men have to have something given to them [in mortality] to make them saviors of men, but not mothers, not women. [They] are born with an inherent right, an inherent authority, to be the saviors of human souls . . . and the regenerating force in the lives of God's children."[10]

Under the oppressive yoke of Communism, a young Croatian was also influenced by his mother—a mother who had a divine nature and an inherent right and authority to care for his soul, even though she did not have the blessing of the fulness of the gospel of Jesus Christ. Kresimir Cosic, a great BYU basketball center and pioneer for the Church in Yugoslavia and Croatia, once described what happened when the gospel penetrated his heart and his conversion began, saying: "Within my heart, there began to burn familiarities—feelings that I had known as a child. The comfort and peace of eternal truths—truths I had been taught by my mother and by my grandmother, for under communism it was the women who kept the faith alive."[11]

As the darkness gathers while Satan does all he can to lead astray more of our Father's children and those in Lehi's spacious building (1 Nephi 8:26–28) mock and persecute the true followers of Christ, we must keep the light of the gospel burning brightly in our hearts and homes as we keep our hands firmly on the iron rod. We must keep the faith alive. As the world slides dangerously farther away from the Lord's standards, we cannot be content to be just a little bit better than the world. A match may be a bit better than no light at all, but when the true Light is brighter than the noonday sun, being a match in the darkness doesn't quite measure up. Christ said, and I paraphrase, "Therefore, what manner of [women] ought ye to be? Verily I say unto you, even as I am" (3 Nephi 27:27).

I also know that with all our potential, we women can be very hard on ourselves. We rejoice in the words of the prophets regarding our divine natures and roles, but we are sometimes unsure and tentative about our capacity and our performance—perhaps feeling that we are often short of the mark. Prophets also know about this tendency in women. President Hinckley has counseled and reassured us, "I do not ask that you reach beyond your capacity. Please don't nag yourselves with thoughts of failure. Do not set goals far beyond your capacity to achieve. Simply do what you can do, in the best way you know, and the Lord will accept of your effort."[12]

We have an awe-inspiring legacy of valiant sisters who have risen and still rise to the divinity within; sisters who did what they could do, in the best way they knew. Think of the influence a single, elderly German sister now has on the entire membership of the Church because she invited Elder Dieter F. Uchtdorf's grandmother to attend the LDS branch in Zwickau, East Germany.[13]

President Boyd K. Packer recalled a group of sisters who were rising to their divine natures despite oppressive obstacles by doing what they could in the best way they knew. He said: "Some years ago Sister Packer and I were in Czechoslovakia, then behind the Iron Curtain. It was not easy to obtain visas, and we used great care so as not to jeopardize the safety and well-being of our members, who for generations had struggled to keep their faith alive under conditions of unspeakable oppression.

"The most memorable meeting was held in an upper room. The blinds were drawn. Even at night, those attending came at different times, one from one direction and one from another, so as not to call attention to themselves.

"There were in attendance 12 sisters. We sang the hymns of Zion from songbooks—words without music—printed more than 50 years before. The Spiritual Living lesson was reverently given from the pages of a handmade manual. The few pages of Church literature we could give to them were typed at night, 12 carbon copies at a time, so as to share a few precious pages as widely as possible among the members.

"I told those sisters that they belonged to the largest and by all measure the greatest women's organization on earth. . . .

"I told them that upon our return I was assigned to speak at a Relief Society conference; could I deliver a message from them? . . . I shall never forget what one sister wrote: 'A small circle of sisters send their own hearts and thoughts to all the sisters and begs the Lord to help us go forward.'"[14]

In a time of unlimited options and voices, we can choose to hear the voice of God, through our beloved prophet, calling us to "rise to the divinity within." I testify Christ will strengthen us (Philippians 4:13). I testify that He loves us and that He holds a place for each of us in His heart.[15] I know we can, as suggested by those dear sisters in Czechoslovakia, beg the Lord to help us go forward with faith and confidence, that we might fulfill our divine missions as His daughters in the latter days.

NOTES

1. Richard G. Scott, "The Sanctity of Womanhood," *Ensign*, May 2000, 36.

2. Emily H. Woodmansee, "As Sisters in Zion," *Hymns of The Church of Jesus Christ of Latter-day Saints* (Salt Lake City: The Church of Jesus Christ of Latter-day Saints, 1985), no. 309.

3. Joseph Smith, *History of The Church of Jesus Christ of Latter-day Saints*, ed. B. H. Roberts, 2d ed. rev., 7 vols. (Salt Lake City: The Church of Jesus Christ of Latter-day Saints, 1932–51), 4:605.

4. Heber J. Grant, *Improvement Era*, May 1935, 276.

5. James E. Faust, "Womanhood: The Highest Place of Honor," *Ensign*, May 2000, 95.

6. Gordon B. Hinckley, "Each a Better Person," *Ensign*, November 2002, 99.

7. Gordon B. Hinckley, "Live Up to Your Inheritance," *Ensign*, November 1983, 84.

8. Gordon B. Hinckley, "The Light within You," *Ensign*, May 1995, 99.

9. Dennis Rasmussen, *The Lord's Question* (Provo: Keter Foundation, 1985), 63–64.

10. Matthew Cowley, *Matthew Cowley Speaks* (Salt Lake City: Deseret Book, 1954), 109.

11. Krisimir Cosic, in Shaun D. Stahle, "National Hero," *Church News*, January 21, 2006, 10.

12. Gordon B. Hinckley, "Rise to the Stature of the Divinity within You," *Ensign*, November 1989, 94.

13. Dieter F. Uchtdorf, "The Opportunity to Testify," *Ensign*, November 2004, 75.

14. Boyd K. Packer, "The Relief Society," *Ensign*, May 1998, 72.

15. See Edward P. Kimball, "God Loved Us, So He Sent His Son," *Hymns*, no. 187.

"THOU ART AN ELECT LADY, WHOM I HAVE CALLED"

Julie B. Beck

In July of 1830, just a few months after the Church of Jesus Christ was formally organized, the Lord told Emma Smith that she was "an elect lady, whom [He had] called" (D&C 25:3). The Lord added that what He said to her, He said to us all (D&C 25:16). The concept of being elect teaches about our identity as children of God. It talks about our purpose in life and what we are supposed to do. That statement goes back to the first teachings given to Adam and Eve and encompasses the plan of happiness. The blessings and privileges for the chosen are rarely comprehended fully.

What does it mean to be elect? Who are the elect? How does one become elect? What are the responsibilities of the elect? How do the elect carry out their responsibilities? What are the blessings the elect receive if they are faithful?

I would like to share today with you some of what I have learned as I have studied the scriptures about being elect and chosen.

WHAT DOES IT MEAN TO BE ELECT?

To be elect means to be formally chosen, singled out, or ordained. The Lord told Emma Smith that she had been formally singled out to do a

---

Julie B. Beck is currently serving as first counselor in the Young Women general presidency. She is a graduate of Dixie College and Brigham Young University. She and her husband, Ramon, have three children and five grandchildren.

great work in the Lord's kingdom. She was an elect lady because she would have the opportunity to receive ordinances and make sacred covenants.

The Lord has told His people throughout time that He has a chosen people, that His people are "peculiar" or special, they are selected for a purpose. He has used other words and phrases with similar meaning—children of the prophets, or a chosen, royal generation, or the seed of Abraham—but they all mean the same thing. It means being singled out or chosen for a special assignment or purpose. Those who are elect are expected to be leaders, more specifically to lead out in following the example of Jesus Christ and spreading His gospel and church on the earth.

WHO ARE THE ELECT OF GOD?

We learn in the scriptures that we were elected or "chosen . . . before the foundation of the world was" (Ephesians 1:4; 2 Timothy 1:9), to be part of the great latter-day work of the Lord. Those who are of the house of Israel are given special assignments to carry the gospel into all the world. When we receive our patriarchal blessings and have our lineage declared, we are being told that we are elect of God. We are designated to be part of the latter-day work.

The elect of God are those who have heard the gospel, been baptized, and have made temple covenants with the Lord under proper priesthood authority. Temple covenants are a key to our election and are a natural outgrowth of honoring our baptismal covenant.

Essentially, each of us who have made covenants could put our name in that verse of scripture in the Doctrine and Covenants which was given to Emma Smith and say, "Julie (or your name), you are an elect lady, whom the Lord has chosen."

Election is not based upon gender but is available to all who fulfill the qualification of harkening to the gospel and receiving ordinances and covenants.[1]

The temple is an important key to our election. President Hinckley has said that the temple is the reason for everything we do.[2] The ordinances of the temple are part of our natural progression as we seek to fulfill our election or calling here on earth. The booklets *For the Strength of*

Youth, Personal Progress, and *Duty to God* all have the temple as the cover illustration. These books are written for youth who have made their first covenants with God and are being prepared to make temple covenants. Those books are like a preparation course which points young men and young women to the temple as the next most important step in their lives. As a leader of young women, I am often asked how a girl prepares for the temple. If she honors and keeps the covenant she has already made at baptism, she is then preparing to make more covenants.

Any single adult woman who qualifies for a temple recommend should be preparing to receive her own endowment if she has not already done so. There is no "super" qualification for those ordinances. Some women postpone those crucial and empowering covenants, thinking that they are somehow tied to a mission or to marriage. In reality, a mission or marriage is an outflow of the endowment and not the other way around. If they are worthy and living the gospel, they should receive the election that can be theirs through the temple endowment.

WHAT ARE THE RESPONSIBILITIES OF THE ELECT AND CHOSEN?

Election is really an opportunity to serve. As the elect of God, we are elected to serve in our own homes and families first and then in the Church and the world. Those who belong to the house of Israel have a special assignment or election to carry the work of the Lord into all the world.

Years ago my husband was elected to serve in our city government. When he won that election, the people of our city expected that he would actually *do* something and *serve* the people while he held that office. It was a trust that he carried with him during his term of service.

We have each been elected, elected by the Lord to serve in His kingdom. We must honor our own election. If we do not fulfill the terms of our election then it could be said that we have been elected in vain. Anyone who is elected to anything is expected to *do* something in return for their election. The purpose of our election is to serve and lead.

When we know we are elected we cannot, we must not, be passive observers of life. We participate actively and work to make a difference on the earth.

In my scripture study, I have been particularly interested in the Lord's first instructions to Adam and Eve. Adam and Eve were the first "elect" people on the earth. They were the first to make covenants and commitments to follow the Lord's plan. To get them started in living His plan, the Lord told them to "be fruitful, and multiply, and replenish the earth, and subdue it: and have dominion" (Genesis 1:28). When He placed them in the garden, He told them to "dress it and to keep it" (Genesis 2:15). Did you hear the action words? Replenish! Multiply! Subdue! Dominate! Dress! Keep! There is nothing passive about those words. The Lord never rescinded those instructions. He expected Adam and Eve and all their posterity to *do* something to justify their election. Adam and Eve honored those instructions. They were personally obedient, and then they freely taught those things to their children (Moses 6:58).

How Do the Elect Lead and Serve?

1. Plan with vision. We cannot lead well unless we have a vision of what we need to be doing. When we know we are the elect of God, we have a plan for our work. Our vision defines *why* we are leading and what our goal is. Without goals or a vision of where we are going, it is difficult to replenish, multiply, subdue, and dominate.

My Grandmother Bangerter summed up her personal vision in one scripture which became the standard for her family: "As for me and my house, we will serve the Lord" (Joshua 24:15). Everyone who knew her understood that about her.

My own parents had a plan for their family. When they got married, they went on a long car trip for their honeymoon. Because my mother is an elect lady and knew that she had responsibilities connected with her calling, she wanted to establish some goals for her new family. As they drove along, my mother started asking my father some questions: "What will our family be like? What do you want our children to do and accomplish? What kind of home will we have?" These were searching questions for a honeymooning couple. She made her first notes about that conversation on a paper sack, which was the only paper she had close at hand.

During their honeymoon, my parents set goals about Church activity and service. They decided that they would take their children to church every week. They would teach their family the principles of the gospel in their home. They set a goal for their children to be married in the temple. They set a goal for them to all graduate from a university. They decided that all of their children would learn to play the piano. They wanted to teach their children table manners and social skills. They desired a house of order and neatness. They began their marriage with a vision for their family.

Well, the years went by and the family grew to include ten children and sixty-three grandchildren. Did the goals change because the number of family members multiplied? No! The goals stayed the same. They did not lose sight of their original vision. Just like Adam and Eve, they were busy multiplying, replenishing, subduing, dominating, dressing, and keeping. It has taken a lot of work to fulfill the vision they had established for their family.

2. Lead by example. Next, we cannot fulfill our election unless we are willing to first be an example. The Savior knew the power of example. He said, "Follow me, and do the things which ye have seen me do" (2 Nephi 31:12). We fulfill the call of an elect person as we exemplify righteousness so others can see what we do and what we are about.

Years ago the Sunday schedule for meetings was different than it is now. There was an early-morning priesthood meeting, then Sunday School in midmorning, and sacrament meeting later in the evening. Relief Society, Primary, and youth lessons and activities were held on weekdays. It was often the custom for women to send their husbands and children to priesthood meeting and Sunday School while they stayed home to cook the Sunday dinner. My mother was not one of those women. She believed in going with her family to church meetings.

One Sunday my mother fell behind schedule. She had succeeded in getting my father out the door to his meetings and the children were ready, but she would obviously be late because she was not yet dressed for church. She thought maybe, just this one time, it would be a good idea to stay home, calm down, and get herself and the family dinner prepared so everything would be well organized when the family came home. As she was ushering us out the door, my four-year-old brother resisted and did not want to go with us. Finally my mother resorted to a tactic she had used before. She would help him choose between right and wrong! She said, "Do you want to go to church and be on Heavenly Father's side, or stay home and be on the devil's side?" To which my brother answered, "I want to stay home and be with *you!*"

I suppose you know what happened next. She quickly put on her dress and went to church with us. She said that she never again thought of staying home to fix Sunday dinner. She knew that an elect lady honors her election when she is an example.

In the world today many people forget the power of example. How I wish more women understood what it meant to be on "Heavenly Father's side and not on the devil's side." There are so many ways that mothers, sisters, aunts, and friends can lead by example. They can honor their election by the books they read, by the movies they watch, by the music they listen to, by the tithing they pay, by the way they use their leisure time, by the way they dress, by the way they speak to and about their husbands and children, by the respect they show for priesthood and other leaders.

Do others see by your example the "mutual respect, affection, trust and love"[3] between you and your husband? Do others know by your actions that your eternal companion is your highest priority? Can the youth in your ward observe "worthiness, loyalty, sacrifice and honoring of covenant in [your] marriage?"[4]

Does your example of dress and appearance show that you know you are chosen of the Lord? Years ago a friend taught me an important lesson about dress and appearance. She was the mother of a large family, yet she was always very well kept. Her clothes were clean. There was nothing casual or ragged in her appearance. (Casual means "without serious intent.") I would describe her as being "dressed up" for her day. I asked her why she always took such care about her appearance although she was only going to the store, cleaning the house, tending children, and cooking food. She said that the people in her home were the most important people in her life. She was sealed to them forever. She wanted to be in her best clothes and on her best behavior when she was with them. She said, "Why would I reserve my best appearance only for the public? The people in my home are the most dear to me. I dress up for them." She knew that she was elect and that the people in her charge were also elect. She was not casual in her approach to her responsibilities. She was serious about her influence and example, and she dressed for it.

Much is said today about modesty and proper covering of the body, but the woman who truly knows she is elect will live that principle to its fullest extent. She will be the example of neatness also. A mother who understands that her daughter is also an elect lady will never pay for any clothing that would demean her daughter. She would do all in her power to honor that election and see that it was not in vain.

President Hinckley has said: "It is the mothers who set the tone of the home . . . [and] most directly affect the lives of their children. It is mothers who teach infants to pray, who read to them choice and beautiful literature from the scriptures and other sources. It is mothers who nurture them and bring them up in the ways of the Lord. Their influence is paramount."[5]

3. Teach the gospel. As the elect of God, we have a responsibility to teach and share the gospel message. Adam and Eve did this in their family. They made the gospel and the Lord's plan "known unto their sons and their daughters" (Moses 5:12). When we have done all we can in our personal lives and families, then we have an obligation to speak up and lead out in what is right and true in the world around us.

We can fulfill our election as we make our communities better places. Our influence is needed in the world. Are the schools our children attend better because of us? Are the dances our children attend of a higher standard because of our influence? Is our neighborhood safer because we live there? Our example and service in our communities will help bless the earth.

We also have the responsibility to share the gospel with the world. This is as easy as opening our mouths and is not as difficult as we make it. As the Lord told Jeremiah, we need not be afraid of the faces of those who do not know the gospel. He has promised to put words in our mouths (Jeremiah 1:8–9).

The Lord said: "And your whole labor shall be in Zion, with all your soul, from henceforth; yea, you shall ever open your mouth in my cause, not fearing what man can do, for I am with you" (D&C 30:11).

As the years have gone by, I feel increasingly honored to be able to share my testimony of the Savior at every opportunity. Wherever I go, I always ask to visit young women who are less active. These are girls who have been forgotten and for one reason or another have stopped coming to church. Some of the choicest experiences of my life have been meeting with these girls. Sometimes they are in large apartment complexes in crowded cities. Sometimes they are tucked away on hillsides in obscure little huts. But as I ask each young woman to share her testimony, and then share my own, the Spirit of the Lord descends on us. I am able to say with boldness that it is time for her to come back. I have never been turned down on that invitation. The girls are always ready to come back.

In Moses we are told that in these last days the Lord would cause "righteousness and truth . . . to sweep the earth, as with a flood, to gather out [the Lord's] elect from the four quarters of the earth" (Moses 7:62). That is now happening. The elect are being gathered, and we can be part of that sweeping up or be swept aside. We are living in a wonderful season when the gospel is going forth at an amazing rate. The opportunities for the elect and chosen to fulfill their election have never been greater.

Conclusion

When we know what it means to be the elect of God, when we know who the elect are and our responsibilities, then we can move forward to fulfill that election.

This is the season for each of us to *do* what we have been elected to do. But there are also many, many priceless blessings attached to those who do what they were elected to do. The Lord has said that He has chosen us "to be his peculiar [or elected] people," and He has promised to make us "high above all the nations . . . in praise, and in name and in honour" (Deuteronomy 26:18–19). If we are faithful, we are promised "all that [Heavenly] Father hath" (D&C 84:38).

In holy temples, elect men and women are "endowed with power from on high" (D&C 38:32, 38; 95:8). The Lord says, "For whoso is faithful unto the obtaining these two priesthoods of which I have spoken, and the magnifying their calling, are sanctified by the Spirit unto the renewing of their bodies. They become the sons [and daughters] of Moses and of Aaron and the seed of Abraham, and the church and kingdom, and the elect of God" (D&C 84:33–34).

The gospel of Jesus Christ is *true!* We are living the plan we joyfully accepted. We have a Savior in Jesus Christ who came and showed the way we should live and established His church and kingdom on the earth. We are privileged to be part of His great work. It is my prayer that we can have it said of us: "Thou art an elect lady, whom I have called" (D&C 25:3).

NOTES

1. LDS Bible Dictionary, s.v. "Election," 662.
2. See Russell M. Nelson, "Personal Preparation for Temple Blessings," *Ensign,* May 2001, 32: "The temple is the house of the Lord. The basis for every temple ordinance and covenant—the heart of the plan of salvation—is the Atonement of Jesus Christ. Every activity, every lesson, all we do in the Church, point to the Lord and His holy house. Our efforts to proclaim the gospel, perfect the Saints, and redeem the dead all lead to the temple. Each holy temple stands as a symbol of our membership in the Church, as a sign of our faith in life after death, and as a sacred step toward eternal glory for us and our families.

   "President Hinckley said that 'these unique and wonderful buildings, and the ordinances administered therein, represent the ultimate in our worship. These ordinances become the most profound expressions of our theology.'"
3. David A. Bednar, "Marriage Is Essential to His Eternal Plan," *Ensign,* June 2006, 86.
4. Bednar, "Marriage Is Essential to His Eternal Plan," 86.
5. Gordon B. Hinckley, "Standing Strong and Immovable," Worldwide Leadership Training, January 10, 2004, 21.

GIFTS: WORTH AND WORTHINESS

Virginia H. Pearce

I pray for the Spirit of the Lord to help each one of you rise above my clumsy words as I attempt to talk about some of the grandest truths of eternity.

HIS GIFT OF WORTH

The first grand truth is that in the eyes of God we are precious. We are worth everything to Him. He knows us completely. He loves us with His infinite and unending love. In fact, His work and His glory is our eternal welfare—not collectively, but individually. His love is for you—and for me—and for every other soul who has ever lived or will ever live on this earth. He will never stop loving us, precisely because He is our Father. We actually carry His spiritual DNA. Our divine attributes came from Him. That cannot change.

President Hinckley has said: "You are His child all the time, not just when you are good. You are His child when you are bad. You have within you . . . a portion of divinity that is real and tremendous and marvelous and wonderful."[1]

Stop for a moment with me and simply allow yourself to feel His great love for you—to *really feel* that you belong to Him. This connection is real

---

Virginia H. Pearce has served as a counselor in the Young Women general presidency. An author, she is also a wife, mother, and grandmother.

and, just like a testimony of Joseph Smith, a testimony of our own worth is revealed by "the spirit, [which] speaketh the truth and lieth not" (Jacob 4:13). If you do not have a witness of this important truth, seek it. But remember that when we ask for this testimony, we may have to give up some of the negative stories we tell ourselves about our own worth. Much as we dislike them, sometimes we insist on keeping them alive. Let go of your history and plead with the Lord to let you know how precious you are. Concentrate on the divinity within yourself and leave the assaults of the past behind.

When we receive a testimony of His love for us, we automatically feel a reciprocal love for Him. "We love Him, because He first loved us" (1 John 4:19). Furthermore, when we recognize our own divine worth and feel His soul-satisfying love, we recognize the worth of every other creature and can't help but reach out in love. We are filled with songs of praise and thanksgiving. Life is abundant. Life is good.

You and I are not alone in wanting to live in the circle of His love, to live with a strong spiritual connection to Him. A large sample of women in the United States were asked to look at fourteen life goals, choosing the three that were most important to them. It may surprise you that their number one choice was believing in God or a higher power, with 69 percent of women in America listing it first on their list. The number two choice was being part of a happy family (63%) and number three was having a good marriage (43%). Financial and career goals were way down on the list.

In this same study, 95 percent of the women believe in prayer and 92 percent believe that God or a higher power knows them personally and is mindful of them. Also, 70 percent believe they have an inner voice, and the majority of them believe that this is very important when making life decisions.[2]

Have you noticed the amazing success of radio and TV talk show hosts who are interested in spirituality? It seems clear that their programming is a response to the heartfelt desires of their audience.

You and I know so many outside our faith who have rich spiritual lives, who are, in fact, kinder, more helpful, more Christlike than many of us who are Latter-day Saints. So how can we talk about the necessity of keeping commandments, seeking ordinances, and making covenants? In other words, how can we talk about the value of specific behavior to those good people in the world who are already experiencing His love?

OUR GIFT OF WORTHINESS

Let's begin with the word *worthiness*. What does it mean to you? Is there some shriveling when I say it? Does it bring to mind judgment, guilt, comparison, constraints, feelings of "I don't quite measure up"? Do these feelings seem inconsistent with the preciousness of the individual soul that we have just spoken of?

Now you can see why preparation for today became almost paralyzing. I *want* to talk about worthiness. I *want* to talk about worthy behavior. I want to talk about a more profound relationship available to those who keep covenants with God through what we call "saving" ordinances. But I *don't want* to diminish the reality of His love even when worthy behavior isn't present. I am praying to be understood, but even more than that, I pray not to be misunderstood. If you feel a bit prickly, would you be willing to set those feelings aside and listen to a few stories, allowing me to share some personal views on covenants, commandments, and their profound power to change and deepen a relationship with God?

First story: The story is told of a woman who was married to a powerful man. At least, he was powerful in her life. Every Monday morning he would hand her a long list of things she was to do that week. The lists came with an unspoken assumption that things would not go well between them if she didn't perform. So, because she wanted a good marriage, every week she would work her way through the list. As the years went by she became increasingly tired. She continued obediently, but she lost the love which she had felt for her husband in the beginning and then began to resent him—finally growing to actually hate him and eventually seeking a divorce.

Several years went by and she married again. This time the man was quite different. He truly cared about her well-being and cherished her in every way. He respected her and her talents and she flourished, falling more deeply in love with him as each year passed. One day, as she was thinking about his goodness, she thought of her life before. She began to chuckle, then to laugh. It suddenly occurred to her that every week she was doing the exact same things that she had so resented doing in her first marriage. But her daily tasks were no longer onerous; rather, they were joyful and reciprocal expressions of love.

God does not compel us to obey Him. We keep His commandments because we love Him. Our worthy behavior is a freely given gift to Him. We want to please Him because we love Him, not because we feel coerced or manipulated into obedience. "For this is the love of God, that we keep his commandments: and his commandments are not grievous" (1 John 5:3). We recognize that His commandments are given as an expression of His love for us. And we keep His commandments as an expression of our acceptance of and gratitude for His love.

Korihor interpreted covenants as a way to bind people down, accusing Alma of behaving like our friend's first husband: "[You] teach this people to bind themselves down under the *foolish ordinances and performances* which are laid down by ancient priests, to usurp power and authority over them, to keep them in ignorance, that they may not lift up their heads, but be brought down according to thy words" (Alma 30:23; emphasis added).

Alma defends the motivation behind a prophet's encouragement of obedience to ordinances. He says that they do not desire to bring power to themselves, as Korihor has accused. Alma points to the hearts of the obedient as a test of the goodness of ordinances and performances. "And now, believest thou that we deceive this people, that causes such joy in their hearts?" (Alma 30:35).

Remember the joy which was the result of our friend's labors when she was choosing to serve someone she loved and who loved her, rather than someone who only loved himself? Our joy is the proof of the goodness of God in asking us to obey His commandments.

Second story: When I was a little girl there were virtually no two-car families in our neighborhood. Each morning, dads got in family cars and drove downtown to offices, leaving mothers and children at home. We waited until Saturdays to do our shopping.

This way of life spawned an industry that is now virtually dead. We had a milkman, we had a Fuller Brush man, and we had the Jewel T man.

One summer morning when I was about five or six years old, I was playing outside with some of my siblings and friends. We spotted the Jewel

T truck parked in front of our house. It was like a milk truck—no windows, but painted a dark brown with yellow writing across it: "Jewel T." The door was open, the salesman was in the house with Mother, and it was irresistible. We all scrambled to see what was inside. And it was wonderful! Behind the driver's seat there was an aisle that went from the front of the truck to the back and on each side there were shelves from floor to ceiling with groceries—cereal, baking powder, Jell-O, sugar—boxes and boxes.

I was entranced with this miniature grocery store when suddenly someone said, "He's coming! Let's get out. Quick!" There was a great deal of jostling, and as I turned to go out the side of the truck I knocked an open bag of jelly beans onto the floor. They were right by the driver's seat and I assume he had been snacking on them as he drove from house to house. I leaned down to gather them up and put them back in the bag when someone said, "Hurry, he's coming!" I left and ran with the other kids to hide behind the house next door.

It didn't work very well. Within a few seconds the Jewel T man came around the corner of the house. "Someone's been in my truck. Who spilled the jelly beans?"

As if orchestrated by a maestro, in one smooth motion all of my friends turned, pointed at me, and took a step back, leaving me standing alone in the middle of a half circle facing a threatening driver. He then moved in and shook his finger at me, saying that it was against the law to get into his truck and he was coming back that afternoon with the sheriff! Then he turned around, went back to his truck, and drove away.

There was a bit of silence and then everyone went back to playing—everyone, that is, except me. In those few seconds, my world suddenly changed. I had never entertained anything other than the thought that I was completely safe—that everyone around me could be trusted to take care of me. But that evaporated like a drop of water on a hot iron. I waited until I was sure no was looking, then crept around to my own backyard, found a bridal wreath bush, and made my way to the inside where I sat completely hidden and waited for the sheriff. I sat there until dinnertime came and it was clear that, for whatever reason, I was probably safe again.

That's a long way of telling you how important I think the concept of *trust* is and how frightening the world can be without it. I believe that one of the most significant blessings of covenant living is that we enter a circle of trust. When we make covenants, we, in essence, say to the Lord: I trust you and you can trust me. I trust you so completely that I will try to do the things that you ask of me, knowing that you have my best interests at heart. Making covenants is a concrete way I express my belief that the Lord will support and prosper me—that sooner or later all things will work together for my good. With this promise from us, He gives us His word: "I, the Lord, am bound when ye do what I say; but when ye do not what I say, ye have no promise" (D&C 82:10).

George Q. Cannon said: "No matter how serious the trial, how deep the distress, how great the affliction, [God] will never desert us. He never has, and He never will. He cannot do it. It is not His character [to do so]. He is an unchangeable being; the same yesterday, the same today, and He will be the same throughout the eternal ages to come. We have found that God. We have made Him our friend, by obeying His Gospel; and He will stand by us. We may pass through the fiery furnace; we may pass through deep waters; but we shall not be consumed nor overwhelmed. We shall emerge from all these trials and difficulties the better and purer for them, if we only trust in our God and keep His commandments."[3]

Does this mean that He only comes through if we are perfect in keeping His commandments? No. That isn't possible. I believe that it means that my *desire* is to keep His commandments and that entering into a covenant relationship means that I enter that holy cycle of repentance, forgiveness, and growth—repentance, forgiveness, and growth—an ever-continuing and upward circle to become like Him, which He can offer me through His atoning power.

When we cannot trust or be trusted we are just as surely immobilized as I was sitting in the middle of the bridal wreath bush. Not once during that long afternoon do I remember feeling sorry for getting into the truck. Fear and lack of support made it impossible for me to even entertain thoughts about my own behavior and desire to be a better person—to recognize that I indeed had done something wrong by getting into someone's truck uninvited. I was immobilized and unable to change or grow because of the experience. On the other hand, when I live in God's circle of trust, I can continually repent, be forgiven, and change, within the safety of His love and promises. Repentance is the doorway into covenants and the ongoing lifeblood of covenants.

Third story: Like most young girls, Janet grew up expecting and longing to be married and have a family. But as her friends and acquaintances seemed to move into marriage quite easily, it just didn't happen for her. There certainly was pain and disappointment, but nonetheless her life was full. She felt directed by the Lord as she pursued an avenue of study that created a great deal of fulfillment. As she approached her forties, the sense of loss became more pronounced, but once again, the Lord gave her clear confirmations that let her know that this was the life He intended for her. She was at peace and went forward with a happy spirit, putting the idea of marriage behind her and contributing in unique and rewarding ways.

Then there appeared a wonderful man and a marriage proposal that seemed good. It was confusing, but she loved the man and took the leap. One of the things about the idea of marriage that worried her a great deal was the fact that because of her busy career, she just couldn't imagine having someone in her rare, private spaces. She needed time away from people. She needed to be able to go home every night and close the door in order to regroup and heal. But she tucked the worry away and they were married.

Sometime within the first year she remembered her fear about losing alone time, and it now seemed ridiculous. She mentioned it to her husband. His response was that perhaps she didn't need as much time alone because when you are completely accepted you are somehow more whole together—a kind of peaceful completeness.

I like that thought. If that is so with a good marriage, think how peaceful it is to live within the completeness of a relationship with God. Within a covenant relationship, we are perfected by His love (1 John 2:5)—in other words, made whole and complete by His love.

Fourth story: In the book of Hosea—a book full of symbolism— Hosea is the betrayed husband whose rebellious wife leads the life of a harlot while her husband remains consistently faithful and forgiving. After incomprehensible strains on the marriage promises, the wife chooses to return to her first husband, "for then was it better with me than now" (Hosea 2:7). Through her repentance and his great mercy and loving kindness, he takes her back. "And I will say to them which were not my people, Thou art my people; and they shall say, Thou art my God" (Hosea 2:23). You see, Hosea and his bride are metaphors for God and His covenant people.

Elder Eyring, in speaking about Hosea, gives us this stunning insight: "All my life I had heard explanations of covenants as being like a contract, an agreement where one person agrees to do something and the other agrees to do something else in return, [but upon studying Hosea] I felt something new, something more powerful. This was not a story about a business deal between partners, nor about business law. . . . This was a love story. This was a story of a marriage covenant bound by love, by steadfast love."[4]

You will notice that in this metaphorical story, even though the husband remained steadfast in his love for his bride, her wanton and unworthy behavior kept her from enjoying the blessings of his love. Even though he loved her, her behavior precluded the possibility of him blessing her, until she repented and returned.

Elder Neal A. Maxwell said: "Thus the hard, cold fact is that how we use our moral agency does not result in a withdrawal of God's love, but does determine the ways and the degrees to which a loving God can express His love of us. Only the most righteous will receive His praise, His approval, and enjoy His presence. . . . If we are unrighteous, 'the spirit of the Lord is grieved. He is grieved (D&C 121:37),' . . . precisely because He loves us so deeply, but do we love Him enough to set things right? This is the continuing test."[5]

Worth, worthy behavior, and ultimate worthiness. There are significant differences, aren't there?

I'm aware that I have used marriage stories several times in this talk as metaphors to help us understand our relationship with God. In the scriptures, the Lord does the same, often referring to Himself as the bridegroom. I think it is helpful imagery. Within a good marriage we experience types and shadows of our more important relationship with God—things like companionship, trust, support, service motivated by love, and an abundance of other blessings. Within a difficult and broken marriage we experience betrayal, distrust, fear, and unhappiness. *We also experience these things when we break our covenants with God.*

Each of us hopes, prays, and works for a happy and fulfilling marriage with a spouse who will love and care for us. Some of us are denied that blessing, but every one of us has the opportunity to make and keep covenants with the Lord. Through baptismal and temple covenants He assures me that He will love and take care of me. And I promise Him, by covenant, that I will always trust Him to do so—and that my trust will be evidenced by my behavior: then, now, and always.

Do you remember the story of Esau? He was hungry. He sold his birthright because it seemed less relevant to his immediate and critical need than was a mess of pottage. The lesson for each of us is to stay within the covenant circle even when there are things outside that may seem better able to relieve our immediate suffering. In contrast to Esau, I promise that when problems come, I will look to Heavenly Father as a partner in solving them. I will choose to see life and its difficulties through eyes of faith.

I am grateful, beyond measure, for commandments and a lifetime of experiences that have led me to rely on Him. I know that I can trust Him. I have confidence that He will stand by me—support me, forgive me, consecrate my experiences to the welfare of my soul, bless and prosper me. Knowing this motivates me to work, repent, and work some more—unencumbered by the terror of going it alone.

Yes, God loves and responds to each of His children, but I am overwhelmed with gratitude for the added opportunity of a covenant relationship with Him. He said: "Be faithful and diligent in keeping the commandments of God, and I will encircle thee in the arms of my love" (D&C 6:20). The process is *so very* simple: A testimony of our divine worth leads us to joyfully repent and enter into a covenant relationship with our Father. Encircled by that relationship of trust and love we perform worthy works—striving to do good continually. When we fail, we repent, are forgiven, and experience growth—over and over and over again. You and I are doing this. And we will keep doing it. We are becoming like Him. And on one distant and longed-for day, in the words of John the Revelator, "[we] shall walk with [Him] in white: for [we] are worthy" (Revelation 3:4).

NOTES

1. Gordon B. Hinckley, *Teachings of Gordon B. Hinckley* (Salt Lake City: Deseret Book, 1997), 160.
2. Wirthlin Worldwide unpublished data projectable to the entire population of women plus or minus 3.5%.
3. George Q. Cannon, as quoted by Jeffrey R. Holland, "Come Unto Me," *Ensign*, April 1998, 17.
4. Henry B. Eyring, "Covenants and Sacrifice," CES Symposium on the Old Testament, August 15, 1995, 2.
5. *The Neal A. Maxwell Quote Book*, ed. Cory H. Maxwell (Salt Lake City: Bookcraft, 1997), 137–38.

DIVINE DOCTRINES, DIVINE REALITY

Barbara Day Lockhart

True doctrines give us a greater sense of "personal identity, personal accountability, and personal joy."[1] I testify that the doctrines of The Church of Jesus Christ of Latter-day Saints are the true teachings of Jesus Christ. These doctrines teach us of our divine reality, who we really are, who we were, and who we will be.

Divine reality is just that: truths from God, which are eternal, unchanging. We obviously don't create divine reality; we are not the source. Our role is to discover these truths, embrace them, and live by them. To do this it is imperative that we connect to the source, that we make a direct connection with God. We may have a knowledge or awareness of these truths, but there is so much more to it.

Once in awhile experiences happen that challenge our view of things. This is a true story. Ben, a handyman, came over to my friend Connie's home to repair a light fixture on her fifteen-foot-high stucco ceiling. He climbed up his ladder and worked for a time repairing the light. When Connie came back into the room, Ben was descending the ladder. She looked at him aghast, her eyes not believing what she saw. His eyes met hers and he grabbed his head. Simultaneously they both reluctantly looked up at the ceiling, and there, hanging from the ceiling, was his hair!

Barbara Day Lockhart is a professor of exercise sciences at Brigham Young University. She is a member of the Relief Society general board.

He scrambled back up the ladder, snatched his toupee, plopped it on his head, and, with his ladder and tools, was out the door in seconds.

What does Ben's hair have to do with his divine reality? How do we keep from losing sight of who we really are? What can we learn about our divine reality that will help us keep from "leaving it behind" or, more appropriately in this case, from "leaving it above"!

The challenge is for each one of us to have enough faith in Christ to believe these doctrines are telling me who I really am and to feel these so deeply that they are a great power in my life. What are these doctrines that teach us our true reality, and how do they become a foundation, a governing power, in our lives? As we analyze these doctrines, are you thinking, *I believe that about me with all my heart?*

Beloved Child of God

First is the doctrine that we are literal children of our Heavenly Father. This truth was proclaimed by the prophet and all the apostles in 1995 in "The Family: A Proclamation to the World": "All human beings, male and female, are created in the image of God. Each is a beloved spirit son or daughter of heavenly parents, and, as such, each has a divine nature and destiny."[2]

Elder Parley P. Pratt wrote: "An intelligent being, [that is each of us] in the image of God, possesses every organ, attribute, sense, sympathy, affection of will, wisdom, love, power and gift, which is possessed by God himself. . . . These attributes are in embryo, and are to be gradually developed."[3] Isn't it amazing to realize that we are composed of the same organs and attributes as God!

Of course, the adversary does not want us to know that we are the same species as God, that we are God's children. However, it is up to us to choose what we will believe. I know that Heavenly Father is my father. And knowing I am His daughter is a fact that continually gives me strength and courage and a belief in my potential so that I don't give up on myself or on Him. Are you also enjoying great happiness because you know you are a child of God? Does knowing that you are Heavenly Father's child make all the difference in how you think of yourself and how you live, pray, and relate to Heavenly Father?

SACRED SOUL, BODY AND SPIRIT

A second aspect of our divine reality is the sacredness of both body and spirit, which constitute the soul (D&C 88:15). The body is "a sign of our royal birthright,"[4] an essential part of our being that is requisite to a fulness of joy (D&C 93:33). Being embodied, we are like our heavenly parents, who have bodies of flesh and bones (D&C 130:22). Both body and spirit are matter, created to coexist in harmony with each other (D&C 131:7). Because of the atonement of Christ, each person is born innocent (D&C 93:38).

Many philosophies through the centuries have taught that the body is evil, that it is an enemy to the spirit. However, the Prophet Joseph Smith has taught that the body is sacred and is a complement to the spirit. "The great principle of happiness consists in having a body. . . . [Those] who have bodies have power over those who have not."[5] We know that after we die, our own body will be reunited with our own spirit. Resurrection is universal for all mankind. The body is the temple of our spirits (see 1 Corinthians 3:16–17). And just as temple ordinances are required for exaltation, so likewise is our body required for exaltation. That alone should teach us how sacred the body is.

President Hinckley has testified, "These remarkable and wonderful bodies are [God's] handiwork. Does anyone think that he can deliberately injure and impair his body without affronting its Creator?"[6] Why is it important that we know this aspect of our divine reality, that our body is a sacred part of our whole soul? Because our body is such an integral aspect of our soul, if we don't like our bodies, how can we like ourselves? If we are disparaging toward our own body, it makes it extremely difficult to know and trust our divine reality and to therefore derive great happiness and strength from it.

I marvel at the phenomenal sacrifice made by the Savior so that we may have our bodies for eternity, so that we may be eligible for a celestial resurrection and exaltation, for a fulness of joy. I am so grateful for my body. Do these beautiful doctrines help you appreciate the sacredness of your body? Can you muster a modicum of gratitude for your body, just as you are? We are not asking for a 10K run, here—just an attitude! An attitude of gratitude!

WORTH OF SOULS

A third aspect of our divine reality is the worth of each soul. The Book of Mormon prophet Jacob assured his flock that "one being is as precious in his sight as the other" (Jacob 2:21). This means that the worth of each soul is a universal truth. The value of each human life is great in the sight of God. The value, importance, or worth of each one of us is a priceless aspect of our divine reality. Literally, each one of us is precious. That is the state of our being. That is the nature of our whole soul. Our body and our spirit are precious to God.

"Remember the worth of souls is great in the sight of God;

"For, behold, the Lord your Redeemer suffered death in the flesh; wherefore he suffered the pain of all men, that all men might repent and come unto him" (D&C 18:10–11).

This scripture teaches us that our value is great and also gives us convincing evidence that this is so. Christ suffered death because He loves each one of us greatly. And God so loved each one of us that He sent His only begotten Son to die for us (John 3:16).

President Hinckley teaches us that God's love is a gift to each one of us. God's love is like the polar star. It is constant. "Love of God is the root from which spring all other types of love; love of God is the root of all virtue, of all goodness, of all strength of character, of all fidelity to do right. . . . Whenever other love fades, there will be that shining, transcendent, everlasting love of God for each of us and the love of His Son, who gave His life for us."[7]

The adversary is delighted when we think we are of little worth. Elder Maxwell, in his inimitable way, said, "Self-contempt is of Satan; there is none of it in heaven."[8] To Heavenly Father, we are precious. How could it be any other way? "God is love" (1 John 4:8). God is our perfect parent who loves us perfectly (Matthew 5:48). To help us understand and embrace our divine worth, Elder Holland explained that "the first and great commandment on earth is for us to love God with all our heart, might, mind, and strength (see D&C 59:5; Matt. 22:37) because surely the first and great promise in heaven is that he will always love us that way."[9]

Feeling and trusting that Heavenly Father loves me and that I am precious to Him is the most humbling thing I have experienced. I've known His love now for over thirty years, and every day I still marvel to know that the God of the whole universe knows me, loves me, and cares for me. This incredible relationship redefines humility. Elder Maxwell taught, "Humility is not the disavowal of our worth; rather, it is the sober realization of how much we are valued by God."[10] When you know you are precious to God, you realize that every person is precious to Him, and people become precious to you too.

God's love is what keeps me going through all of life's challenges; His love is the source of my happiness and peace. I ache to have everyone seek after and receive His love (Moroni 7:48). Is God's love blessing your life? Do you really know how precious you are to Him?[11]

IMPACT OF THESE TRUTHS

What does knowing that we are literal children of God—that our whole soul, body and spirit, is sacred and that we are precious to Him just as we are—what does this do for our lives? We see ourselves as we really are. It keeps us from being defined by others or by our circumstances. Just think of the significance of that! Living by our divine reality makes us personally secure; what would possibly constitute a threat to our being? When you know you are validated by Christ, what more do you need? Being yoked to Him takes stress, anxiety, and worry out of our lives. The Savior makes good on His promise that our hearts will not be troubled, that we need not be afraid (John 14:27). When we are certain that we are the child of Heavenly Father and that He loves us, we can cope with anything. It is crucial to know from Him that we are His and that He loves us.[12]

One of the barriers to having these truths influence our lives is the human tendency to think that we somehow determine our reality, our worth. We feel as if this is all in our own hands, which puts great stress in our lives. Then we erroneously conclude that our worth is not great, that we are not important, or are of little value. We might even think that God cannot love us, that we are not worthy of His love. Thinking this way only reflects that we don't understand God, and we don't understand His doctrines.

Worth and worthiness are very distinct in nature. The gifts of worth are the gifts of our divine reality. It is imperative to realize that the gifts of worth, of our divine reality, are not in our hands, they are inherent. However, worthiness is in our hands. And we will be most apt to choose Christ and choose to be worthy when we accept without a doubt that our worth is great to Him. When we know that we are truly precious to God, we don't want to do anything to let Him down. If we do disappoint Him, we want to repent. We feel godly sorrow because we know He is disappointed in us. Without this intimacy with Heavenly Father, what is the point? What are we doing with our lives?

RISE TO THE DIVINITY WITHIN US

Why does President Hinckley challenge us to "rise to the divinity within" us?[13] If we do know our divine reality, it is the most powerful motivation for good.

President Hinckley explains it like this: "Can you imagine a more compelling motivation to worthwhile endeavor than the knowledge that you are a child of God, the Creator of the universe, our all-wise Heavenly Father who expects you to do something with your life and who will give help when help is sought for? . . . Respect for self is the beginning of virtue in men. That man who knows that he is a child of God, created in the image of a divine Father and gifted with a potential for the exercise of great and godlike virtues, will discipline himself against the sordid, lascivious elements to which all are exposed."[14]

Considering the enormous impact that knowing our divine reality has for good, it is no wonder that the adversary has focused much of his efforts to keep us in the dark. But doesn't it make us unsettled to think we can be misled? Doesn't it lead us to question why these aspects of our divine reality are so difficult to believe about ourselves?

ATONEMENT

Elder Ballard explained that the Atonement is the key: "I believe that if we could truly understand the Atonement of the Lord Jesus Christ, we would realize how precious is *one* son or daughter of God. . . . Our

Heavenly Father has reached out to us through the Atonement of our Savior. He invites all to 'come unto Christ, who is the Holy One of Israel, and partake of his salvation, and the power of his redemption' (Omni 1:26). . . . What possible thing in the whole world is remotely as important as to know this? . . . Brothers and sisters, never, never underestimate how precious is the *one*."[15]

Elder Holland has taught us: "My desire today is for *all* of us . . . to have a more straightforward personal experience with the Savior's example. Sometimes we seek heaven too obliquely, focusing on programs or history or the experience of others. Those are important but not as important as personal experience, true discipleship, and the strength that comes from experiencing firsthand the majesty of His touch. . . .

"[Christ] is saying to us, 'Trust me, learn of me, do what I do. . . . If you will follow me, I will lead you out of darkness.'"[16]

WALKING IN DARKNESS AT NOONDAY

If we take our eye off of Him and let the world define us, it is as if we are "walking in darkness at noon-day" (D&C 95:6). The Lord rebuked the Saints in Kirtland, Ohio, in 1833 for not following His direction concerning the building of the temple. The Lord taught these Saints that when they ignore Him, they are "walking in darkness at noon-day." They are looking to other sources for direction. When we look to the world and worldly values for a sense of our value or worth, for our reality, we are "walking in darkness at noon-day."

We lose sight of our true reality and think we have to create a reality or an identity. Instead of living the plan of salvation (the plan of happiness) we may feel as if we are living a "giant reward system." We feel compelled to somehow earn love or to give ourselves worth or importance. We tend to compare and compete with others rather than be content with what we have been given. And our attempts to create reality are so futile. For example, many today are unhappy with their bodies and are using surgery to recreate their appearance. In the eternal scheme of things, can people really refashion their own bodies? Which body will be resurrected, the one they made or the one Heavenly Father made?

COMPREHENDING DIVINE REALITY

We can get so lost without God, "walking in darkness at noon-day." I know; I was there for half my life. When I was in my twenties, I skated in several Olympic Games as a speed skater for the United States. At that time, I thought my value came from my accomplishments. When I achieved a great deal and nothing changed within me, I was really confused. I loved what I could do but didn't really like myself. And no amount of success changed my negative self-talk and self-contempt. I had so much to hide. I felt that if anyone were to really get to know me, they wouldn't like me.

It was only when I pled with Heavenly Father in a most fervent prayer to know if He loved me that my heart was changed. And that change didn't come immediately. I knew He loved me; He told me so. He gave me a powerful answer to my most earnest prayer, "Of course I love you. You are my daughter." But my negative self-talk had become so habitual that even though I knew He loved me, I still could not bring myself to feel love for myself. I couldn't stand the disparity, the darkness, the loneliness I felt inside. With faith in God that He could change me, I pled with Heavenly Father night and day for some six months, and He eventually changed my heart.

The change was that I sincerely felt a tremendous gratitude for my life—grateful to be me. I honestly had never remembered feeling that I liked me, that I liked who I was. This newfound respect for myself enabled me to see myself as distinct from my behavior and my circumstances. The darkness, the negativism, the self-abasement were gone for good. He totally changed my life. No longer was I emotionally needy, no longer worried about myself, that I was never good enough, obsessed with getting others' approval. Instead of being so self-absorbed, I became secure in my divine reality, that I am God's child, that He loves me, that I am precious to Him. No trial, no rejection, no circumstance has ever caused me to doubt or question His acceptance of me. This is reality. Life now is filled with finding ways of giving rather than being obsessed with getting.

ENCIRCLED ETERNALLY IN THE ARMS OF HIS LOVE

I feel as did Lehi of old: "The Lord hath redeemed my soul from hell; I have beheld his glory, and I am encircled about eternally in the arms of His love" (2 Nephi 1:15).

There is no question that the source of our true reality is divine. Some of the marvelous fruits of living according to our divine reality are peace, happiness, and being blessed by God's love every day. I wouldn't trade these for anything.

We can do this. It is in the realm of possibility for each one of us. Each of us has a divine reality that is already there, already present. We just need enough faith in Christ to believe that these truths actually pertain to us. I can't think of anyone who was born other than as a child of God. I can't think of anyone whose body is not sacred. And I know without a doubt that the worth of each soul is great!

I testify that Jesus is the Christ. He is my strength, my joy, my happiness. His love and power in my life have completely changed me, changed my nature. I testify that He provides for us every opportunity pertinent to becoming like Him. He is "the way, the truth, and the life" (John 14:6). It is through His merits that we are saved. He, alone, will keep us from "walking in darkness at noon-day." I pray that we will "come unto Christ," yoke ourselves with Him, receive His great love for us, and live according to our true divine reality. In this way, we will "rise to the divinity within us."

NOTES

1. See Neal A. Maxwell, *A Wonderful Flood of Light* (Salt Lake City: Bookcraft, 1990), 40–41.
2. "The Family: A Proclamation to the World," *Ensign*, November 1995, 102.
3. Parley P. Pratt, *Key to the Science of Theology*, 4th ed., in James E. Talmage, *The Articles of Faith* (Salt Lake City: Deseret News, 1909), appendix 8, 48.
4. James E. Talmage, in Conference Report, October 1913, 117.
5. Joseph Smith, *Teachings of the Prophet Joseph Smith*, sel. Joseph Fielding Smith (Salt Lake City: Deseret Book, 1938), 181.
6. Gordon B. Hinckley, "The Scourge of Illicit Drugs," *Ensign*, November 1989, 50.

7. Gordon B. Hinckley, *Teachings of Gordon B. Hinckley* (Salt Lake City: Deseret Book, 1997), 319.

8. Neal A. Maxwell, *The Neal A. Maxwell Quote Book*, ed. Cory H. Maxwell (Salt Lake City: Bookcraft, 1997), 306.

9. Jeffrey R. Holland, "Look to God and Live," *Ensign*, November 1993, 14.

10. Maxwell, *Neal A. Maxwell Quote Book*, 165.

11. See John H. Groberg, "The Power of God's Love," *Ensign*, November 2004, 11.

12. See Neal A. Maxwell, "The Pathway of Discipleship," *Ensign*, September 1998, 7.

13. Gordon B. Hinckley, "Each a Better Person," *Ensign*, November 2002, 99.

14. Hinckley, *Teachings of Gordon B. Hinckley*, 158.

15. M. Russell Ballard, "The Atonement and the Value of One Soul," *Ensign*, May 2004, 86–87; emphasis in original.

16. Jeffrey R. Holland, "Broken Things to Mend," *Ensign*, May 2006, 70, 69; emphasis in original.

WHAT DOES THE ATONEMENT MEAN TO YOU?

Cecil O. Samuelson

It is wonderful to be with you and to consider together President Hinckley's challenge to "rise to the divinity within us."[1] It is my judgment that we can most effectively do this by knowing, understanding, and incorporating into our lives the special assets and blessings of the atonement of Jesus Christ.

As with our Nephite brothers and sisters of 2,500 years ago, "we talk of Christ, we rejoice in Christ, we preach of Christ, we prophesy of Christ" (2 Nephi 25:26). Even with all the current falsehoods and distractions about Jesus Christ created by the adversary, as well as the many misunderstandings expressed by others regarding our theology, it has always been the case, as taught by the Prophet Joseph Smith, that "the fundamental principles of our religion are the testimony of the Apostles and Prophets, concerning Jesus Christ, that He died, was buried, and rose again the third day, and ascended into heaven; and all other things which pertain to our religion are only appendages to it."[2]

Elder Cecil O. Samuelson, twelfth president of Brigham Young University, is a member of the First Quorum of the Seventy for The Church of Jesus Christ of Latter-day Saints. Prior to his call to full-time LDS Church service, he was senior vice president of Intermountain Health Care. In addition to his career as a physician of rheumatic and genetic diseases, he served at the University of Utah as a professor of medicine, dean of the School of Medicine, and vice president of health sciences. He and his wife, Sharon Giauque Samuelson, have five children and five grandchildren.

These fundamental principles are grounded in the atonement of Jesus Christ. As we read in the Bible Dictionary, "The word [Atonement] describes the setting 'at one' of those who have been estranged, and denotes the reconciliation of man to God. Sin is the cause of the estrangement, and therefore the purpose of atonement is to correct or overcome the consequences of sin."[3] I believe it is also possible to become estranged from God for many reasons other than overt sin. For example, when a disaster or disappointment strikes, there may be the temptation to ask, "Why me?" or to say, "It isn't fair!"

The risks of our establishing or stretching an unnecessary distance from our Father in Heaven and the Savior are significant and constantly around us. Happily, the Atonement was meant for all of these situations as well. That is why Jacob, the brother of Nephi, described the Atonement as "infinite" (2 Nephi 9:7), meaning without limitations or externally imposed constraints. That is why the Atonement is so remarkable and so necessary. Little wonder, then, that we not only need to appreciate this incomparable gift but also to understand it clearly.

Jesus Christ was the only one capable of performing the magnificent Atonement because He was the only perfect man and the Only Begotten Son of God the Father. He received His commission for this essential work from His Father before the world was established. His perfect mortal life devoid of sin, the shedding of His blood, His suffering in the garden and upon the cross leading to His voluntary death, and the resurrection of His body from the tomb made possible a full atonement for people of every generation and time.

As we know, the Atonement makes the Resurrection a reality for everyone without qualification. With respect to our individual transgressions and sins, however, there are conditional aspects of the Atonement that require our faith in the Lord Jesus Christ, our repentance, and our compliance with the laws and ordinances of the gospel.

Much of our understanding and knowledge of the Atonement comes from the Restoration scriptures. While the Old Testament is replete with atonement references, only one verse in the New Testament mentions Christ's atonement using this very word. The word *atonement* is used more than thirty times in the Book of Mormon—small wonder that it is "another testament of Jesus Christ." In addition to atonement insights in the Book of Mormon, some of which I will mention shortly, the doctrinal depths of the Atonement are also plumbed with sacred perspective in the Doctrine and Covenants and the Pearl of Great Price.

Perhaps the most oft-quoted verse in our Latter-day Saint meetings and writings is this wonderful clarifying and summarizing verse from the Book of Moses:

"For behold, this is my work and my glory—to bring to pass the immortality and eternal life of man" (Moses 1:39).

Because of the Resurrection, all of us will have immortality. Because of the Atonement, those who have sufficient faith in the Lord Jesus Christ to take upon themselves His name, who repent and live in accordance with His gospel, who keep covenants made with Him and His Father, and who participate in the saving ordinances made available in sacred ways and places will experience and enjoy eternal life.

I don't know about you, but I cannot recall ever encountering a person with professed strong faith in Jesus Christ who was very worried about the Resurrection. Yes, all of us may have questions about the details, but we understand that the fundamental promise is all-inclusive and sure.

Because eternal life is conditional and requires our effort and compliance, most of us do struggle from time to time, perhaps regularly—even constantly—with questions related to living the way we know we should. As Elder David A. Bednar has asked, do we "mistakenly believe we must make the journey from good to better and become a saint all by ourselves, through sheer grit, willpower, and discipline"?[4] In other words, to achieve the complete and promised blessings of Jesus' Atonement, do we need to do it on our own?

If it is the case that our salvation is only a matter of our own effort, then we are in serious trouble, since we are all imperfect and unable to comply fully in every way all of the time. If we are not fully independent in our quest for eternal life, then how do we achieve the help and assistance we require? Nephi clarified the dilemma of the relationship between grace and works as he testified, "For we know that it is by grace that we are saved, after all we can do" (1 Nephi 25:23).

Unlike the word *atonement*, the word *grace* appears frequently in the New Testament. The Bible Dictionary reminds us that *grace* means a divine mechanism or device that brings strength or help through the mercy and love of Jesus Christ made available by His atonement.[5] Thus, it is through the grace of Christ that we are resurrected, and it is His grace, love, and atonement that help us accomplish the good works and make the necessary progress that otherwise would be impossible if left solely to our own capacities and resources.

Given all that has been said, let me now ask each of us these questions: What does the Atonement mean to you? What are the implications of the Atonement for the problems and challenges you face? How can we access the happiness we have been promised in our mortal lives and gain a comfortable assurance that we will achieve eternal life? How may I narrow the gap between who I am and the person I want and need to become? These are tough questions, but necessary queries if we are really serious in our discipleship of the Savior and in our quest to be like Him and eventually be with Him.

Among the many things I admire about Nephi was his attitude. Let me mention an example or two that I believe bear on the questions we have about incorporating the Atonement into our lives. As we know, Nephi's life was not an easy one, particularly in comparison with the comfort most of us take for granted today. He and his family lived for years in the wilderness before arriving in the promised land. There were periods of hunger, thirst, and danger. He had to deal with serious family problems exacerbated by Laman and Lemuel. Finally, about thirty years after leaving Jerusalem, Nephi and the family members trying to keep the commandments of the Lord needed to separate themselves from those relatives siding with Laman and Lemuel in their iniquity. That meant once again starting over in the wilderness.

In the face of all these privations and difficulties, Nephi was able to say, "And it came to pass that we lived after the manner of happiness" (2 Nephi 5:27).

He understood that there is a pattern for living that results in happiness, independent of the difficulties, challenges, and disappointments that come into all of our lives. He was able to focus on the "big picture" of God's plan for him and his people and was thus able to avoid being brought down by his frustrations or by the accurate observation that life is not fair. It isn't fair and, in spite of this truth, he and his people were happy. They understood an atonement would take place, and they had confidence it would include them.

This is not to represent that Nephi was unaware of his serious problems or that he was devoid of disappointment. Think of the tender period that occurred for Nephi and his family at the time of the death of father Lehi. You recall that Lehi called all of his children together and gave his sons specific counsel and blessings. We can easily imagine that it was difficult for Nephi as a younger son to be appointed as a leader for his older brethren. It was even more difficult for Laman and Lemuel to be subject to their younger brother, and they were grossly cruel to Nephi as he attempted to keep all of the family on the straight and narrow path.

Not only was Nephi saddened by the conduct and attitudes of his brethren, he was painfully aware of his own inadequacies. Listen to some of his words:

"Behold, my soul delighteth in the things of the Lord; and my heart pondereth continually upon the things which I have seen and heard.

"Nevertheless, notwithstanding the great goodness of the Lord, in showing me his great and marvelous works, my heart exclaimeth: O wretched man that I am! Yea, my heart sorroweth because of my flesh; my soul grieveth because of mine iniquities" (2 Nephi 4:16–17).

If I were to continue to read his account, you would hear of his appreciation to God for his blessings. You would hear his testimony about the ministering of angels he had experienced as a result of his prayers. You would hear of the wonderful and magnificent things he had been shown. I will now return to Nephi's words as he asks himself important questions that we might ask ourselves as we consider the place of Christ's atonement in our own lives:

"O then, if I have seen so great things, if the Lord in his condescension unto the children of men hath visited men in so much mercy, why should my heart weep and my soul linger in the valley of sorrow, and my flesh waste away, and my strength slacken, because of mine afflictions?

"And why should I yield to sin, because of my flesh? Yea, why should I give way to temptations, that the evil one have place in my heart to destroy my peace and afflict my soul? Why am I angry because of mine enemy?" (2 Nephi 4:26–27).

After his lament, he then answered his own questions, knowing the approach to his problems that he must take. Said he: "Awake my soul! No longer droop in sin. Rejoice, O my heart, and give place no more for the enemy of my soul. . . . O Lord, I have trusted in thee, and I will trust in thee forever" (2 Nephi 4:28, 34).

Does this mean that Nephi no longer had problems? I don't think so. Does it mean that he fully understood all that was happening to him? Again, I'm convinced he did not. Remember the answer that Nephi gave to an angel several years before when he was asked a very important question related to the atonement of Christ that was yet to occur in the future.

Nephi said, "I know that he [meaning God] loveth his children; nevertheless, I do not know the meaning of all things" (1 Nephi 11:17).

We also can't and won't know the meaning of all things, but we can and must know that the Lord loves His children and that we can be the beneficiaries of a full measure of Christ's grace and atonement in our lives and in our struggles. Likewise, we know and must remember the foolishness and danger of giving "the evil one place in our hearts."

Even when we fully understand and commit to excluding evil and the evil one from our hearts and from our lives, we fall short because we are too often "natural" men and women. Thus, we must be grateful for and also practitioners of the principle of repentance. While we often speak of our repentance as an event, which it sometimes is, for most of us it is a constant, lifelong process.

Of course, there are sins of both omission and commission for which we can immediately begin the repentance process and never again visit a particular kind of iniquity or mistake. We can, for example, be absolutely perfect full-tithe payers for the rest of our days, even if that has not always been the case. But there are other dimensions of our lives that require our continual improvement and constant attention, such as our spirituality, our charity, our sensitivity to others, our consideration for our family members, our concern for our neighbors, our understanding of the scriptures, the quality of our personal prayers, our temple participation, and the like.

We can be grateful that the Savior, understanding us better than we understand ourselves, instituted the sacrament that we might regularly renew our covenants by partaking of the sacred emblems with the commitment to take upon ourselves His holy name, to always remember

Him, and to keep His commandments (D&C 20:77). As we follow the pattern that causes us to "live after the manner of happiness," our repentance and our performance assume a higher quality, and our ability to understand and appreciate the magnificence of the Atonement increases.

In the weeks prior to the organization of the Church in 1830, the Prophet Joseph Smith received a remarkable revelation that adds to the rich store of our understanding about the Atonement because it was the Savior Himself who was speaking and teaching. He described Himself as "the Redeemer of the world" (D&C 19:1) and acknowledged that He was following the will of the Father.

Said He: "Wherefore, I command you to repent, and keep the commandments which you have received" (D&C 19:13).

This simple pattern of repentance and obedience, repeated in clarity so many times, really is the basis for "living after the manner of happiness." We know this is what we need to do. Sometimes we might forget why it is that we need to do so. Let me continue with more of the Savior's words from the same revelation:

"Therefore, I command you to repent—repent, lest I smite you by the rod of my mouth, and by my wrath, and by my anger, and your sufferings be sore—how sore you know not, how exquisite you know not, how hard to bear you know not.

"For behold, I, God, have suffered these things for all, that they might not suffer if they would repent;

"But if they would not repent they must suffer even as I;

"Which suffering caused myself, even God, the greatest of all, to tremble because of pain, and to bleed at every pore, and to suffer both body and spirit—and would that I might not drink the bitter cup, and shrink—

"Nevertheless, glory be to the Father, and I partook and finished my preparations unto the children of men" (D&C 19:15–19).

What a remarkable lesson. I am sure that none of us can imagine the significance and the intensity of the Lord's pain as He accomplished the great Atonement. I seriously doubt that Joseph Smith at that time had a complete sense of the suffering of the Savior. The Prophet did gain greater appreciation and understanding from his own trials and torture in later years. Think of the corrective instruction given by Jesus Himself as He counseled and comforted Joseph in the dark hours of his Liberty Jail incarceration. After enumerating not only all that had happened to the Prophet Joseph and his associates, but also all that could yet befall them, the Lord simply said: "The Son of Man hath descended below them all. Art thou greater than he?" (D&C 121:8).

This question to Joseph is also a question to each of us in our personal and unique struggles and challenges. None of us should ever be in doubt as to the correct answer.

That Jesus experienced what He experienced, not because He couldn't avoid it but because He loves us, is sobering indeed. And not only does He love us, but He loves and honors His Father with a depth and loyalty that we can only begin to imagine. While this might be sufficient in its own right, we must never forget, if we feel to honor and love Him, that Jesus Christ did what He did for us that we might not suffer to the same degree that justice alone would require of us.

As some of you might know, I have a background in medicine. For many years, articles have appeared in the medical literature that have discussed the Savior's suffering and the pain that He experienced. I'll not detail any that have been written. I will report, however, that those most conversant with the realities of pain understand better the enormity of His sacrifice. The scourging, the privations, the abuse, the nails, and the inconceivable stress all led to His experiencing excruciating agony that could not be tolerated by anyone without His powers and without His determination to stay the course and suffer all that could be meted out. Bleeding from every pore is most uncommon but is also well documented. It occurs only under very unusual conditions of almost unimaginable stress—the stress Jesus necessarily suffered for us to make His atonement in our behalf possible.

As we consider the comprehensiveness of the Atonement and the Redeemer's willingness to suffer for all of our sins, we should gratefully acknowledge that the atoning sacrifice also covers so much more! Listen to these words of Alma to the faithful people of Gideon almost a century before the Atonement was actualized:

"And he [meaning Jesus] shall go forth, suffering pains and afflictions and temptations of every kind; and this that the word might be fulfilled which saith he will take upon him the pains and the sicknesses of his people.

"And he will take upon him death, that he may loose the bands of death which bind his people; and he will take upon him their infirmities, that his bowels may be filled with mercy, according to the flesh, that he may know according to the flesh how to succor his people according to their infirmities.

"Now the Spirit knoweth all things; nevertheless the Son of God suffereth according to the flesh that he might take upon him the sins of his people, that he might blot out their transgressions according to the power of his deliverance; and now behold, this is the testimony which is in me" (Alma 7:11–13).

Think of a full and comprehensive remedy for our pains, afflictions, temptations, sicknesses, sins, disappointments, and transgressions. Can you imagine any alternative to Jesus' atonement? Then add to that the incomparable Resurrection and we begin to understand just enough to sing, "I stand all amazed at the love Jesus offers me."[6]

What does the Atonement mean to you and to me? It means everything. As Jacob explained, we can "be reconciled unto [the Father] through the Atonement of Christ, his Only Begotten Son" (Jacob 4:11). This means that we can come into full harmony and complete acceptance with Him. It means that we can avoid the mistakes or misunderstandings that "denieth the mercies of Christ, and setteth at naught the atonement of him and the power of his redemption" (Moroni 8:20).

We avoid dishonoring and disrespecting the Savior's atonement by heeding the counsel of Helaman, which is as pertinent today as it was in the years immediately preceding the Lord's earthly advent. Said he:

"O remember, remember, my sons, the words which king Benjamin spake unto his people; yea, remember that there is no other way nor means whereby man [meaning women and men] can be saved, only through the atoning blood of Jesus Christ, who shall come; yea, remember that he cometh to redeem the world" (Helaman 5:9).

His atonement does indeed cover the world and its people from the beginning to the end. Let us not forget, however, that in its comprehensiveness and completeness it is also intensely personal and uniquely crafted to fit perfectly and address perfectly each of our own individual circumstances and situations. The Father and the Son know each of us better than we know ourselves and have prepared an atonement for us that is fully congruent with our needs, challenges, and possibilities.

Thanks be to God for the gift of His Son and thanks to the Savior for His atonement. It is true and is in effect and will lead us where we need and want to be.

Remember the wise advice and counsel from the Proverbs:

"Trust in the Lord with all thine heart; and lean not unto thine own understanding. In all thy ways acknowledge him, and he shall direct thy paths" (Proverbs 3:5–6).

His path, via the atonement of Jesus Christ, which must be our path, leads us back to Him.

NOTES

1. Gordon B. Hinckley, "Each a Better Person," *Ensign*, November 2002, 99.
2. Joseph Smith, *Teachings of the Prophet Joseph Smith*, sel. Joseph Fielding Smith (Salt Lake City: Deseret Book, 1976), 121.
3. LDS Bible Dictionary, s.v. "Atonement," 617.
4. David A. Bednar, "In the Strength of the Lord," Brigham Young University–Idaho Devotional, January 8, 2002.
5. LDS Bible Dictionary, s.v. "Grace," 697.
6. "I Stand All Amazed," *Hymns of The Church of Jesus Christ of Latter-day Saints* (Salt Lake City: The Church of Jesus Christ of Latter-day Saints, 1985), no. 193.

THE ENABLING POWER OF THE ATONEMENT: BASK IN HIS LIFE-GIVING LIGHT

Carolyn J. Rasmus

I am a convert to The Church of Jesus Christ of Latter-day Saints, having been baptized in my early thirties. But when I was about five years old I had an experience that became a "defining moment." I was outside with my mother. While she was hanging clothes on the clothesline, I was in the backyard swing, singing a song I'd learned in Sunday School.

"Jesus loves me this I know, for the Bible tells me so. Little ones to Him belong, we are weak, but He is strong." I did not fully recognize all that was happening to me, but I literally felt His love. I began pumping and singing—harder and harder. "Yes, Jesus loves me, Yes, Jesus loves me, Yes, Jesus loves me, the Bible tells me so."[1] I was so filled with His love for me, I felt I could do anything—even go all the way over the top of the swing if I pumped hard enough! That didn't happen, but what did happen was much more significant: I felt Christ's love and I knew He knew me. I hope you have felt the reality of His love and especially that you might experience it today and have it confirmed again and again.

Elder David A. Bednar, while serving as president of Brigham Young University–Idaho and prior to his calling to the Quorum of the Twelve, said, "I suspect [we] are much more familiar with the nature of the

---

Carolyn J. Rasmus is a retired institute instructor. She is a former administrative assistant to the Young Women general presidency. A popular author, she has recently served a mission to New Zealand.

redeeming power of the Atonement than we are with the enabling power of the Atonement."

He suggested that most of us understand that Christ came to earth to die for us, to pay the price for our sins and to make us clean; to redeem us from our fallen state and to enable every person to be resurrected from the dead. In other words, we know the Atonement is for sinners.

But, Elder Bednar added, "I frankly do not think many of us 'get it' concerning this enabling and strengthening aspect of the Atonement, and I wonder if we mistakenly believe we must make the journey from good to better and become a saint all by ourselves, through sheer grit, willpower, and discipline, and with our obviously limited capacities."[2]

Well, that's me! I'm the first to admit my guilt in believing that through "sheer grit, willpower, and discipline" I can manage just about anything. Preparing this chapter is an example. I searched the scriptures, scanned articles and books, followed links on the Church Web-site, and labored over an outline. I felt a tremendous burden as I struggled along working with "sheer grit." I think this is not an uncommon feeling among women. We have a tendency to believe that we have to do everything all by ourselves. I know that nothing is further from the truth; I have repeatedly experienced the enabling power promised by the Savior, but I so easily forget and am so slow to remember.

As the deadline approached, I experienced increased stress, and stress drives away the Spirit. I came to a point where I knew I could not do this alone; I desperately needed His help. I prayed for guidance, understanding, wisdom, and the enabling power of Jesus Christ. "Why is this so difficult?" I prayed.

With force and power these words came streaming into my mind: Because Satan does not want you to teach of the atonement of Jesus Christ. He knows that when we understand the enabling power of the Atonement, we will be changed; we will have strength beyond our natural abilities, our weakness will be turned to strength, and we will know that "in the strength of the Lord [we] canst do all things" (Alma 20:4). Christ will heal our feelings of fear, distrust, anger, self-doubt, sorrow, discouragement, and inadequacy. He will help us get through difficult days and trying times—if we but come unto Him. But if Satan can prevent us from learning the doctrine of and drawing upon the enabling power of Christ's atonement, he will leave us crippled, weak, and ineffective—basically, "miserable, like unto himself" (2 Nephi 2:27).

My prideful thinking had led me to believe that I could prepare this talk without His help. However, as I sought forgiveness, a feeling of peace flooded over me. I felt great relief, and scriptures and thoughts came into my mind. I began to write, knowing I was being "enabled" by Christ's promised grace. I determined I would do everything within my power, relying upon the enabling power of Christ to foil Satan's intent.

I know many of you deal with things much more difficult than writing a chapter. In sharing my experience, I in no way want to minimize Christ's power to enable, empower, and strengthen us to deal with much harder things—things such as divorce, disease, death of loved ones, depression, violence, children who choose not to follow the gospel plan, abuse of a variety of kinds (emotional, physical, spiritual, and sexual), tragic accidents, infidelity, and much, much more. To quote Carlfred Broderick, LDS family therapist and author: "The gospel of Jesus Christ is not insurance against pain. It is a resource in event of pain, and when that pain comes (and it will come because we came here on earth to have pain among other things), when it comes, rejoice that you have a resource to deal with your pain."[3]

I have come to know many incredible women who have struggled under very difficult circumstances and who have each prevailed by coming to rely on Christ, which has enabled them to carry on when burdens seemed too heavy and pain too intense to bear.

A dear friend lovingly cared for her brilliant husband who experienced early-onset Alzheimer's disease. He also suffered physical illnesses. She was widowed at age fifty-five. She told me, "There are times when the sadness is overwhelming. I get on my knees and plead, 'You have to carry this for a while. I can't do this alone.' And I feel His strength—strength enough to allow me to move forward and face each day, one at a time. To me, this is the power of the Atonement. I know He will not change my situation; the only thing I can change is me—I have to humble myself and depend on Him for help. Through this experience, I am coming to know the Savior as a person—not just someone I read about in the scriptures, but someone with whom I am developing a comforting relationship."[4]

There are many Latter-day Saints who have experienced the great anguish that accompanies a child choosing a path that leads him or her away from the Church. A mother, reflecting on her family of eight children, shared: "My awkward attempts to help my children solve their problems are often interpreted as an intrusion. The defenses go up as the lines of communication come crashing down. Then I blame myself for what I did or didn't do over the years. Such thoughts bring feelings of despair and helplessness. It is so easy to forget that before they were ever our children, they were (and are) His. I have come to believe that Christ's love will do what ours alone cannot. His love will break down all barriers and overcome all obstacles, as it heals and makes whole their broken hearts. And, in that moment, our hearts will be healed as well."[5] That is the power of the Atonement.

Some time ago I became acquainted with a woman in an institute class I was teaching. Frequently, she would stop by my office after class. Over a period of many months, she shared bits of her life story. It was not pretty. As a child she had been ritually and sexually abused. She had spent years in therapy, at times institutionalized because she could not cope. I remember the day she came to my office pleading for help. I could see her pain, but I had no training in how to handle such things, and I pled with the Lord to know how I might help. I played Church hymns and after a time, when she had finally calmed down, I invited her to sit in my office chair. On the wall, at eye level, was a painting of Christ. I invited her to look into His eyes as I began reading to her from the scriptures:

"Fear not, little flock. . . . Look unto me in every thought; doubt not, fear not" (D&C 6:34, 36).

"The Lord hath comforted his people, and will have mercy upon his afflicted. . . . For can a woman forget her sucking child, that she should not have compassion on the son of her womb? . . . Behold, I have graven thee upon the palms of my hands" (1 Nephi 21:13, 15–16).

"Behold, he suffereth the pains of all men, yea, the pains of every living creature, both men, women, and children, who belong to the family of Adam" (2 Nephi 9:21).

"Look unto God with firmness of mind, and pray unto him with exceeding faith, and he will console you in your afflictions, and he will plead your cause. . . . O all ye that are pure in heart, lift up your heads and receive the pleasing word of God, and feast upon his love" (Jacob 3:1–2).

As I read to her, without question, I knew I had been blessed by the love and mercy of Jesus Christ to do and say things beyond my natural ability. For my friend, it was a new beginning. Years later she wrote of that day, "I felt an overwhelming feeling of love and peace. Intellectually, I knew about the Atonement, but that day I came to a 'heart knowledge' as I *felt* His healing power. Over time I came to know that ultimately true healing can only come from the Master Physician, Jesus Christ."[6] The healing which she experienced that day was only a beginning. Challenges still remain, but she is learning to trust in His promises as she turns to the scriptures and seeks His help through prayer.

Recently, I became acquainted with a young mother with two active boys under the age of three. Her husband is in college and works two jobs. Both hold responsible callings in the ward. I don't ever remember seeing her without a smile on her face and a warm greeting for everyone. You can imagine my surprise when I learned that she suffers from the painful and debilitating disease of rheumatoid arthritis.

"How do you manage?" I asked her.

"Well," she hesitated, "I'm trying to learn to submit to His will, especially when every joint aches and I only have energy enough to lie on the couch and watch my boys play."

"But you never miss church and are always so pleasant," I said. "How do you do it?" I was not prepared for the simplicity of her answer.

"We try to do what we are asked—to hold family home evening, read the scriptures every day, and pray. I am so grateful for prayer. Several months ago I wanted so badly to have a party for my son's first birthday. I prayed to Heavenly Father, 'You know how to help me. This isn't for me; it's for my son.' When I finished that prayer, I knew I would be sustained."[7] This young mother understood the enabling power of the Atonement.

I think of so many I know who have not yet come to believe all that Christ promises. My heart goes out to them, and I share with them Christ's assurance and invitation: "Peace I leave with you, my peace I give unto you. . . . Let not your heart be troubled, neither let it be afraid" (John 14:27). Of this invitation, Elder Jeffrey R. Holland made this thought-provoking statement, "I submit to you, that may be one of the Savior's commandments that is, even in the hearts of otherwise faithful Latter-day Saints, almost universally disobeyed; and I yet I wonder whether our resistance to this invitation could be anymore grievous to the Lord's merciful heart."

He added: "In [this] same spirit, I am convinced that none of us can appreciate how deeply it wounds the loving heart of the Savior of the world when he finds that his people do not feel confident in his care or secure in his hands."[8]

Do we fully understand how sincere the Savior is when He offers to help us? He stands ever ready to have us come unto Him that He might strengthen us and embrace us in the arms of His love. The scriptures bear record of this:

The Lord has promised: "I have heard thy prayer, I have seen thy tears: behold, I will heal thee" (2 Kings 20:5).

To the people at Zarahemla, Alma declared, "Behold, [Christ] sendeth an invitation unto all men, for the arms of mercy are extended towards them, and he saith: Repent, and I will receive you" (Alma 5:33).

The Savior invites us all to "be faithful and diligent in keeping the commandments of God, and I will encircle thee in the arms of my love" (D&C 6:20).

In the ninth chapter of 3 Nephi, Christ says, "Behold, mine arm of mercy is extended towards you, and whosoever will come, him will I receive; and blessed are those who come unto me" (3 Nephi 9:14).

Will you, for a moment, see yourself standing before Christ's outstretched arms as He waits for you to "come unto Him" and be encircled in the arms of His love? It is here you will be healed, nourished, loved, enabled, strengthened, and made whole. We need to learn to let the Savior carry our burdens and to go to Him regularly to seek His "enabling power." To the faithful, Christ has declared: "I will also ease the burdens which are put upon your shoulders, that even you cannot feel them upon your backs, . . . that ye may stand as witnesses for me hereafter, and that ye may know of a surety that I, the Lord God, do visit my people in their afflictions." In fulfillment of that wonderful promise, "the Lord did strengthen them that they could bear up their burdens with ease, and they did submit cheerfully and with patience to all the will of the Lord" (Mosiah 24:14–15).

Please ponder the words of two hymns, each written as if Christ Himself were speaking to us:

Lean on my ample arm,
O thou depressed!
And I will bid the storm
Cease in thy breast.
Whate'er thy lot may be
On life's complaining sea,
If thou wilt come to me,
Thou shalt have rest.[9]

In another familiar hymn, Christ also speaks to us, saying:

Fear not, I am with thee; oh, be not dismayed,
For I am thy God and will still give thee aid.
I'll strengthen thee, help thee, and cause thee to stand,
Upheld by my righteous, omnipotent hand.

When through fiery trials thy pathway shall lie,
My grace, all sufficient, shall be thy supply.
The flame shall not hurt thee; I only design
Thy dross to consume and thy gold to refine.[10]

Did you notice the phrase, "my grace, all sufficient, shall be thy supply"? The Bible Dictionary teaches that "the main idea of the word [grace] is divine means of help or strength, given through the bounteous mercy and love of Jesus Christ.

"It is through the grace of the Lord Jesus, made possible by his atoning sacrifice, that mankind will be raised in immortality, every person receiving his body from the grave in a condition of everlasting life."

Please consider these next sentences:

"It is likewise through the grace of the Lord that individuals, through faith in the atonement of Jesus Christ and repentance of their sins, receive strength and assistance to do good works that they otherwise would not be able to maintain if left to their own means. This grace is an enabling power."[11]

These are heady thoughts, but true doctrine—doctrine that, if understood, will not only bless our daily lives but help us withstand the challenges and pressures of our time. But how do we begin to allow the

Atonement to work in our lives? What do we need to do? It is more simple than most of us think.

When we feel troubled, unsure, afraid, or discouraged, we need to remember the things that are taught in Primary: First, we must believe in Christ and all He has promised to do for us. Obeying His commandments and partaking of the sacrament bring us strength beyond our own. Prayer, fasting, study of the scriptures, and temple worship also bring us close to Him where we can feel His love and know of His promises.

Most of all we need to recognize our need for His grace—both for our ultimate salvation and also for His enabling power every day of our lives. Through His grace, each of us can be uplifted and strengthened (see Proverbs 3:34; 1 Peter 5:5; D&C 88:78; 106:7–8).

I love this statement from the Church publication, *True to the Faith: A Gospel Reference*, "If you ever become discouraged or feel too weak to continue living the gospel, remember the strength you can receive through the enabling power of grace."[12] This is the very knowledge Satan does *not* want you to know, understand, or apply in your life!

To each of you, I bear testimony that Christ stands ever ready to respond to our feelings of grief, despair, inadequacy, discouragement, pain, and temptation. He constantly offers us His comfort, peace, hope, love, and strength. I know this from personal experience. There are times when I feel a direct answer from the Lord. At other times I sense He allows me to wrestle for a time so that I might learn and grow.

Jesus loves us! This we know, for the scriptures tell us so. All of us "to Him belong; we are weak, but He is strong."

I pray that we might realize the truth of Christ's promise to each of us and that we will come to learn of and apply the essential doctrine of Christ's enabling power in our lives.

NOTES

1. Anna B. Warner, "Jesus Loves Me, This I Know," 1860.
2. David A. Bednar, "In the Strength of the Lord," Brigham Young University–Idaho Devotional, January 8, 2002.
3. Carlfred Broderick, "The Uses of Adversity," in *As Women of Faith*, 1988 Brigham Young University Women's Conference (Salt Lake City: Deseret Book, 1989), 172–73.
4. Personal interview with author, February 27, 2006.

5. Personal e-mail to author, March 14, 2006.

6. Personal correspondence to author, March 28, 2006.

7. Personal interview with author, February 27, 2006.

8. Jeffrey R. Holland, "Come unto Me," *Ensign*, April 1998, 19.

9. "Lean on My Ample Arm," *Hymns of The Church of Jesus Christ of Latter-day Saints* (Salt Lake City: The Church of Jesus Christ of Latter-day Saints, 1985), no. 120.

10. "How Firm a Foundation," *Hymns*, no. 85, verses 3 and 5.

11. LDS Bible Dictionary, s.v. "Grace," 697; emphasis added.

12. *True to the Faith: A Gospel Reference* (Salt Lake City: The Church of Jesus Christ of Latter-day Saints, 2004), 78.

STAND ON YOUR FEET AND GO FORWARD AS SONS AND DAUGHTERS OF GOD

◆

Janine T. Clarke

We have been counseled many times and in different ways to *stand*. We are asked to "stand . . . in holy places and be not moved" (D&C 87:8); "to stand as witnesses of God at all times and in all things, and in all places" (Mosiah 18:9); to "stand fast in the faith" (1 Corinthians 16:13); to "stand in the place of thy stewardship" (D&C 42:53); to "stand and testify" (Alma 5:44); and to "Stand for Truth and Righteousness."[1]

Standing requires strength, especially if you do it for a long time. To stand means to remain stable or intact, to withstand, to endure, to be firm and unwavering. Standing implies that one has a purpose, that one is undaunted and courageous in a cause.

The questions that I have been pondering for the last few months have been these: How can we as women be valiant and courageous? How can we, in our individual circumstances, thrust in our sickles and join in the work to bring to pass the Lord's eternal purposes? How can we conquer roadblocks and move forward? How can we stand fast in the faith with so much wickedness around us?

As I thought about these questions, and possible answers to them, I remembered a family home evening lesson that my daughter gave many years ago when she was in Primary. Her lesson was on the Godhead. She talked about each member of the Godhead and their individual attributes.

Janine T. Clarke has served as a stake Young Women president and on the Salt Lake Area Day of Celebration Committee. She is a wife and mother.

At the end of her lesson, she gave us a three-day challenge. She said that on the first day we were to express appreciation in our private prayers for Heavenly Father. On the second day we were to express appreciation and gratitude for the Savior, and on the third day, in our private prayers, we were to express appreciation for the Holy Ghost. I accepted her challenge. Usually, my prayers are full of many different things that I am happy about and grateful for. But on that day I knelt down and had just one thing on my mind. I expressed gratitude to my Heavenly Father for Him. Tears quickly sprang to my eyes as I realized how strongly I felt about Him and how much I appreciated His love, His care, and His support. I did as my daughter asked for those three days and the experience gave me a stronger testimony of the three members of the Godhead and helped me realize the depth of my love and appreciation for each of them.

Every Sunday thousands of young women across the world stand and repeat the Young Women's Theme, which begins, "We are daughters of our Heavenly Father, who loves us, and we love Him."[2] Isn't that the most simple and beautiful doctrine? We are daughters of a loving Heavenly Father, and we love Him in return.

In the 2005 October general conference, Elder Jeffrey R. Holland said, "You are literally a spirit daughter of heavenly parents with a divine nature and an eternal destiny. That surpassing truth should be fixed deep in your soul and be fundamental to every decision you make. . . . There could never be a greater authentication of your dignity, your worth, your privileges, and your promise. Your Father in Heaven knows your name and knows your circumstance. He hears your prayers. He knows your hopes and dreams, including your fears and frustrations. And He knows what you can become through faith in Him."[3]

There is a wonderful book entitled *True to the Faith: A Gospel Reference*. In it is a section entitled "God the Father." From that section we read, "Our Heavenly Father is a God of judgment and strength and knowledge and power, but He is also a God of perfect mercy, kindness, and charity. Even though we 'do not know the meaning of all things,' we can find peace in the sure knowledge that He loves us (see 1 Nephi 11:17). . . .

"From time to time, ponder the beauties of creation: trees, flowers, animals, mountains, the waves of the ocean, a newborn child. Take time to gaze into the heavens, where the courses of the stars and planets are evidence of 'God moving in his majesty and power' (see D&C 88:41–47). . . .

"Seek to know your Father in Heaven. He loves you, and He has given you the precious opportunity to draw near to Him as you pray."[4]

> *Heavenly Father, are you really there?*
> *And do you hear and answer every child's prayer? . . .*
> *Pray, he is there; Speak, he is listening.*
> *You are his child; His love now surrounds you.*[5]

If every young woman and every woman in the world knew that they were a beloved daughter of God, what a difference that would make! That knowledge would affect their decisions, increase their self-esteem, and give them a vision of who they are and who they can become. I have been blessed with a loving earthly father, and so it has not been difficult for me to envision while I pray the face and the voice of my loving Heavenly Father. I know that there is a God in heaven who loves and watches over each one of us.

Jesus stands with open arms to receive us (Mormon 6:17). Jesus "standeth up to plead" for each of us (2 Nephi 13:13).

"Through the Atonement of Jesus Christ, we can be reconciled to our Heavenly Father. . . . We can ultimately dwell in His presence forever, having been 'made perfect through Jesus' (see D&C 76:62, 69). . . . The Atonement is the supreme expression of our Heavenly Father's love for us (see John 3:16). . . . It is also the greatest expression of the Savior's love for the Father and for us. . . .

"Without the Atonement, spiritual and temporal death would place an impassable barrier between us and God. . . .

"In addition to offering redemption from the pain of sin, the Savior offers peace in times of trial. As part of His Atonement, Jesus took upon Himself the pains, sicknesses, and infirmities of all people (see Alma 7:11–12). He understands your suffering because He has experienced it. With this perfect understanding, He knows how to help you. You can cast 'all your care upon him; for he careth for you' (1 Peter 5:7)."[6]

Isn't it a marvelous feeling to know that Jesus Christ knows how we feel and that He can succor us? There is no heartache that He has not felt, no sorrow that He has not experienced. We can lay our burdens at His feet and He will help us carry them. Some of the most sacred and meaningful moments of my life have been when, on my knees, with a heavy heart, I have poured out my soul to my Heavenly Father. The healing balm of those emotional and often painful moments was in knowing that the Savior knows and feels what I feel and helps me to carry my burdens. Sometimes I have prayed for certain trials to be taken away, and though that has not always happened, I have felt in every instance, that the trial has been softened and that I have been strengthened to handle it. The Savior gives each of us the strength to steadfastly stand. He fortifies us—He fills in for our weaknesses and shortcomings.

Elder Russell M. Nelson has said, "Thanks to Him, no condition is hopeless. Thanks to Him, brighter days are ahead, both here and hereafter. Real joy awaits each of us—on the other side of sorrow."[7]

I love the words of a song entitled "Behold the Wounds in Jesus' Hands" by John V. Pearson:

> *Behold the wounds in Jesus' hands,*
> *The marks upon His side,*
> *Then ponder who He meant to save*
> *When on the cross He died.*
> *We cannot see the love of God*
> *Which saves us from the fall,*
> *Yet know that Christ from wood and nails*
> *Built mansions for us all.*
>
> *Behold the outstretched hands of Christ,*
> *Our God, who came to save,*
> *Whose love and grace redeems our souls*
> *And lift us from the grave.*
> *Through bruised and battered as we stray*
> *His guiding hands caress,*
> *He washes and anoints with oil*
> *Then in His arms we rest.*
>
> *Behold the wounds in Jesus' hands.*
> *Look to your Lord and live.*
> *He yearns to bless you with His love*
> *And all your sins forgive.*

Oh, empty is the heart of man
When it is filled with sin.
Come, open wide your broken heart
And let your Savior in!

Behold His wounded hands and feet!
Come touch, and see, and feel
The wounds and marks that you may know
His love for you is real.
Then as you fall to worship Him
And wash His feet in tears,
Your Savior takes you in His arms
And quiets all your fears.[8]

I know that we have a loving brother, even Jesus Christ, who has paid the price for each of us. He is our example and the light that we hold up. How He loves us!

The Holy Ghost " 'witnesses of the Father and the Son' (2 Nephi 31:18), and reveals and teaches 'the truth of all things' (Moroni 10:5)." He guides you and protects you. "He is the Comforter (John 14 :26). As the soothing voice of a loving parent can quiet a crying child, the whisperings of the Spirit can calm your fears, hush the nagging worries of your life, and comfort you when you grieve.

"As you bring your life in harmony with God's will, you gradually receive the Holy Ghost in great measure. . . . Keep yourself clean. Fill your life with goodness so you can be worthy of the constant companionship of the Holy Ghost."[9]

We live in a world of temptation and spiritual darkness. The gift of the Holy Ghost is the gift that we need more than any other gift. The Holy Ghost will guide us toward the light. I want to bear testimony of the reality of the Holy Ghost. Countless times I have felt His promptings. The quiet voice of the Holy Ghost pierces my soul, and I have learned, and am still learning, to listen to and heed those promptings. Recently, as I read the Book of Mormon, I felt the Holy Ghost nudge me as I read certain passages. He instructed and tutored me. As I read the book, I humbly came to realize that there were many things that I needed to work on.

There are three distinct members of the Godhead, each with individual attributes but united in purpose. Do we recognize and appreciate each of them? Do we realize what they do for us and how they love us?

I recently re-read the personal history of my great-grandmother Armenia Willey Lee. Armenia, at the age of nineteen, married a man who had recently lost his wife. He had five children. They moved to Canada and settled in Cardston where she gave birth to an additional five children. After nine years of marriage, Armenia's husband died suddenly. She writes, "Now, ten I have to mother, and without an earthly father, my burden seems heavy—hard to bear, but God will hear my feeble prayer. . . . Sometimes the responsibilities of family, the businesses, sickness, poverty, quarantines, trying to comfort the bereaved when often my own heart is breaking, loneliness . . . all seem to[o] much, but the power of the Priesthood is continually manifested in my behalf." She writes of the temple, music, Church callings, service, good friends, as things that helped her along the way. She also testifies of the divinity of Jesus Christ and the sustaining power that she felt as she stood and pressed forward. Armenia Willey Lee later served as the matron of the Cardston Alberta Temple for over twenty years. I have a legacy passed on to me of standing fast in the faith and relying on the Lord.[10]

We have but a few short years here on earth. Our eternal destiny is dependent on how we spend this time. Life has many layers, we are stretched in different directions, time is limited, and our lists are long. What are our priorities? What are the most important things in life? May I submit to you a foundation—a layer of life that should be paramount: Take the time to draw near to Heavenly Father, come to know and love the Savior, and live worthy of the constant companionship of the Holy Ghost. Live your life in such a way that you feel close to the members of the Godhead. After this foundational layer, other important layers are added such as family, callings, and so on, but we are responsible first and foremost for our own personal salvation and each of us needs to be anchored in Christ.

As we press forward, trying our best to be obedient and live righteously, a real spiritual power comes into our lives and lifts us. Have you felt it? This spiritual power gives us confidence. We can do anything that we are asked to do with the help of the Lord. Ammon gloried in the strength of the Lord. In Alma 26:11–12 he says, "I do not boast in my own strength, nor in my own wisdom; but behold, my joy is full, yea, my heart is brim with joy, and I will rejoice in my God. Yea, I know that I am nothing; as to my strength I am weak; therefore I will not boast of myself, but I will boast of my God, for in his strength I can do all things; yea, behold, many mighty miracles."

I bear testimony to you that the gospel of Jesus Christ is true. Stand confidently in the strength of the Lord. Numerous people, some who have gone before and some who are yet to come, are cheering you on. You know the truth, you have "the breastplate of righteousness, . . . the helmet of salvation, and the sword of the Spirit." The "shield of faith" will help you "to quench all the fiery darts of the wicked" (Ephesians 6:14–17). You can do it! May I end with a few favorite scriptures:

"But who may abide the day of his coming? And who shall stand when he appeareth?" (Malachi 3:2); "The house of the righteous shall stand" (Proverbs 12:7); "The Word of our God will stand forever" (Isaiah 40:8); "The wicked shall not stand" (D&C 29:11); "And the rain descended, and the floods came, and the winds blew, and beat upon that house; and it fell not, for it was founded upon a rock" (3 Nephi 14:25); "The Lord will give strength unto his people, the Lord will bless his people with peace" (Psalm 29:11).

NOTES

1. Young Women Theme, *Young Women Personal Progress: Standing As a Witness of God,* (Salt Lake City: The Church of Jesus Christ of Latter-day Saints, 2001), 6.
2. Young Women Theme, *Young Women Personal Progress,* 5.
3. Jeffrey R. Holland, "To Young Women," *Ensign,* November 2005, 28.
4. *True to the Faith: A Gospel Reference* (Salt Lake City: The Church of Jesus Christ of Latter-day Saints, 2004), 74–75.
5. Janice Kapp Perry, "A Child's Prayer," *Children's Songbook of The Church of Jesus Christ of Latter-day Saints* (Salt Lake City: The Church of Jesus Christ of Latter-day Saints, 1989), 12–13.
6. *True to the Faith,* 14–15, 20.
7. Russell M. Nelson, "Jesus Christ—the Master Healer," *Ensign,* November 2005, 88.
8. © 1997 John V. Pearson, "Behold the Wounds in Jesus' Hands." Used by permission.
9. *True to the Faith,* 82–84.
10. Personal history of Armenia Willey Lee, compiled by her daughter Caroline Lee Pitcher.

SERIOUS REFLECTION
PRECEDES REVELATION

Maurine Jensen Proctor

LATE NIGHT BLESSING

One night several years ago, we had an older teenaged daughter who did not arrive home at her 12:00 A.M. curfew. One o'clock came and she still wasn't there. We did what any good parent would do. We panicked. We prayed. We made those awkward middle-of-the night calls to her friends. 2:00 A.M. Our imaginations were flying with the dangers she could be in. We prayed harder. I cried with worry. The minutes seemed like hours. 2:30 A.M. 2:45 A.M. The world was asleep, but not us—two parents so concerned about their precious daughter.

At last, at 3:00 A.M., we heard the front door quietly open. We had decided on a plan to divide and conquer. My husband, Scot, stayed up in our bedroom and prayed for me while I went down to greet our daughter. The conversation was just as you might expect. I pounced on her—not literally, but there was an edge in my voice. I reminded her of her curfew, told her of the dangers and temptations abroad in the late hours of the night, described our painful worry. She was defensive. She asked if we didn't trust her. She told me she was too old for a curfew. The more she resisted my teaching, the more tension you could feel between us. I badly needed help to turn this divisive conversation into a sweet moment of

Maurine Jensen Proctor is the Editor-in-Chief of Meridian Magazine, *a daily Internet magazine for Latter-day Saints, and an author of several books. She and her husband are the parents of eleven children.*

love and teaching. Just then I felt the influence of my husband's prayers for me, and an impression came into my mind. I had been praying much for this daughter of ours whom I had been worried about, and just a few days earlier the Spirit had whispered something about her to me.

I stopped my lesson on curfews for a moment. I was still and knew that this was the moment to tell her that message. "Last week," I said, "the Spirit told me something about you." Her defensiveness began to fall from her. It was the first time she really heard anything I said. "Tell me," she said with real eagerness. I answered, "The Spirit told me not to worry so much about your life because all things would work out for you, that everything would be OK."

"You heard that, Mom?" she asked eagerly. "What else did the Spirit tell you about me?" Listen to the faith in her questions. She believed that God had heard my prayers and answered them. She believed that He knew her and loved her. When I saw her as a daughter pushing the limits by coming in late, He knew her heart and the faith that resided there that maybe she didn't even know. Our conversation became sweet as I told her of the confidence that God had in her and His personal knowledge of her heart and goodness.

Before, she had been eager to escape my presence and lecture. Now, she was all ears and we talked until 4:00 A.M. I count it as a treasured hour in my mothering experience.

Dark Stones Filled with Light

Our life is like the journey the Jaredites anticipated across the stormy sea, where the mountain waves would dash them, they would be carried here and there by the winds, and they would be tossed by strong currents. This is a journey they could not survive in the dark.

Was there anything really wrong with the way I began talking to my daughter? Given the situation, I was fairly calm, I was clear, I was also right. The problem was, until the Spirit stepped in with His light, I was also totally ineffective.

The brother of Jared sought a remedy for the darkness. Putting his mind and muscle to the solution, "[he] did molten out of a rock sixteen small stones; and they were white and clear" (Ether 3:1). I have tried to imagine the work and ingenuity it would take to melt stones. What kind of grueling labor in those times was required to create a heat source that can melt stones, sweat dripping from your brow?

Yet still, after all the brother of Jared could do, after hard labor and effort, and the best solutions of his own mind, still he had only 16 dark stones. They were only able to shine when they were touched by the finger of God.

So often we are troubled and hurried, wearied and overworked. We create the equivalent of 16 stones in our lives, and that is where we leave it. The world is so much with us that we do not take the journey to the mountaintop and let the Lord touch all our dizzying effort with His finger and fill it with light. Until He does, however, we are still traveling in the darkness.

Busy and hurried, too often we take "natural man" solutions, rushing from one task to another, checking off the items on our lists to do in a mad frenzy without the transforming power that spiritual insight always brings. The alarm rings in the morning, and we are off and running, too often without climbing the mountain to have the stony pieces of our lives touched with light.

THE TRUE MEANING OF BLINDNESS

The scriptures have a phrase for this hurry in the darkness. They speak of people who suffer from "the blindness of their minds" (Alma 13:4). The original Greek translation of this word "blindness" yields some profound understanding. The word is *po'-ro-sis*, which means: "the covering with a callus; obtrusiveness of mental discernment, dulled perception."[1]

Paul, before his conversion, had this kind of blindness. He went around with great zeal doing the wrong thing, spewing out anger and persecuting Christians. Then, after his vision on the road to Damascus, he literally lost his sight. He was blind until he received a blessing and the scales fell from his eyes.

Then there was the man, blind from birth, whom the Lord healed on the Sabbath. Of course there was a ruckus and the Pharisees called the man before them, wanting to know how he had received his sight. They said, "[The man who has done this] is not of God, because he keepeth not the sabbath day." Healing was not a Sabbath day activity to their way of thinking. The healed man answered, "Whether he be a sinner or no, I know not: one thing I know, that, whereas I was blind, now I see" (John 9:15, 25).

Is there anything greater than those moments in our own lives where the scales fall from our eyes, when we can say, "whereas I was blind, now I see"?

Alma says the Spirit enlightens our understandings and expands our minds (Alma 32:28, 34). Conversely, you can feel the lack of the Spirit sometimes when you wander along, dulled and shrunken, blind and blunted in your mind and heart.

FROM BELIEF TO ENLIGHTENMENT

King Benjamin said, "Believe in God; believe that he is, . . . believe that he has all wisdom, and all power, both in heaven and in earth; believe that man doth not comprehend all the things which the Lord can comprehend" (Mosiah 4:9).

He comprehends the answers to every question we have. It isn't His will that we travel in the dark. He knows how to spring us from our limitations and lift the roadblocks. Don't you wonder: How can I love effectively and open my heart to bless those whose lives touch mine? How do I choose between all the possibilities and make the best use of my life? How do I find sustenance for the dry times? What is the song I came to sing? How can I overcome the things that hurt? Who am I? And dear Lord, who art thou?

The Lord offers us His solutions to all of our questions, and He tells us, "I am more intelligent than they all" (Abraham 3:19). There is not a problem we can pose to Him or a challenge so perplexing that He does not already have the answer. How can some of that light be shed into our own minds?

The scriptures reveal a pattern for receiving enlightenment—and it is not one we usually talk about: *Serious reflection precedes revelation.*

Lehi tells his sons about his vision of the tree of life, and they have vastly different reactions. Laman and Lemuel went into a tent and fought about its meaning, but Nephi turned his mind to serious reflection. His mind became a fertile field in which the Lord could plow. He says, "As I sat pondering in mine heart I was caught away in the Spirit of the Lord, yea, into an exceedingly high mountain, which I never had before seen, and upon which I never had before set my foot" (1 Nephi 11:1).

Laman and Lemuel's debate in the tent did not lead to revelation. Nephi's pondering opened the door to an expansive revelation that has blessed us all. Serious reflection was Nephi's way of being, for he tells us later, "My heart pondereth continually upon the things which I have seen and heard" (2 Nephi 4:16).

SERIOUS REFLECTION

In October of 1918, Joseph F. Smith received a glorious vision of Christ coming to the host of the dead. The record of that vision is now found in section 138 of the Doctrine and Covenants. In this vision he saw the joy and gladness of the innumerable company of spirits who had been faithful in the testimony of Jesus Christ. What opened his eyes to receive this powerful experience? He said, "I sat in my room pondering over the scriptures," and again, "As I pondered over these things which are written, the eyes of my understanding were opened" (D&C 138:1, 11).

Joseph Smith tells us that before he received his First Vision of the Father and the Son, his "mind was called up to serious reflection" (Joseph Smith—History 1:8). What is serious reflection? It is focused and concentrated thought, like sunlight through a magnifying glass that will burn a hole in paper. It is not superficial. It does not flit around from one distraction to another. It does not leap off course or waver like the waves of the sea.

We receive further insight on this from Oliver Cowdery's description of Joseph the night that Moroni first visited him. Oliver writes, "On the evening of the 21st of September, 1823, previous to retiring to rest, our brother's mind was unusually wrought up on the subject which had so long agitated his mind—his heart was drawn out in fervent prayer, and his whole soul was so lost to every thing of a temporal nature, that earth to him had lost its charms, and all he desired was to be prepared in heart to commune with some kind messenger who could communicate to him the desired information of his acceptance with God.

"At length the family retired, and he, as usual, bent his way, though in silence, where others might have rested their weary frames 'locked fast in sleep's embrace,' but repose had fled, and accustomed slumber had spread her refreshing hand over others beside him—he continued still to pray—his heart, though once hard and obdurate, was softened, and that mind which had often flitted, like the 'wild bird of passage,' had settled upon a determined basis not to be decoyed or driven from its purpose."[2]

I love that image of our thoughts as a "wild bird of passage." How often they are! And how often we wish they were not that way.

When I think of a wild bird of passage, I remember the day that a bird flew into our office through an open window. It could not find its way out, and in its panic it flew from one side of the room to the other in useless flutterings. We watched it swoop from corner to corner, dashing about and making no progress. That sort of panic is in great contrast to Joseph's determined prayer that would not be decoyed or driven from its purpose.

DISTRACTIONS KEEP US FROM REVELATION

Prayer and spirituality demand mental discipline and focus. Is it any wonder that this kind of prayer does not lead to revelation: "Dear Heavenly Father, Thank thee for . . . did I thaw the meat for dinner? Bless us to . . . I hope this won't take long. I have so much to do. And please bless . . . Is the party Friday or Saturday night?"

Distractions are the enemy of pondering and serious reflection. It doesn't always take a major sin to leave us blind. Enough little things that turn our heads will do. C. S. Lewis captures this idea in his book *The Screwtape Letters*. The premise is that these are a series of letters from Screwtape, a senior devil to a junior devil teaching him the best way to tempt the mortal to whom he is assigned.

Screwtape explains, "I once had a patient, a sound atheist, who used to read in the British Museum. One day, as he sat reading, I saw a train of thought in his mind beginning to go the wrong way." In other words, this sound atheist considered for a moment that there might be a God. He had a moment of serious reflection about the divine and eternal.

Screwtape says, "Before I knew where I was I saw my twenty years' work beginning to totter. If I had lost my head and begun to attempt a defence by argument I should have been undone. But I was not such a fool. I struck instantly at the part of the man which I had best under my control and suggested that it was just about time he had some lunch. [God] presumably made the counter-suggestion . . . that this was more important than lunch. At least I think that must have been His line for when I said 'Quite. In fact much *too* important to tackle at the end of a morning,' the patient brightened up considerably; and by the time I had added 'Much better come back after lunch and go into it with a fresh mind,' he was already half way to the door." Of course, Screwtape reported with satisfaction, the distraction worked, and by the time the man was out the door and had seen a No. 73 bus and a newsboy, he was back to what he called "real life" and the thought of God never returned to his mind.[3] Why tempt us with dark deeds, when our heads can be so easily turned from eternal things by a distraction?

OF DEEP IMPORT

Not only are our lives riddled with distractions, too often we think the distractions are what life is all about. We become "caught in the thick of thin things."[4] In fact, should we have a moment of quiet, too often we actively seek to fill it with more distractions. We turn on radios in cars, or work to the background of the television's blare. We stay on the shore playing with plastic beach toys instead of wading into the deep water where so much waits to be discovered.

Joseph Smith said, "Deep water is what I am wont to swim in" (D&C 127:2), and he also said, "The things of God are of deep import; and time, and experience, and careful and ponderous and solemn thoughts can only find them out. Thy mind, O man! if thou wilt lead a soul unto salvation, must stretch as high as the utmost heavens, and search into and contemplate the darkest abyss, and the broad expanse of eternity—thou must commune with God."[5] He said this in the context of saying that in too many of our classes and gatherings we have been light-minded, "vain and trifling," and unfocused in our direction.

We cannot understand the answers to questions we have not asked.

God cannot share His deep knowledge with those who are not interested in the elementary curriculum. In the journey to understand the vast expanse that God would teach us about our own lives and the universe beyond, vista leads to another vista. Impressions come to minds open to be taught, not those already rattling with trifles.

But, we want to cry out: "My life is fragmented and torn to pieces by obligations and duties, all the nits and gnats of mortality. I cannot help it. It's the condition and jangle of the modern world." I say, we must help it. We are the people of God. He has things to tell us that are only accessible to a mind that can often be given to serious reflection. We did not come here to forget our divine destiny under a clutter of random thoughts.

BUZZING FLIES A BLESSING

Once as a young mother I needed an answer to prayer. I got a baby-sitter, took my scriptures and journal and hiked a trail to the top of a mountain where I overlooked a wondrous vista. I sat down, opened my scriptures and journal, and began to pray. Suddenly I heard a buzzing noise, lots of buzzing noises. Flies were everywhere, circling my head, landing on the pages of my scriptures, obliterating my reading. I tried to continue, but it was hard. The flies buzzed and dive-bombed around me, and in great frustration I gathered up my things and went home, thinking I had not received an answer. In reality, I received an answer that has stayed with me my whole life.

I realized that the flies were a symbol. They were like the distractions that too often kept me from a spiritual focus when I needed it so badly. Just as I would have liked to read verse one, a fly landed in the middle of the second sentence. Verse two had two flies. I would love to ponder, to focus on the deep things of the Spirit, but distractions kept me from it. I was like Martha, "careful and troubled about many things" (Luke 10:41), but spiritual focus was the better part, which too often daily life allowed little time for.

It does not surprise us to find out that in order to learn to play a musical instrument to perfection it requires the utmost concentration, thought, and practice. Why then do we suppose that having the mysteries of God unfolded to us would somehow require little mental energy?

We must decide if we will travel this mortal journey tangled in distractions or find time on a daily basis for the serious reflection and pondering that leads to revelation, whether we will travel in dark barges or have them lit by stones touched by the finger of God. These times are so dangerous we simply cannot afford to travel blindly.

A PATH TO PERSONAL REVELATION

What kind of pondering leads to revelation and answered prayers, to throwing open doors of understanding in our minds?

Nephi helps us here. He gives us clues as to what he was thinking just before he was caught up to that high mountain. First, he says, "I, Nephi, was desirous also that I might see, and hear, and know of these things, by the power of the Holy Ghost" (1 Nephi 10:17). We ponder because we have a real question or challenge. We ponder because we really want to know the truth about something. We want to know things as they really were, "as they really are and of things as they really will be" (Jacob 4:13). *Desire burns in us for heavenly knowledge.*

Abraham left the residence of his fathers in Ur because he said, "Finding there was greater happiness and peace and rest for me, I sought for the blessings of the fathers . . . desiring also to be one who possessed great knowledge and to be a greater follower of righteousness" (Abraham 1:2).

There's that word *desire* again. For Abraham it flung open the door to a new dispensation of gospel light.

Listen to the pitch of desire that led Lucy Mack Smith to ponder and seek for the true religion. She said that "in the anxiety of my soul to abide by the covenant which I had entered into with the Almighty, I went from place to place to seek information or find, if possible, some congenial spirit who might enter into my feelings and sympathize with me.

"At last I heard that one noted for his piety would preach the ensuing Sabbath in the Presbyterian church. Thither I went in expectation of obtaining that which alone could satisfy my soul—the bread of eternal life. When the minister commenced, I fixed my mind with breathless attention upon the spirit and matter of the discourse, but all was emptiness, vanity, vexation of spirit, and fell upon my heart like [a] chill, untimely blast. . . . It did not fill the aching void within nor satisfy the craving hunger of my soul. I was almost in total despair, and with a grieved and troubled spirit I returned home, saying in my heart, there is not on earth the religion which I seek. I must again turn to my Bible, take Jesus and his disciples for an example. I will try to obtain from God that which man cannot give nor take away. I will settle myself down to this. I will hear all that can be said, read all that is written, but particularly the word of God shall be my guide to life and salvation, which I will endeavor to obtain if it is to be had by diligence in prayer."[6] Lucy's words are an expression of serious reflection. Her desire expressed with great emotion "the aching void" and the craving void of my soul.

A GRADUAL TRANSFORMATION OF OUR THINKING

Do you think it was wanting too much for Nephi to desire to see and hear the vision that his father Lehi had told them about? Do you think it was self-important for Abraham to leave home because of his intense desires for righteousness? Was Lucy's desire just too much?

No—they were all answered with profound revelation and blessings on their heads. Their desires for heavenly knowledge were linked to the unwavering sense that God was able to guide them to answers. Too often we are not creatures of too many desires, but shallow, vapid souls wanting too little, refusing to think too deeply.

We live in a universe, as Elder Neal A. Maxwell said, "drenched in divine design,"[7] where wonder is added to wonder. God and His Son Jesus Christ are willing to share the secrets of the universe if we are only willing to receive their gifts (and "not become offended by Their generosity"[8]).

Pondering the scriptures leads to revelation. Joseph Smith had been pondering James 1:5 when he went to the Sacred Grove and John 5:29 when he received section 76 of the Doctrine and Covenants. Joseph F. Smith had been pondering scriptures from 1 Peter 3:18–20 and 1 Peter 4:6 when he received his vision of the spirit world.

Pondering deep things leads us closer to God. The Lord has told us, "For my thoughts are not your thoughts, neither are your ways my ways" (Isaiah 55:8). Yet, He desires our thoughts to gradually become like His thoughts and our ways to become His ways.

As Elder Maxwell said, "All knowledge is not of equal significance.

There is no democracy of facts! . . . As we brush against truth, we sense that it has a hierarchy of importance. . . . Some truths are salvationally significant, and others are not."[9]

What can we ponder? We can ponder what the scriptures mean. We can ponder what the real questions are we need to pray about. Sometimes before I pray, I write my questions down in a notebook, so I don't forget them. Too often something urgent and obvious blinds us to the real issue at hand. What is it that I need to see that I'm not seeing?

We can ponder how the Lord sees our challenges and how He would solve them. We can ponder the tender mercies of the Lord in our lives and what it teaches us about His attributes. Pondering leads us to truths beyond what the "natural man or woman" can find, stability when the world around is reeling, light when we have been traveling blindly. A world of invitation awaits. So many things about our lives we cannot choose, but we can decide where our minds travel.

SURROUNDED BY ENEMIES AND YET . . .

One of my favorite passages is the record of a sleepless night spent by Lucy Mack Smith guarding the chest that held the manuscript of the Book of Mormon. This was during the time the Book of Mormon was being printed in Palmyra. Guards were posted around her home, because enemies of the new Church hoped to steal the manuscript and burn it. That night she could not sleep for pondering. As she said, "I fell into a train of reflections which occupied my mind until the day appeared. I called up to my recollection," she said, "the past history of my life, and scene after scene seemed to rise in succession before me." During that night she thought of her family, of her intense search to find the truth of salvation. She remembered her confidence that God would raise up some-one who would bring the truth to "those who desired to do his will at the expense of all other things." She remembered with "infinite delight" the truths that Joseph had taught her.

She said, "My soul swelled with a joy that could scarcely be height-ened, except by the reflection that the record which had cost so much labor, suffering, and anxiety was now, in reality, lying beneath my own head—that this identical work had not only been the object which we as a family had pursued so eagerly, but that prophets of ancient days, angels, and even the great God had had his eye upon it. 'And,' said I to myself, 'shall I fear what man can do? Will not the angels watch over the precious relic of the worthy dead and the hope of the living? And am I indeed the mother of a prophet of the God of heaven, the honored instrument in performing so great a work?' I felt that I was in the purview of angels, and my heart bounded at the thought of the great condescension of the Almighty.

"Thus I spent the night surrounded by enemies and yet in an ecstasy of happiness. Truly I can say that my soul did magnify and my spirit rejoiced in God, my Savior."[10]

May our ponderings give us light in our journeys, perspective for the moment, and enlightenment in both big things and things that are big to us. One night years ago, when I had been pondering and praying about how to help my daughter, I was given just the right thing to say at the right moment. It was a big thing to me.

NOTES

1. *Strong's New Testament Greek Lexicon*, entry number 4457.
2. Oliver Cowdery, "A Remarkable Vision," *Latter-day Saints' Millenial Star* 1, no. 2 (May 1840–April 1841): 42.
3. C. S. Lewis, *The Screwtape Letters* (New York: HarperCollins, 2001), 2, 3.
4. Robert L. Millet, *When a Child Wanders* (Salt Lake City: Deseret Book, 1996), 11.
5. Joseph Smith, *Teachings of the Prophet Joseph Smith*, sel. Joseph Fielding Smith (Salt Lake City: Deseret Book, 1976), 137.
6. Lucy Mack Smith, *The Revised and Enhanced History of Joseph Smith by His Mother*, eds. Scot Facer Proctor and Maurine Jensen Proctor (Salt Lake City: Bookcraft, 1996), 48, 49–50.
7. Neal A. Maxwell, "Called and Prepared from the Foundation of the World," *Ensign*, May 1986, 36.
8. Neal A. Maxwell, *Neal A. Maxwell Quote Book*, ed. Cory H. Maxwell (Salt Lake City: Bookcraft, 1997), 222.
9. Neal A. Maxwell, "The Inexhaustible Gospel," *Brigham Young University 1991–92 Devotional and Fireside Speeches* (Provo, UT: Brigham Young University Publications, 1992), 141.
10. Smith, *Revised and Enhanced History of Joseph Smith*, 208, 210, 211.

"Thou Didst Hear Me"

Wayne Brickey

Perhaps you heard about the kindergarten teacher who walked about the classroom as the children did their artwork. She stopped beside one little gal who was concentrating very hard. "My, my, Chelsea," the teacher said. "You look pretty serious about your drawing. What is it?"

Chelsea replied, "I'm drawing God."

The teacher paused and said, "But I didn't think anyone knew what God looks like."

Without even looking up from her work, Chelsea replied, "They will in a minute."

Well, Chelsea had a point there. It is our business to know God. As Jesus said in His prayer at the Garden of Gethsemane, it is life eternal to know the Father and the Son (John 17:3). In certain ways, we can actually become better acquainted with God while we are here in this world than we could when we lived in His presence. Of course, as Chelsea and the rest of us learn more about Him, we find that the lessons can't be drawn with a pencil or a crayon. And they aren't learned or taught in a minute.

In fact, this business of getting acquainted with Him—life's main business—is very time-consuming. Which is perfectly all right, of course. From the moment of birth to the moment of death, it is one business

---

Wayne Brickey has been an instructor in the Church Educational System for thirty years and the author of numerous books. He is also the father of a large family.

worth spending our lives on. And it is this business that helps us understand why we have to wait for answers to our prayers.

Permit me to say something obvious about the long, faithful wait: When His answer *seems* to be getting further away, it is actually getting closer. Now that is a simple fact, but a very important one that we sometimes forget. I repeat it in different words: The longer we wait, the more ready we are for the best possible answer. And the more ready we are, the more determined He will be to grant an answer that will surpass our greatest hopes. That is not just a fact about prayer and answers. It is a fact about Him. Knowing this can keep our hopes bright during the long wait. Remember what Joseph Smith declared: "Since the beginning of the world have not men heard nor perceived by the ear, neither hath any eye seen, O God, besides thee, how great things thou hast prepared for him that waiteth for thee" (D&C 133:45).

Not only is the long wait worth it, but it makes a difference. By the time the answer finally comes, we have matured in patience. Oh, how patient our Father is. And oh, how vital it is that we become patient, too. We are learning about Him on the inside, you might say. Instead of just learning what He looks like, we are learning what it feels like to be as He is.

The long, faithful wait also teaches us to put things into his hands, to treat him as a perfectly reliable, living friend. As He sees our long-standing trust in Him, He accepts it as a token of absolute loyalty, a sign of our lasting, durable friendship with Him. When He sees to His satisfaction that we trust Him, and He finally answers, our joy is too great for words. Our relief and gratitude is nearly infinite, not just because we got an answer. We overflow with joy because we staked everything on our belief that He is a true friend, and it turned out that He was all that and more. When the long wait is over, when we contemplate the careful engineering and customizing and timing and thoughtfulness and generosity of His answer, we see that He had not once forgotten us all along.

So it isn't surprising to find our heroes in the scriptures saying things like, "Thou didst hear me." They say this with relief and joy, usually after a long wait. Here is how Alma said it: "And thou didst hear me because of mine afflictions and my sincerity" (Alma 33:11).

He doesn't speak as if the answer came right away. For him and all of us, there is usually this matter of a trial of faith. The trial may be before we pray or it may come after or during, or all of these. But during the trial our Father draws closer to us, and we draw closer to Him.

Notice Alma's words: "because of mine afflictions." Affliction makes a life very interesting, to us and even to the Lord. Alma's prayers were interesting to the Lord because there were important things going on. There was some drama. There was a struggle, a battle for good. Things were at stake. Alma was giving his all. People were in need. What kind of story is it where there is no need, no emergency, no problem, no toil, where there is no place for integrity or heroism or courage? The word for that might be "boring." Alma's situation called for divine help, it called for miracles. Now that was interesting. He was heard because of his afflictions.

But he also mentioned another thing: "Thou didst hear me because of mine afflictions and my *sincerity*." You've probably heard teachers encourage their students to ask questions by saying there is no such thing as a stupid question. There may be one exception to that general rule: the *insincere* question, the fake question, the one asked just to get credit or just to make an impression, the question asked by someone who doesn't really care about the answer. Most teachers don't like that kind of question. They don't like pretended questions or pretended sincerity. They love to answer students who care.

Parents are the same way. Parents love it when a child comes sincerely asking, sincerely conversing, sincerely honoring the connection with Mom or Dad. Most parents would die to honor that kind of seeking. Some parents *have* gladly died for it. In fact, the most dramatic death in all of history was intended to inspire and honor and answer that kind of sincerity in the Father's children.

Alma wasn't guilty of casual prayers or routine, boring, thoughtless prayers. He was hungry. He pled. He begged. You see this in every case where the faithful say that God heard them.

Matthew mentions a lady from across the Palestine border in Canaan. She was a borderline person in the sense that she was not of Israel. Her people were surely to be taught, though not until later in the schedule. But she got Jesus' attention. The eyewitness account says that she *"cried unto him."* Here was a mother. She wasn't asking something for herself. She came begging a blessing upon her daughter who, she said, was "vexed"

(Matthew 15:22). Her cry may or may not have been accompanied by tears. But it was a cry because it came forth from her hungry, unselfish soul. It was sincere—sincere to the bone.

That word "cried" brings to mind the famous case of Enos. He was heard by His Maker when he came to that point of sincerity where, as he says it, "I cried unto him" (Enos 1:4).

And there was the father of Enos, Jacob. He had spent so *long* watching and aching and working and praying and waiting while his loved ones wandered from the truth. When they finally did turn around, his comment is simply, faithfully this: "Now, this thing was pleasing unto me, Jacob, for I had requested it of my Father in heaven; for he had heard my cry and answered my prayer" (Jacob 7:22).

And the list goes on. The list includes Sarah and Abraham, Hannah and her husband, Elkanah, Nephi, Joseph Smith, Elisabeth and Zacharias. . . . You and I could make a list of hundreds we know from the scriptures and from our acquaintances. But our Father could add to the list the names and stories of millions, literally billions of His children whom He has individually heard and individually answered because of their sincerity.

It is interesting that wherever there is selfish insisting and pushing and demanding in our prayers, the sweet tone of sincerity is missing. If we are cajoling God, trying to force His hand, whining and teasing out of our strong ego, we aren't really asking. We are telling. We are somewhat foolishly getting the roles of parent and child mixed up, acting as if He were the servant and we were the god.

Childlike sincerity often increases as our afflictions go on for a time. We finally discover who is the child around here, who is the dependent and needy one. At some point in the long, faithful wait we finally say to Him, "I think I'm getting it now. I think I'm ready, ready not for my will, but Thine. I no longer demand that things be done my way. I no longer insist on what I want. Now I just want to do Thy will. I apologize that I spent so long trying to get my way. But now, please, Father, please just let it be Thy will that is done."

Have you noticed that this can take time, this coming to ourselves, this becoming as a child? Have you noticed that the great Parent in Heaven waits patiently while we go through that change?

Here is a little statement found in our LDS Bible Dictionary in the back of our scriptures. It's under the heading "Prayer." It says: "Prayer is the act by which the will of the Father and the will of the child are brought into correspondence with each other. The object of prayer is not to change the will of God."[1]

If we misunderstand prayer, we may look upon it as an opportunity to talk God into things, to introduce to Him a new idea, to give Him some pointers, or to get Him to change His calendar. You know, like, "Couldn't we hurry things up a little bit here?"

But if I think He is waiting, it may well be that He is waiting for someone to catch up—perhaps someone like me. And He would far rather wait than grant a blessing poorly timed.

Sometimes you come around an aisle in the grocery store and see somebody just standing there, looking back, waiting. It usually turns out that this person isn't doing this for fun. No, when you take a closer look you see they are waiting for a dawdling little child. Now, one kind of parent will be waiting there patiently, maybe even with a bit of a smile on her face. She might explain things this way: "I might as well be patient. I might as well relax while I wait, because this child of mine doesn't move fast, at least not when I want him to. Everything is fascinating and novel to him. He is absorbing it all, or trying to. This is his job as a child, and his job takes time. He's just doing his job. I brought him into this big interesting place. I knew very well what would happen. So I'm not surprised or offended if I have to wait in the aisles." And the mother might even add this: "Besides, my child is still on some sort of schedule he brought from heaven. I guess up there they don't care much about clocks or even calendars."

Or, on the other hand, we might find another kind of parent waiting in the aisle, the kind that stands there fuming, rolling his or her eyes, getting kind of crazy with impatience, saying those familiar words, "Can't you just hurry *up*?" (By the way, that edgy question sounds hauntingly like what we sometimes say to God in our prayers: "Can't you just hurry *up*?")

So, which kind of parent resembles our Eternal Father? He spends a lot of His time, or rather His eternity, doing what? Waiting. He's good at it. He is used to it. He's the one who put us here. He knew we would take time to absorb, to get used to things, to grow, to try and try again. That's our job. By His design, our job takes time.

I repeat: When I am impatiently waiting for Him, it is more likely the case that *He* is waiting for *me,* or for one of His other dawdling children. Here is a little more from that entry in the Bible Dictionary: "The object of prayer is not to change the will of God, but to secure for ourselves and for others blessings that God is already willing to grant, but that are made conditional. . . . Blessings require some work or effort on our part before we can obtain them."[2]

When our Father is kind enough to wait for us, we might want to be courteous about the situation. We might consider showing friendship for Him and trust in Him by being patient with His patience, by loving His love for us, by appreciating His good judgment in matters that we don't understand, by being cheerful toward this grand being who is letting us slowly mature.

I'd like to share with you some words spoken by Lorenzo Snow. He had lived long, and he knew about those long, silent periods that sometimes stretch on before a prayer is answered. As the Lord's mouthpiece on the earth, President Snow said this just a short time before his death:

> My hopes in reference to the future life are supremely grand and glorious, and I try to keep these prospects bright continually; and that is the privilege and the duty of every Latter-day Saint. I suppose I am talking now to some Latter-day Saints that have been sorely tried. . . . Everything sometimes becomes dark to us and we almost forget the relationship that we stand in to the Lord and begin to feel as though it was not what we expected.
>
> I wonder if there are a few here within the sound of my voice that have feelings of this kind, like old Job had, for instance. A poor man who wondered why his children were taken from him; why his herds were destroyed and why his houses, his dwelling, went up in flames, and why he was left without anything. He formerly was a very wealthy man, then was left without anything. . . . The Lord had a certain position in which He sought to place Job in the future at some future time when years and years had rolled away perhaps, and He wanted to try him. He wanted to educate him so that he would not complain, no matter how illy he thought himself treated by the Lord. . . .

. . . We should seek to be calm and cool as Job learned to be calm and cool.[3]

It sounds as if we'd better keep before ourselves a bright, day-by-day, unwavering hope in the future life. It is our privilege and our duty. It will make the long wait go by more smoothly and sweetly. It helps us be uncomplaining, to be pleasant, and as President Snow put it, "calm and cool as Job learned to be." Maybe there is no other way to learn except by having to wait between the time that we feel a great need and the time that it is met.

Let me mention a specific need. I don't know about you, but many of us have been waiting a long time for our bodies to get better—to become more comfortable, more graceful, more functional and . . . well, if we must be honest, to be nicer to look at. You will understand if I say that "the weight drags on." Our poor bodies actually seem to get worse, not better. Maybe some of us haven't actually prayed for a better body, but most of us do long for one. The fact is that, as we said earlier, the longed-for blessing is getting closer every day. And if we live faithfully in the meantime, that body will be wondrous, even to the point of being celestial, with infinite glory and power. I want to read with you more of what President Snow said. He was in the twilight of life, confined to a more and more frail physical body.

> Think of what superior blessings we actually possess. We know that in the future after we have passed through this life, we will then have our [spouses] and our children with us. We will have our bodies glorified, made free from every sickness and distress, and rendered most beautiful. There is nothing more beautiful to look upon than a resurrected man or woman. There is nothing grander that I can imagine that a man can possess than a resurrected body. There is no Latter-day Saint within the sound of my voice but that certainly has this prospect of coming forth in the morning of the first resurrection and being glorified, exalted in the presence of God, having the privilege of talking with our Father as we talk with our earthly father.[4]

Between now and the time when we will converse with our Father face to face, we can beseech Him—our wonderful, faithful friend—in prayer. I testify that He is always waiting to hear from us. He rejoices to do so. He hears every sincere word. He remembers every sincere prayer. I testify that He will pour out blessings such as our eyes have not yet seen, blessings such as our ears have not yet heard, blessings that are too wondrous to have entered into our little imaginations. It will be so, for those who live and pray and wait—faithfully.

NOTES

1. LDS Bible Dictionary, s.v. "Prayer," 752–53.
2. LDS Bible Dictionary, s.v. "Prayer," 753.
3. Lorenzo Snow, in Conference Report, October 1900, 4.
4. Snow, in Conference Report, October 1900, 4.

Centering in the Peace of
Private Prayer

~

Barbara Bradshaw

At the conclusion of the school year my early-morning seminary class presented me with a book. On the inside cover they all wrote loving messages expressing their testimonies and gratitude for a great year together. I would like to share what one girl wrote. In class I had always appreciated her "get to the point" attitude. She wrote:

"Sister Bradshaw, Thanks for a great year of seminary. I'll never forget what I learned"—and then in parenthesis she wrote—"(well I'll forget some of it, but not the important stuff)."

My hope is that what I share with you will be the important "stuff" that you will never forget.

If I could sit knee to knee with you and ask you to tell me about yourself, what would you say?

Would you tell me you are married or never married or widowed or divorced? Would you tell me about your children or your longing to have a child? Would you tell me about late nights and difficult tests because you are a student? Would we share stories about our "perfectly perfect" grandchildren and the joy of grandmothering? Would you tell me you are the Young Women camp director or the Relief Society president or the nursery

---

Barbara Bradshaw is currently serving as a Church service missionary. She has served as a ward and stake Relief Society president, Young Women president, and early-morning seminary teacher. She is married to Cal W. Bradshaw and they have three children and three grandchildren.

leader? Or would you tell me you are investigating the Church or strug-gling to come back into activity?

Would you tell me what you do in your spare time? Do you enjoy reading or running? Do you like to garden or crochet? Would you ask, "What is spare time?" Would you tell me about babies and bottles and changing diapers and wiping noses and picking up toys and tucking little ones in bed at night? Would you share with me how clean and quiet your home is because your children have all grown up? What would you tell me about who you *really* are?

A few weeks ago a dear friend asked this question, "When did you know you were a child of God?" That caused me to pause and think about the past thirty years since my baptism into the Church. I would like to share with you my personal experience about who I *really* am and when I found out that I am a child of God.

As a senior in high school I was invited by a friend named Julie to lis-ten to the missionary discussions. Every Sunday night Julie and I met with the Seventies in her ward, and they taught me the discussions. They taught me just enough of the gospel for me to know it was familiar and it was true. Growing up I didn't have much self-confidence or self-esteem or feelings of self-worth. I had often wondered, who was I? What was my place in the world? At the very first sacrament meeting I attended as a brand new member of the Church, the sacrament hymn answered in a very real way those questions. We sang, "God Loved Us, So He Sent His Son." I would like to share with you the words of the third verse:

> *Oh, love effulgent, love divine!*
> *What debt of gratitude is mine,*
> *That in his off'ring I have part*
> *And hold a place within his heart.*[1]

At the *very moment* of singing those words I *knew* who I was. I knew where my place was. And it changed everything in my life!

Today I would pose a question to each of you: When did you know you are a child of God? Was it when you were baptized? Perhaps you have always had a sure knowledge of being His child. Have you received that assurance during a quiet moment of prayer or a time of great trial in your life? Or are you today wondering who you are and where your place is?

One of the first songs we teach children at home and in Primary is "I Am a Child of God."[2] I think of my two granddaughters Emma and Natalie singing that song at the top of their voices and believing every word of it. When we as women sing those words do we believe every word we sing? Do you know you are a child of God? Do you understand that He knows you best, which is precisely why He loves you the most?

President Gordon B. Hinckley said this, "Believe in God the Eternal Father. He is the great Governor of the universe, but He is our Father and our God to whom we may go in prayer. We are His sons and daughters. Have you ever really thought that you were a child of God and that you have something of divinity within you?"[3]

"He rules over all, but He also will listen to your prayers as His daughter and hear you as you speak with Him."[4]

"To call upon the Lord for wisdom beyond our own, for strength to do what we ought to do, for comfort and consolation, and for the expression of gratitude is a significant and wonderful thing."[5]

To know that we can communicate with Him who rules over all and yet who knows our name, who knows our thoughts and the intents of our heart is an awesome thing to ponder.

We pray for wisdom, for inspiration, for understanding. We pray for protection and we pray for strength in moments of temptation. We pray for family and for friends and for ward members. We pray for missionaries and those who serve our country. We pray over our church assignments and responsibilities. We pray about our jobs and our goals. Amulek counseled us as to what we should pray about: "Yea, cry unto him for mercy; for he is mighty to save. Yea, humble yourselves, and continue in prayer unto him. Cry unto him when ye are in your fields, yea, over all your flocks. Cry unto him in your houses, yea, over all your household, both morning, mid-day, and evening. Yea, cry unto him against the devil, who is an enemy to all righteousness. Cry unto him over the crops of your fields, that ye may prosper in them. Cry over the flocks of your fields, that they may increase. But this is not all; ye must pour out your souls in your closets, and your secret places, and in your wilderness. Yea, and when you do not cry unto the Lord, let your hearts be full, drawn out in prayer unto him continually for your welfare, and also for the welfare of those who are around you" (Alma 34:18–27).

Would you, for a moment, ponder on the blessings of talking *and* listening with the One who knows us best and loves us most? Those blessings are innumerable, and for each blessing you have received I am certain you could share a sweet experience.

I would like to focus on just three blessings that come into our lives when we have genuine and contemplative prayer:

1. To *know* the will of the Lord for us individually. Last May I was released from my calling as stake Relief Society president. That calling had come to me at my release as the ward Relief Society president. I loved serving the women in my ward and stake. But after eight-and-a-half years I was looking forward to a less time-demanding calling. My plan was simple. I would teach the sixteen-year-old Sunday School class. My plan was to have bright, sunny mornings to work in my yard during the summer and beautiful, cloudless days to ski in the winter. My plan was to have long afternoons to organize the countless boxes in my basement and work on my missionary's scrapbook. That was *my* plan.

As I knelt down to pray the night of my release, I asked the Lord to put me where He wanted me. I told Him I would do His will if He would direct me to the place He needed me to serve Him. I offered this same prayer every day. And then I got a phone call from the director of Church Building Hosting where I had been serving a service mission. She asked if I would take on the added responsibility to supervise hosting in the Relief Society Building. I accepted. I had asked for the Lord to place me where He needed me and I would do His will.

As I told my husband of my new assignment—I complained! What about *my* plan? What about the wonderful goal I had set to organize and clean out boxes? What about all the things I was finally going to be able to have the time to do?

A few days later I excitedly went to the mailbox (as mothers of missionaries do) and found a letter from Brigham Young University. It took me several minutes before I even dared to open it. Inside was an invitation from President Cecil Samuelson to serve on the BYU Women's Conference Committee. I had asked the Lord to place me where He needed me and I would do His will.

As I told my husband of my new assignment—I complained! I am just an ordinary person! I am a convert to the Church! What could I possibly add to BYU Women's Conference? That was not in *my* plan.

That night as I knelt at my bedside I asked the Lord for His forgiveness for my complaints and my doubts. Hadn't I told Him I would do *His* will and be where *He* wanted me to serve? During that prayer I got the quiet, unmistakable assurance that the Lord's will for me was to serve Him as the hosting supervisor in the Relief Society Building and to serve Him here at Women's Conference. And He has blessed me with abilities beyond my own. He has taken an ordinary convert, and just as He has in every calling and assignment that has come to me, He has put me in extraordinary circumstances to help me rise to the divinity within me.

This leads me to my second suggestion for the blessings that come from genuine, contemplative prayer.

2. The strength and assurance and time and ability to *do* the will of the Lord. I had the opportunity to serve the young women of my ward in Redmond, Washington, several years ago. We decided to have a Talent Share for Mutual one evening. As we prepared for this event, we encouraged each young man and young woman in the ward to participate. We held it in the cultural hall. We had a spotlight on the stage to illuminate those who were performing. Around the cultural hall were the displays of those who were artistic and creative.

We had youth who sang, played the piano, displayed paintings, shared crafts they had made, read poetry, and told jokes (yes, that *is* a talent!). It was turning out to be a very successful night. In the audience were the youth, the Young Men and Young Women leaders, and the bishopric. And on the back row in the corner, leaning back on their chairs were the Priest-age boys of our ward. Six or seven young men who were less than thrilled about being at a Talent Share activity!

As we neared the end of our evening, someone tapped me on the shoulder, "Sister Bradshaw, I decided to do something, is it OK?" I turned around to see Christine, a brand new Beehive. "Of course, Christine, we would love to hear from you," I responded, assuming that she would be singing. She came from a family of 11 children who loved to sing! And so I passed the word to our emcee that our final performer would be Christine.

Now, I would like you to picture in your minds Christine—4 foot 10 inches tall, seventy pounds soaking wet, long red hair. As she approached the stage the lights in the cultural hall were dimmed. I sensed groans from the back row of Priests who had to sit through one more number. Christine surprised all of us when she walked out onto the stage with a music stand in one hand and a *trumpet* in the other! I didn't know Christine played the trumpet, and as it turned out she had only been taking lessons for a few weeks.

As she raised the trumpet to her lips, there was silence in the cultural hall. As she blew into the instrument, there was still silence! She tried again—silence. She tried again—still silence. She tried once more and this time something close to a few notes came out. Her face began to match her red hair. I wanted to do something but wasn't quite sure what it was I should do. I glanced back into the dark at the row of boys and hoped they caught my glare. I didn't want anyone to laugh or tease or cause Christine more discomfort than she was already having.

As she continued to try to blow air into that trumpet and make something come out, she looked into the dark cultural hall where the audience was seated. And then one of those boys sitting in the dark corner, leaning back on his chair called out, "Hey, Christine! Come on—you can do it!" I knew by the look on Christine's face that she recognized the voice of her sixteen-year-old brother, David. "Come on, I know you can do it!" he repeated. David then got out of his seat and walked right up to the stage so she could see his face. Christine then put that trumpet to her lips and played the most beautiful trumpet solo any of us had ever heard.

We too have an Older Brother who is cheering us on. He encourages us, "Be of good cheer, little children; for I am in your midst" (D&C 61:36); "Be of good cheer, and do not fear, for I the Lord am with you, and will stand by you" (D&C 68:6); "Be of good cheer, for I will lead you along" (D&C 78:18); "In the world ye shall have tribulation: but be of good cheer; I have overcome the world" (John 16:33).

He carries our burdens. We are told in Psalms, "Cast thy burden upon the Lord, and he shall sustain thee" (Psalm 55:22). In Matthew we are taught and comforted by these words, "Come unto me, all ye that labour and are heavy laden, and I will give you rest. Take my yoke upon you, and learn of me; for I am meek and lowly in heart: and ye shall find rest unto your souls. For my yoke is easy, and my burden is light" (Matthew 11:28–30).

He sets the example of *doing* the Father's will, "For I came down from heaven, not to do mine own will, but the will of him that sent me" (John 6:38).

In the April 2006 general conference, Elder Henry B. Eyring shared his personal experience about praying to know and do Heavenly Father's will. "Once . . . I prayed through the night to know what I was to choose to do in the morning. I knew that no other choice could have had a greater effect on the lives of others and on my own. I knew what choice looked most comfortable to me. I knew what outcome I wanted. But I could not see the future. I could not see which choice would lead to which outcome. . . .

"I prayed, but for hours there seemed to be no answer. Just before dawn, a feeling came over me. More than at any time since I had been a child, I felt like one. My heart and my mind seemed to grow very quiet. . . .

"Somewhat to my surprise, I found myself praying, 'Heavenly Father, it doesn't matter what I want. I don't care anymore what I want. I only want that Thy will be done. That is all that I want. Please tell me what to do.'

"In that moment I felt as quiet inside as I had ever felt. And the message came, and I was sure who it was from. It was clear what I was to do. I received no promise of the outcome. There was only the assurance that I was a child who had been told what path led to whatever He wanted for me."[6]

The third blessing I would suggest to you that comes from praying to our Heavenly Father is:

3. To *feel* His love. In the Doctrine and Covenants we read that if we pray always, the Lord will pour out His Spirit upon us and great shall be the blessing that comes to us (D&C 19:38). Kathleen Hughes, first counselor in the Relief Society general presidency, teaches us about this blessing: "One of the most sublime experiences is to feel in prayer the warmth of the Spirit—a clear manifestation to us that Heavenly Father hears us and loves us. Equally sweet is the recognition as we go about the activities of our lives that a prayer has been answered, that we have

experienced a miracle in our lives. Once again we have received a manifestation of His love for us."[7]

Shortly after Bonnie Parkin was sustained as the Relief Society general president, I was speaking to a group of students at Utah State
University. I was speaking about "Belonging to Relief Society." I told those
students of Sister Parkin's desire that all Relief Society sisters feel the love
of the Lord daily. I then asked them to share with me a time they had felt
the Lord's love for them personally. They told of moments during scripture reading and moments during prayer when they felt His love. One
young woman told of receiving her patriarchal blessing and knowing that
she was loved by the Lord.

I will never forget the reply of one soft-spoken girl who told me the
only time she had ever felt the Lord's love was when she went to the
temple, dressed in white and surrounded by others dressed in white. She
felt He really loved her and was mindful of her. She then went on to say
that when she left the temple and went out into the world that "the
world" made her feel unloved and unappreciated and unworthy, but for
those precious hours spent in the Lord's house she felt His love for her.

I challenge you to write down these words: "I feel the love of the Lord
for me when" and fill in the blank space. And then when you kneel to
pray to close the day just give thanks. Don't ask for anything. Just thank
Heavenly Father for your family, for your friends, for safety, for health, for
your body, for the beauty of this earth, for service given, for service
received, for clean water, for a warm bed, for clothes to wear and a washing machine to wash them in, for eyes to see and ears to hear and hands to
do good for others, and especially give thanks for our Savior, Jesus Christ.
For His atonement, for His love, for His example, for His willingness to
provide the way for you and me to return to our heavenly home. When
you pray a prayer of gratitude, I promise that you will feel the love of the
Lord for you.

May each of us "center in the peace of private prayer." I testify to you
that blessings will come to you as you communicate with the One who
knows you best and loves you most.

NOTES

1. Edward P. Kimball, "God Loved Us, So He Sent His Son," *Hymns of The Church of Jesus Christ of Latter-day Saints* (Salt Lake City: The Church of Jesus Christ of Latter-day Saints, 1985), no. 187.
2. Naomi Ward Randall, "I Am a Child of God," *Children's Songbook of The Church of Jesus Christ of Latter-day Saints* (Salt Lake City: The Church of Jesus Christ of Latter-day Saints, 1989), 2.
3. Gordon B. Hinckley, "Inspirational Thoughts," *Ensign*, March 2006, 3.
4. Gordon B. Hinckley, *Discourses of President Gordon B. Hinckley, Volume 2: 2000–2004* (Salt Lake City: Deseret Book, 2005), 219.
5. Gordon B. Hinckley, *Discourses of President Gordon B. Hinckley, Volume 1: 1995–1999* (Salt Lake City: Deseret Book, 2005), 57.
6. Henry B. Eyring, "As a Child," *Ensign*, May 2006, 16.
7. Kathleen Hughes, "Feeling the Love of the Lord through Prayer," *Ensign*, July 2004, 61.

ACCORDING TO YOUR PRAYERS

—◆—

Margaret Lifferth

In the early days of the Church, my great-grandmother, Johanna Hansen, joined the Church in Denmark, causing great sorrow to her parents. One day her father found her in the back of the house among the trees, pouring out her heart to God in prayer. For him, that was the last straw. He disowned her and sent her out into the streets. She eventually immigrated to Utah, married, and raised five faithful children, including my grandfather. A few lines of testimony written on her tombstone to all of her posterity begins with these words: "My children remember your prayers/And daily live thereby."

The act of prayer that so enraged her father and caused her to be forced from her home was the very principle she wanted her children to remember and apply first in their lives.

Primary children all over the world sing a beautiful song entitled "A Child's Prayer." The song begins with these two questions. "Heavenly Father, are you really there? And do you hear and answer ev'ry child's prayer?"[1]

I suspect that at some point each of us has asked those same heartfelt questions. I can imagine my grandmother Johanna asking those questions as she was seeking spiritual truth. And I can almost hear her reply to us

---

Margaret Lifferth serves as a first counselor in the Primary general presidency. A homemaker, she is a wife, mother, and grandmother.

with these words from the song: "Some say that heaven is far away, But I feel it close around me as I pray."

What is prayer and how do we pray? Listen to the next few lines of the song.

> Heavenly Father, I remember now
> Something that Jesus told disciples long ago:
> "Suffer the children to come to me."
> Father, in prayer I'm coming now to thee.[2]

How do we come to the Father? Listen to the words of the Savior:

"And when thou prayest, thou shalt not be as the hypocrites are: for they love to pray standing in the synagogues and in the corners of the streets, that they may be seen of men. Verily I say unto you, They have their reward.

"But thou, when thou prayest, enter into thy closet, and when thou hast shut thy door, pray to thy Father which is in secret; and thy Father which seeth in secret shall reward thee openly.

"But when ye pray, use not vain repetitions, as the heathen do: for they think that they shall be heard for their much speaking.

"Be not ye therefore like unto them: for your Father knoweth what things ye have need of, before ye ask him" (Matthew 6:5–8).

The Pharisees prayed publicly in the synagogues and in the streets. They prayed with vain repetition and much speaking. The Lord withdrew from the crowds and went to solitary places to pray. He taught us to come to the Father with the faith of a child, with humility and a believing heart. Even so, the Savior acknowledges that Heavenly Father already knows our needs and our hearts. So why do we pray?

Prayer is for our benefit. When we kneel down and bow our heads, and ask God for blessings that we need, we are acknowledging our dependence on Him for everything that we enjoy. We recognize Heavenly Father as the giver of all, as the source of power, light, life, and strength. Over and over the scriptures repeat these words of the Savior: "Ask, and it shall be given you; seek, and ye shall find; knock, and it shall be opened unto you" (Matthew 7:7).

Nephi reminds us that "if ye would hearken unto the Spirit which teacheth a man to pray ye would know that ye must pray; for the evil spirit teacheth not a man to pray, but teacheth him that he must not pray" (2 Nephi 32:8). Why? Because when men stop praying, they place confidence in themselves and gradually lose the spirit of God.

Prayer is also a witness that we remember the Lord—morning, noon, and night. We covenant to remember Him every week when we take the sacrament.

In Primary we teach children to pray using the four steps of prayer—addressing our prayer to Heavenly Father, giving thanks, asking for what we need, and closing our prayer in the name of the Savior. Is there anything in this pattern that can help to make our prayers more meaningful? Let's take a look.

Prayer is a communication of a child to his Heavenly Father. Think of the beautiful, pure doctrine that teaches us to simply kneel down and address our Father. When we begin our prayers with "Heavenly Father" we are reminded of who He is. He is a personal, living God who knows our name as well as our heart. We are also reminded of who we are. We are His children, created in His image. He loves us, and we are His "work and his glory" (Moses 1:39).

We thank Him for our blessings. This helps us remember how much He loves us—and how much we, in turn, should do for others.

I have a good friend whose husband was in the hospital a couple of years ago, dying of leukemia. He had had different chemotherapies and a bone transplant and was very ill. Every day she would drive to the hospital to give comfort, encouragement, and support. She told me that one of the most difficult things was anticipating what news would greet her as she arrived each day at the hospital. Sometimes everyone was so hopeful, but often she was greeted with another crisis in her husband's health. The worry and the roller coaster of emotion was wearing her down. Even touching the button for the hospital elevator caused her stomach to wrench with anxiety.

To help her prepare for these daily ups and downs, she decided that during the thirty-minute drive to Salt Lake she would think of as many blessings as she could. She related that it was a wonderful time of reflection. She could feel the Lord's love for her, and in every part of her life she recognized and acknowledged His blessings. Those drives to the hospital regularly turned into prayers of thanksgiving. With prayers of gratitude, she was strengthened to be able to minister to the needs of her husband.

Prayer is also a time to ask for blessings. What are the desires of our heart? For what do we pray? Christ said this, "After this manner therefore pray ye: Our Father which art in heaven, Hallowed by thy name.

"Thy kingdom come. Thy will be done in earth, as it is in heaven.

"Give us this day our daily bread.

"And forgive us our debts, as we forgive our debtors.

"And lead us not into temptation, but deliver us from evil: For thine is the kingdom, and the power, and the glory, for ever. Amen" (Matthew 6:9–13).

Christ's prayer teaches us to pray for daily needs, forgiveness, and strength against temptation. Other scriptures teach us to also pray for crops, fields, households, mercy, comfort, protection, the Holy Ghost, gifts of the Spirit, love, and testimony.

In fact, in Alma we are told that "ye must pour out your souls in your closets, and your secret places, and in your wilderness" (Alma 34:26). Don't you love that image of "pouring out your souls"? That was the phrase my grandmother used to describe her fervent prayer. I know that you can remember times when you have done that. Alma continues that we must "let your hearts be full, drawn out in prayer unto him continually for your welfare, and also for the welfare of those who are around you" (Alma 34:27).

We can and we must ask, knock, and seek for a variety of blessings. But in those moments of pouring out our souls and asking with full hearts, we must remember one very important principle. It is taught in the Lord's prayer with these words, "Thy will be done in earth, as it is in heaven" (Matthew 6:10). This principle was reaffirmed when the Lord prayed, "Remove this cup from me: nevertheless not my will, but thine be done" (Luke 22:42).

Is it possible that sometimes when we pray we are like a hungry child asking only for candy. In our prayers, do we say, "Heavenly Father, this is the blessing I want," when what we really need and what He would give us are the rich experiences that will nourish our souls, increase our growth, and keep us on the path that will bring us home to Him. Many times the answers to our prayers are those refining experiences that we may not recognize as blessings.

Let me illustrate this idea with the story of Alma and Mosiah and their rebellious sons. Alma the Younger and the four sons of Mosiah were literally "seeking to destroy the church" (Mosiah 27:10). And then the angel appeared to them. He spoke with a voice of thunder and shook the earth so that those five young men fell to the earth. And when he had their attention, the angel said, "I come to convince thee of the power and authority of God, that the prayers of his servants might be answered according to their faith" (Mosiah 27:14). Whose prayers? Yes, the prayers of Alma specifically and also his people, and I can well imagine the prayers of Mosiah.

After their miraculous conversion, Mosiah's four sons wanted to go on a mission—to the Lamanites in the land of Nephi, of all places. Mosiah was not thrilled with this prospect; in fact, scripture tells us that the four sons had to "plead with their father many days that they might go up to the land of Nephi" (Mosiah 28:5). If you have teenagers, you know what that's like.

Mosiah bought himself some time by saying he would pray about it. He "inquired of the Lord if he should let his sons go up among the Lamanites to preach the word. And the Lord said unto Mosiah: Let them go up . . . and I will deliver thy sons out of the hands of the Lamanites" (Mosiah 28:6–7).

With that assurance, Mosiah's four sons, Ammon, Aaron, Omner, and Himni, "took their journey into the wilderness to go up to preach the word among the Lamanites" (Mosiah 28:9). On the way they did some praying of their own. They "fasted much and prayed much that the Lord would grant unto them a portion of his Spirit to go with them . . . that they might be an instrument in the hands of God to bring . . . their brethren . . . to the knowledge of the truth" (Alma 17:9). By praying to be an instrument in the hands of God, they were in essence saying, "Thy will be done."

Now listen to the Lord's answer to that prayer. "Go forth among the Lamanites, thy brethren, and establish my word; yet ye shall be patient in long-suffering and afflictions, that ye may show forth good examples unto them in me, and I will make an instrument of thee in my hands unto the salvation of many souls" (Alma 17:11).

We learn that the prayers of the four sons of Mosiah would be granted, but that it wasn't going to be easy.

Well, what happened with those four missionary sons? We know they had great success teaching the gospel. But what did the Lord require of them? Ammon battled at the waters of Sebus and cut off the arms of the enemy. He met the king of the land and was almost slain with the sword. What about Aaron, Omner, and Himni? They were rescued from prison by Ammon. When he found them, "they were naked, and their skins were worn exceedingly because of being bound with strong cords. And they also had suffered hunger, thirst, and all kinds of afflictions" (Alma 20:28–29).

Had I been Mosiah, I don't know if I would have thought my prayers of protection were being answered in quite the way I had hoped. And yet, listen to this testimony when Mosiah's sons return home. "And now behold, Ammon, and Aaron, and Omner, and Himni, and their brethren did rejoice exceedingly, for the success which they had had among the Lamanites, seeing that the Lord had granted unto them according to their prayers, and that he had also verified his word unto them *in every particular*" (Alma 25:17; emphasis added).

This story taught me an important principle when my own daughter left on a mission to a country where living conditions are quite basic. I prayed for her welfare every day. I was so excited to receive her first letter from the mission field—until I read it. Living conditions were beyond "basic" and included a neighborhood outhouse, showers from water in a bucket that she bought off an ox-drawn wagon, dirt floors, neighborhood animals in and out of the house, and a sweet native companion that spoke no English. I could only imagine my daughter's feeling of isolation. Reading the letter, I started to cry.

I knelt down to pray for her, but the thought came to me that all the people in that whole country were also Heavenly Father's children, so He must not be too concerned about daily comforts. So I prayed for her to learn the language, make adjustments, and to be healthy. It wasn't long before we learned that she had contracted a tropical fever and was very ill in the mission home.

But she did get better, and she did learn the language and loved and taught the people. My prayers were being answered. And then, just before she was to come home, a class five hurricane hit the country in which she was serving, and tens of thousands of people lost their lives in mudslides and floods. My prayers became more earnest. The official word from the mission was that all the missionaries had been brought into the city where the mission home was and that everyone was safe.

I had a little nagging feeling of doubt and suggested to my husband that we call the mission home, "just to make sure." He reminded me that surely they had more to do than answer phone calls from worried mothers. But that nagging feeling stayed with me, and I needed to call. One of the elders answered the phone, and when I inquired about Sister Lifferth, there was a short pause. He told me that the missionaries in her district had not been able to get to the mission home before the hurricane hit. But he assured me that the mission president's car was loaded with supplies and as soon as the roads were repaired, he would be on his way to help, hopefully within a week. Of course there was no mail, no phone, no way to get in touch with her either for the mission president, or for me.

I remember going to the temple, the house of prayer, and there receiving the calming assurance that she was safe and would be home at the designated time. That feeling stayed with me, and because of that answered prayer, I was able to be a voice of comfort for the rest of our family and friends.

Within a month our daughter returned home from her mission, just as scheduled. It was then that we learned that the night the hurricane hit, she and her companion were out teaching. As they left one of their appointments early in the evening, they found that the water in the streets had risen to the middle of their calves. They decided they had better return home. Since much of what was in their apartment was wet, her companion slept on the kitchen table, and my daughter pushed the two kitchen chairs together for her bed. Although they made it through the night, they shared those two dry places with a family of rats.

When morning came, they gathered what food and supplies they had and set up a small relief station at the church. About a week later, when the mission president arrived, the missionaries were fine and had given substantial service in the community. When my daughter arrived home from her mission, I could see in her greater confidence, knowledge, faithfulness, and testimony. I could see that the Lord had answered, not the words of my first frantic prayers, but the desires of my heart, in every particular.

Now, the update. Today, this same daughter is expecting her fourth baby. Her oldest child is five. Who can argue that the best preparation for this time of her life may have been that class five hurricane?

Why am I sharing these stories? It is because when you think your prayers are not being answered, I want you to remember that the Lord knows the desires of your heart. Sometimes we receive what we desire most only as we are "long-suffering and patient in affliction." The Lord will refine us.

Remember that the prayer Joseph Smith offered in the Sacred Grove was a miraculous manifestation of the Lord's love for him as well as a revelation of who he was. But it was the prayer in the Sacred Grove that led to the prayer in Liberty Jail, where the Prophet asks in anguish: "O God, where art thou? And where is the pavilion that coverth thy hiding place? How long shall thy hand be stayed, and thine eye, yea thy pure eye, behold from the eternal heavens the wrongs of thy people and of thy servants, and thine ear be penetrated with their cries?" (D&C 121:1–2).

In this prayer of anguish I hear Joseph asking: "Heavenly Father, are you really there? And do you hear and answer ev'ry child's prayer?" And then comes this answer of assurance, "My son, peace be unto thy soul; thine adversity and thine afflictions shall be but a small moment; and then, if thou endure it well, God shall exalt thee on high; thou shalt triumph over all thy foes" (D&C 121:7–8).

Salvation is not cheap, for us or for our loved ones, and is not salvation the most inner desire of our heart? Is it not the plea for eternal life, for ourselves and others, that moves us to "pour out our souls" to God? Let us not think that when life is difficult our prayers are not being answered.

When we are willing to say "Thy will be done," it is an affirmation that we believe and trust the Lord completely when He tells us, "This is my work and my glory—to bring to pass the immortality and eternal life of man" (Moses 1:39). It is a declaration that we know that as our Father, He knows us better than we know ourselves and that we trust Him to lead us home.

Finally, when we close our prayers in the name of the Savior, it reminds us and confirms to Heavenly Father that we know that it is the Atonement that lifts us from our sins and from our troubles and opens the door to the kingdom of God.

The second verse of that beautiful Primary song "A Child's Prayer" confirms the truth to us:

> *Pray, he is there; Speak, he is list'ning.*
> *You are his child; His love now surrounds you.*
> *He hears your prayer; He loves the children.*
> *Of such is the kingdom, the kingdom of heav'n.*[3]

I testify that Heavenly Father hears our prayers, and that at some glorious day we will know that "the Lord had granted unto [us] according to [our] prayers . . . in every particular" (Alma 25:17).

NOTES

1. Janice Kapp Perry, "A Child's Prayer," *Children's Songbook of The Church of Jesus Christ of Latter-day Saints* (Salt Lake City: The Church of Jesus Christ of Latter-day Saints, 1989), 12–13.
2. Perry, "A Child's Prayer," 12–13.
3. Perry, "A Child's Prayer," 12–13.

FAMILIES ANCHORED IN THE SCRIPTURES

Cheryl C. Lant

One of the most profound experiences I have ever had was when my first child was placed in my arms. I remember feeling the weight, the warmth, and the dampness of that tiny body. I remember thinking that there had never been a more beautiful little girl. And I remember the wonder and awe of parenthood.

Since that time—and eight more babies—I have come to realize that those first moments of joy and excitement have gotten me into a lot of trouble. Parenthood, once started, never goes away. And it takes a lot of work.

Seriously, there is nothing more beautiful or wonderful than being part of a family. And there is no greater responsibility. Families are at the core of our Heavenly Father's plan. "The Family: A Proclamation to the World" states, "The family is central to the Creator's plan for the eternal destiny of His children."[1]

Our Heavenly Father intended for families to be eternal, as the proclamation explains: "The divine plan of happiness enables family relationships to be perpetuated beyond the grave. Sacred ordinances and covenants available in holy temples make it possible for individuals to return to the presence of God and for families to be united eternally."

Families, as defined by our Heavenly Father, bring the greatest

Cheryl C. Lant has served as the Primary general president. She is also the co-founder of a private school. She is a wife, mother, and grandmother.

blessings of heaven. But along with those blessings come great responsibilities. The proclamation states, "Parents have a sacred duty to rear their children in love and righteousness, to provide for their physical and spiritual needs, to teach them to love and serve one another, to observe the commandments of God and to be law-abiding citizens wherever they live."

These are the words of our latter-day prophets. They are founded in the scriptures.

In Doctrine and Covenants 93:40 we read: "But I have commanded you to bring up your children in light and truth."

Doctrine and Covenants 68:25–28: "And again, inasmuch as parents have children in Zion, or in any of her stakes which are organized, that teach them not to understand the doctrine of repentance, faith in Christ the Son of the living God, and of baptism and the gift of the Holy Ghost by the laying on of the hands, when eight years old, the sin be upon the heads of the parents.

"For this shall be a law unto the inhabitants of Zion, or in any of her stakes which are organized.

"And their children shall be baptized for the remission of their sins when eight years old, and receive the laying on of the hands.

"And they shall also teach their children to pray, and to walk uprightly before the Lord."

This scripture goes on to list other things we must teach our children, including Sabbath day observance, hard work, and avoiding materialism (D&C 68:29–32). In fact, as we study the scriptures, we find them replete with admonitions to parents to teach their children. The scriptures give us those principles that we are to teach. They are the word of God, and we are responsible to teach from them.

Now, Satan wants to gain power over our children and our families. In Doctrine and Covenants 78:10 we read: "Satan seeketh to turn their hearts away from the truth, that they become blinded and understand not the things which are prepared for them."

But the scriptures can protect us from Satan if we know them and if we use them. In Mosiah 1:5, King Benjamin testifies of the importance of teaching our children out of the scriptures: "I say unto you, my sons, were it not for these things, which have been kept and preserved by the hand of God, that we might read and understand of his mysteries, and have his commandments always before our eyes, that even our fathers would have dwindled in unbelief, and we should have been like unto our brethren, the Lamanites, who know nothing concerning these things, or even do not believe them when they are taught them, because of the traditions of their fathers, which are not correct."

Isn't it interesting that he says our traditions can lead us astray if we do not read and follow the teachings in the scriptures? Do we have any traditions in our homes and families that would draw our children away from the truth rather than towards it? Do we do anything that would make it difficult for them to accept the truth when they learn it?

Many years ago when my husband was a seminary teacher, he was teaching the young people principles of the gospel concerning the Sabbath day. He was using quotes from the latter-day prophets and from the scriptures. In the middle of the class one young woman burst out, with some emotion, and said, "My dad is a good man; you can't tell me different." Upon questioning her, he found that her family, though active in the Church, had certain "traditions" that they always followed on Sunday that were in conflict with what the prophets were saying. These traditions were making it very difficult for her to accept the teachings of the prophets.

When we anchor our lives and teachings in the scriptures, we can be sure we are where we need to be. We can be sure our children have a firm foundation of righteousness.

Now, how do we accomplish this? We may speak of anchoring ourselves and our children in the scriptures, but we know that, in fact, it is often a challenge to keep ourselves engaged in the scriptures, let alone our children. Anyone who has endeavored to have daily scripture study with teenagers can testify of that. But it is worth the effort. In our home we found there were lots of advantages to reading and teaching from the scriptures.

My son who has five young children put it this way: "When we take our children into the scriptures, Jesus can teach them with His own words, through the Spirit."

Children are smart and strong willed. It is not uncommon for them to question everything their parents tell them. But when you are quoting a prophet or reading directly from the scriptures, it is fairly uncomfortable for them to argue. They may question and want to discuss, but it is not easy to disregard the words of the Lord directly. And as parents, we can find in the scriptures direction and answers to every issue: "For behold, the words of Christ will tell you all things what ye should do" (2 Nephi 32:3).

As we teach from the scriptures, it is important that the children have their own set of scriptures so that they can hold them, turn the pages, and read the words of the Lord directly. Having their own scriptures, they can mark them, become familiar with them, and feel the Spirit from them. They need not be expensive books—the simple economy editions contain the same truth as the leather-bound versions—but let them have their own.

As we begin teaching from the scriptures, one of the first things that we must establish is the principle of obedience. Doctrine and Covenants 84:44 teaches, "For you shall live by every word that proceedeth forth from the mouth of God."

In 3 Nephi 12:20 we read, "For verily I say unto you, that except ye shall keep my commandments, which I have commanded you . . . , ye shall in no case enter into the kingdom of heaven."

Next, teach that the words of the latter-day prophets are modern-day scripture. In Doctrine and Covenants 1:38 we learn that "what I the Lord have spoken, I have spoken, and I excuse not myself; and though the heavens and the earth pass away, my word shall not pass away, but shall all be fulfilled, whether by mine own voice or by the voice of my servants, it is the same."

And in Doctrine and Covenants 68:4: "Whatsoever [the prophets] shall speak when moved upon by the Holy Ghost shall be scripture, shall be the will of the Lord, shall be the mind of the Lord, shall be the word of the Lord, shall be the voice of the Lord, and the power of God unto salvation."

Another important principle to remember is that of discovery. If there is a question or an issue at hand, go to the scriptures together, with your children, to find the answer. Turn to the Topical Guide, even if you may already know the reference you want. Let them discover the answers they need.

We can be assured that the Spirit will aid us in our teaching. He will help us know what to teach, how to teach it, and where in the scriptures we can find help. He can also witness to our children that what we are teaching them through the scriptures is true. Turn with your families to Moroni 10 and experience the "test" of the Book of Mormon. This witness will strengthen them in their resolve to live the principles they are learning.

The more we turn to the scriptures, the more comfortable we will become in the scriptures ourselves, and our own personal lives will be purified. The more we take our children to the scriptures, the stronger they will become. They will have their own strength and testimony, and it will help them make correct choices.

As we teach from the scriptures, we can help our children learn how to apply, or "liken," the scriptures to their lives. Nephi explains: "For I did liken all scriptures unto us, that it might be for our profit and learning" (1 Nephi 19:23).

When we read a scripture with our children, we might ask the question, "Therefore, what?" They then can relate it to the things that are happening in their own lives and decide what the Lord would have them do.

As we teach from the scriptures consistently, we set a pattern for our children in their own lives. They learn that when there is trouble, the Lord has the answers. They grow in faith and confidence in the words of the Lord.

My husband and I began this process of teaching through the scriptures when our children were very young. We read the Book of Mormon stories to them and talked about the obedience of Nephi, the courage of the stripling warriors, and the love of the Savior. Then as they grew, we tried to meet our daily challenges by turning to the scriptures. Let me give you some examples.

Perhaps, in your family, children want to stay up late at night. Rather than scolding them every night about bedtime, turn to the Topical Guide under the word *retire*. There you will find a reference to Doctrine and Covenants 88:124, part of which says, "Retire to thy bed early, that ye may not be weary."

Now, that is great. This tells them not only what to do but also why. Your understanding will increase even more as you read those lines in the context of the entire verse: "Cease to be idle; cease to be unclean; cease to find fault one with another; cease to sleep longer than is needful; retire to thy bed early, that ye may not be weary; arise early, that your bodies and your minds may be invigorated."

And greater insight is received as you read the verses before and after it—verses 123, 125, and 126:

"See that ye love one another; cease to be covetous; learn to impart one to another as the gospel requires. . . .

"And above all things, clothe yourselves with the bond of charity, as with a mantle, which is the bond of perfectness and peace.

"Pray always, that ye may not faint, until I come. Behold, and lo, I will come quickly, and receive you unto myself. Amen."

Then comes the question, "Therefore, what?" What do I need to do?

As I read these verses, I recognize that the counsel about going to bed early can help me as a mother as well as my children. These scriptures also teach me that I must work with my children with love and gentleness. I must pray for my Heavenly Father's help and then be consistent in my efforts. I must work to create a peaceful, orderly environment in my home. All of these things will help me be a better mother while at the same time they help my children learn appropriate behavior. The scriptures are comprehensive in blessing our lives.

Maybe the challenge you struggle with in your family is children who are constantly fighting and arguing. There is a whole column of references in the Topical Guide under the word *contention*. Third Nephi 11:29 is just one of the scriptures listed: "For verily, verily I say unto you, he that hath the spirit of contention is not of me, but is of the devil, who is the father of contention, and he stirreth up the hearts of men to contend with anger, one with another."

Though we learn a principle from this scripture, the challenge of how to change out-of-control behavior still remains. A scripture that could help is Proverbs 15:1: "A soft answer turneth away wrath: but grievous words stir up anger."

So we see that soft voices might help. Another idea is expressed in Mosiah 4:15: "But ye will teach them to walk in the ways of truth and soberness; ye will teach them to love one another, and to serve one another."

Serving one another within the family will increase the feelings of love. These are things we can do to overcome contention. Then comes the question again, "Therefore, what?" What do we need to do to have sweeter feelings in our family? Whom are we following when we fight and argue? How can we serve one another in our home? Let the children help figure out the answers to these questions and decide what they will do based on the scriptures you have read with them.

Couple the words of the latter-day prophets with the scriptures. Let me give you an example. I love the book *Stand a Little Taller* by President Gordon B. Hinckley. If I were to speak to my children on the principle of choice and consequence, I might use the scripture Moses 6:33, which reads, in part, "Choose ye this day, to serve the Lord God who made you." I would then follow with this quote from President Hinckley's book:

"Have you ever looked at a great farm gate that opens and closes? If you look at the hinge, it moves ever so little. Just a little movement of that hinge creates tremendous consequences out of the perimeter. That is the way it is with our lives. It is the little decisions that make the great differences in our lives."[2]

What a great way for us to teach the principle of choice and consequence when our children say to us, "Please, just this once. It's no big deal."

This process of solving our challenges in the scriptures fits every time and every age of our lives. Maybe your children are grown and have families of their own. Our responsibility as parents never ends; it just changes. Your children need your love and support as much when they are grown as they ever have. Give it to them through the scriptures.

If you are alone now, you still have questions and challenges regarding your own personal life that can be answered in the scriptures. By feasting upon the words of the Lord, you will find strength, comfort, guidance, and peace.

Anchoring our children in the scriptures will take some time and some effort—especially at first. But as we really make an effort to do this and to be consistent, our testimonies of the blessing it is to our families will increase. We will love the feeling it brings into our homes—the strong and abiding connection with heaven.

Every truth that we need to learn and that we need to teach our children can be found in the scriptures. By teaching from them we lay a foundation for our children that cannot fail them. Even if they stray for a time—and some of them might—they will have that knowledge of the truth to which they can return.

In our family we found a scripture we wanted to use as our family creed. It is found in 3 Nephi 6:14, and we adapted it to read, "[Being] converted unto the true faith . . . [we will] not depart from it, for [we are] firm, and steadfast, and immovable, willing with all diligence to keep the commandments of the Lord."

I truly believe that anchoring ourselves, our children, and our families in the scriptures is the only way we can protect them from the stormy seas of life. It is the only way to get safely back to our Father in Heaven as an eternal family.

I bear my testimony that God lives. He knows us. He loves us. His Son, Jesus Christ, is our Savior. He has given His word, His gospel, to us through the scriptures so that we might find joy in this life and salvation in the life to come. May we anchor ourselves in His scriptures. May we live by every word that proceeds from His mouth.

NOTES

1. "The Family: A Proclamation to the World," *Ensign*, November 1995, 102.
2. Gordon B. Hinckley, *Stand a Little Taller* (Salt Lake City: Deseret Book, 2001), 147.

MAKE YOUR CHILDREN
PARTICIPANTS IN THE SPIRITUAL
GROWTH PROCESS

———◆———

John Bytheway

Whenever I'm asked to talk about the youth, I feel like answering, "I don't know anything about raising teenagers, I just like to talk to them." My children are a "piece of cake." I've got five, from seven years old to three months old, and although our house is often loud and messy, I wish they would remain as easy to take care of as they are now. Fortunately, I married someone who is much wiser than I am concerning how to raise children, so I'm going to have to learn from her.

My grandpa used to say, "Experience is a dear school, and we fools will learn in no other." Well, I feel like I've spent my whole life as a fool playing "catch up." I learned too late the things I wish I'd known in high school, the things I wish I'd known before my mission, the things I wish I'd known when I was single. I wish I could hear your version of "what I wish I'd known before I had teenagers." Well, one of the great things about the gospel is that, while it can't give us instant experience, we can learn from the experiences of others in the scriptures; the gospel can teach us timeless principles.

Recently, two young men who are close to me have come home early from missions. The reasons were not entirely clear, but it was not because of transgression. Perhaps it was because the work was too hard, or perhaps they were not prepared for the emotional and spiritual stamina missionary

John Bytheway is a part-time religious instructor at Brigham Young University. A popular author, he and his wife are the parents of five children.

work requires. Now that I have three sons of my own, their future missionary service is almost all I think about. How can I help them be prepared and eager to serve missions?

Dr. John L. Lund taught me a couple of things which have helped me as a parent. First, "Parenting is not the art of hanging on, but the art of letting go." He elaborated on that idea by explaining that "parenthood is the gradual transfer of responsibility for your children's lives from your shoulders to theirs."[1] These ideas have motivated my wife and me to teach our children what we have called "competencies." Many times a day I find myself trying to teach my children to do for themselves what I might more easily do for them.

Only recently did I realize that I should also be trying to give them "competencies" in their spiritual lives, perhaps even more than in their temporal lives. In other words, I should be helping them to do for themselves spiritually what before I might have tried to do for them. If I could assure you that over at the Brigham Young University Bookstore there were a limited amount of "teenage testimonies" sitting on the shelf available for purchase, there would be a mass exodus that would rival the run on Albertsons the day the shelves were first stocked with caffeine-free Dr. Pepper. There are times when we wish we could just "give" our children a testimony, hand it to them on a silver platter, but we all know that testimonies don't come that way. Each of us must grow our own.

ASSURANCE, ACTION, EVIDENCE

Recently, Elder David A. Bednar gave a talk entitled "Seek Learning by Faith." The principles Elder Bednar taught will forever change me as a parent and as a teacher. He said that we often emphasize "teaching by the spirit," but not its companion principle "learning by faith." He spoke of the larger spiritual pattern and process of teaching and learning as a sequence of "assurance, action, and evidence" and of the learner's part in the spiritual growth process. The words he chose all come from scriptural statements about faith. Paul taught that "faith is the substance [or the assurance] of things hoped for, the evidence of things not seen" (Hebrews 11:1). Joseph Smith in *Lectures on Faith* declared that faith is "the principle of action in all intelligent beings."[2]

Since hearing Elder Bednar's talk, I've thought of a number of scriptural examples where the Lord requires His children to become participants, or to take action, in the spiritual growth process.

For example, in Luke 17 we read about the ten lepers, who obviously had some assurance that Jesus could help them. The lepers "lifted up their voices, and said, Jesus, Master, have mercy on us. And when he saw them, he said unto them, Go shew yourselves unto the priests. And it came to pass, that, as they went, they were cleansed" (Luke 17:13–14).

In other words, the lepers had some *assurance* that Jesus could help them, but Jesus required them to take *action*. Elder James E. Talmage in *Jesus the Christ* teaches that in order for the lepers to be readmitted to fellowship, they would have to show themselves to the priest.[3] Thus, Jesus was asking them to do what they would do if they were already healed, perhaps, as a test of faith. Note the conclusion of the story: "And it came to pass, that *as they went,* they were cleansed." Note the important principle involved—they were cleansed *as they went.* Not "as they just stood there." They took action and received the evidence. *Jesus made them participants in the spiritual growth process.*

A few years ago, my home stake in Salt Lake City held their youth conference at Snow College. I was the Young Men's president in my ward, and I told the youth conference planners that since I would be there, they could use me as much or as little as they wanted. But they were smarter than that. It would have been easier for them to say, "Round up the youth, stick them in a classroom, put a quarter in John Bytheway, and he'll talk to 'em for three hours," which I would have gladly done had they asked. But just *telling* them the gospel doesn't make them part of the spiritual growth process, as Elder Bednar explained. Apparently, the planners in my stake knew that.

Instead, they went to a tremendous amount of work and planned something else. Each of the youth were "called" on a mission. They spent part of the first day learning the first and second missionary lessons, and then they were divided into companionships (you can imagine all the headaches that entailed—kids wanting to be with their friends as a companion, etc). In conjunction with the leaders of some of the wards in Ephraim, families were selected who would allow the youth "missionaries" to come into their homes and teach the lessons. Some of these families were less active—more headaches for the planners.

Well, to make a long story short, they pulled it off. And after these youth missionaries returned to the chapel, we had a testimony meeting which was something extraordinary. What happened there, I'm almost certain, would not have happened had the leaders just decided to let John Bytheway talk to the kids for three hours.

During the missionary activity, the youth suddenly found themselves in the role of teacher. Not as listeners getting yet another list of gospel do's and don'ts, but as actual teachers of the gospel. They taught, they testified, and they came back to testimony meeting with evidence, real evidence in their hearts of the truthfulness of the gospel. What happened? *The youth conference planners made the youth participants in the spiritual growth process.*

As I listened to their testimonies, I was reminded of a statement by President Boyd K. Packer: "It is not unusual to have a missionary say, 'How can I bear testimony until I get one? How can I testify that God lives, that Jesus is the Christ and that the gospel is true? If I do not have such a testimony would that not be dishonest?' . . .

"Oh, if I could teach you this one principle! A testimony is to be *found* in the *bearing* of it. Somewhere in your quest for spiritual knowledge, there is that 'leap of faith,' as the philosophers call it. It is the moment when you have gone to the edge of the light and step into the darkness to discover that the way is lighted ahead for just a footstep or two. . . .

"It is one thing to receive a witness from what you have read or what another has said; and that is a necessary beginning. It is quite another to have the Spirit confirm to you in your bosom that what *you* have testified is true. Can you not see that it will be supplied as you share it? As you give that which you have, there is a replacement, with increase!"[4]

The young people took action. They heard themselves teach the gospel, and I believe the Spirit helped them to discover, "This really is true, isn't it!"

Several months ago, I visited an institute teacher friend of mine in Austin, Texas. He told me that he doesn't teach in the same way that he used to. Rather than teaching the class what he's already learned, he organizes his lessons in such a way that he leads the students to discover for themselves the truths and principles of the gospel in the scriptures. It's having some wonderful results. Which do you think would have more impact on a young person? If you told them a gospel truth, or if they were led to discover it on their own? Which would do more for their spiritual life? Which method, "stand and deliver" or "lead them to discover," really makes them participants in the spiritual growth process? Also, which would more fully allow the Spirit of the Lord to tailor-make an experience for them?

SOLVE YOUR BOSS'S PROBLEMS

I don't know if you know this, but Willy Wonka is a Mormon. ("Right, Brother Bytheway, and I'm an oompa loompa.") I served my mission in the Philippines more than twenty years ago now, and my mission president was a man named Menlo F. Smith. At that time, he operated all the candy companies that made the Willy Wonka candy. He was a hugely successful businessman who began reading a Book of Mormon he found on the shelf one day, which belonged to his less-active wife. As he took action and read, he obtained spiritual evidence, and ten years later, he was my mission president.

One day I walked into his office and said something like, "President, there's a problem in such and such area, what would you like us to do?" I had interrupted him like this before, and I think he'd had enough. He said, "Elder Bytheway, sit down. Elder, do you want to get ahead in business?" Actually, I didn't know what I wanted to do in my post-mission life, but I said, "Yes." President Smith said slowly and with emphasis, "Solve your boss's problems." Never come to your boss with a problem, always come with a solution! Then he showed me what he called the five levels of delegation.

1. Seek problems, solve them, keep it to yourself.
2. Seek problems, solve them, report back.
3. Seek problems, recommend solutions.
4. Seek problems, ask the boss, "What should I do?"
5. The boss finds out about the problem and comes to you!

This little idea has blessed my life, especially when I worked in a position where I was supervising others. President Smith also taught me that a *good* leader *tells* his people what to do, but a *great* leader *trains* leaders as he leads. I learned that lesson personally when President Smith went to Singapore for two weeks for a mission presidents' meeting. I discovered that if I prayed for help and really thought hard about what President Smith would do in a certain situation, I could usually figure it out. President Smith was trying to give me "competencies." What confidence President Smith built in me when he began to ask me for, and to trust in, my recommendations! (Parenthetically, imagine the burdens we could remove from our bishopric's backs if we would more often come to them with solutions instead of problems and complaints.)

You can only imagine my surprise when I noticed the Lord working this way with one of His prophets in the scriptures. The brother of Jared came to his boss, so to speak, with a problem. In pondering how they would be able to breathe in their small barges, he asked the Lord, "What shall we do for air?" And the Lord answered him. Then the brother of Jared came back with another problem, "What shall we do for light?" And the Lord said, in effect, "Mahonri, what would you like me to do?" He put the brother of Jared, Mahonri Moriancumer, in the role of problem solver.[5] Mahonri went back to the books, and perhaps he read the story of Noah (Ether 2:16–3:6). (A footnote in Ether 2:23 takes you to Genesis 6:16, and the footnote to that verse says that "some rabbis believed [that Noah had] a precious stone that shone in the ark.")

However he did it, the point is the brother of Jared worked on the problem himself, because the Lord, rather than telling him what to do, *made Mahonri Moriancumr a participant in the spiritual growth process.*

You may have also noticed how the Lord teaches us to make decisions. Oliver Cowdery was told, "You have supposed that I would give it unto you, when you took no thought save it was to ask me. But, behold, I say unto you, that you must study it out in your mind; then you must ask me if it be right" (D&C 9:7–8). In other words, you come to me with your recommendation and you ask me if it is right.

For another example on the ward level, the Young Women's president in my ward asked the bishop to speak to the young women about modesty, but Bishop Marsh had a different idea. He brought the priests quorum in to talk to the young women about modesty. It was fascinating! He had to get things going, since some priests are not used to stringing many words together, but once he did, the young women listened to the priests in their own ward teach and testify of modesty, and the young women listened differently than they would to their usual leaders. *Bishop Marsh made the priests participants in the spiritual growth process,* and the young women benefited.

WHY HAVEN'T WE EVER DONE THIS?

As I've been trying to teach my own children, I've watched other dads and sons in my neighborhood. Some of the boys, not even preteens but Primary age, are constantly involved in Little League sports. So in my efforts to keep up with the Joneses, I've had my son in Jr. Jazz basketball and T-ball. I want to give him these basic sports competencies and make sure he doesn't have to experience being picked last on the team at recess. In the midst of all this watching and wondering and hoping I'm being a decent dad to my sons and preparing them for this interesting world, I attended a general conference priesthood session by myself. (My oldest boy is only six, so I'll be going alone a while longer.)

Elder Ronald A. Rasband blessed my life greatly that evening. He said, "We must ask ourselves constantly if that extra sporting event, that extra activity or errand outside of the home is more important than families being together at home. . . . When I was first called to the Seventy some years ago, we were assigned to move to Solihull, England, to serve in the Area Presidency. Sister Rasband and I took our two youngest children with us on this assignment. Our daughter was a young single adult and our son a seventeen-year-old who liked American-style football and played it very well. We were very concerned about them. No friends, no extended family, and no American football! I wondered, 'Would this exciting new experience prove to be a serious trial for our family?'

"The answer came in an early assignment I received. I had been asked to speak to the missionaries at the Missionary Training Center in Preston, England. I called President White of the center and was pleased to hear that he knew of my family's situation. He suggested we include our children on our visit to Preston. Once we were there, he even invited our daughter and son to speak to the missionaries! What a thrill for them to be and feel included and share their testimonies of the Lord's work! [Notice they were asked to share their testimonies—"a testimony is found in the bearing of it!"]

"When finished and after tender good-byes to those missionaries, we visited the beautiful Preston England Temple, which was close to the Missionary Training Center. As we walked near the front door, there stood President and Sister Swanney, the temple president and matron. They greeted us and welcomed us into the temple with, 'Elder Rasband, how would you and your family like to perform baptisms for the dead?' What a wonderful idea! We looked at each other and gratefully accepted. After performing the ordinances and while my son and I were still in the font with tears of joy in our eyes, he put his hand on my shoulder and asked, 'Dad, why haven't we ever done this before?' I thought of all the football games, all the movies we had attended together, all of the good times we had shared—certainly happy memories and traditions that are so important to build.

"However, I realized we had an opportunity to add more meaningful spiritual experiences with our children like what we had experienced in Preston that day."[6]

These words of Elder Rasband and the talk of Elder Bednar have given me more motivation than ever before to make my own children participants in their own spiritual growth.

CHOICES AND CONSEQUENCES

How can we help the youth carry on even when things don't go as they planned? I don't know how well this will work, but I'm going to try to change the way I interact with my children when they come to me with problems. I'm going to assure them to keep the faith, then I'm going to ask them to take action and look for evidence.

When problems arise as they get older, I am going to say something like, "I don't really know why that happened. *But, knowing what you know, knowing that God lives, and knowing that He loves us, what are you going to do next?*" I want them to discover the answer. I want them to have personal experience in relying on their spiritual nature. I want them to build spiritual competencies to prepare them for their missions, their marriages, and for raising children of their own.

Often when bad things happen to young people, they wonder why God would let this happen to them. A basic understanding of the doctrines of the gospel is helpful here. We should not look to God as the source of all our problems—so many of our problems come from the Fall, the fall of Adam, the personal fall that each of us experience, living in this fallen world, among fallen beings, who sometimes fall on us! While I believe that God does not cause our problems, He allows us to experience them, and He is the living assurance that helps us through them. The Fall is the sickness and the Atonement is the cure. The Lord doesn't necessarily remove our problems, but with His atoning power He will help us through them (Helaman 5:12; Mosiah 21:15).

My goal is to help my children see that, with the Lord's help, we always learn more from our tough times than from our easy times.

One of the visual aids I often use while teaching the youth is a stick labeled "choice" on one end and "consequence" on the opposite end. I use it to illustrate a statement of Henry Emerson Fosdick: "He who picks up one end of the stick, picks up the other."[7] I hope it illustrates that every choice has a consequence, for good or bad.

Sometimes our young people believe that if they simply try to do what's right, their life will be without problems. They expect good consequences to *immediately* follow their good behavior. But there's a space between "choice" and "consequence," and very often trusting in the Lord means trusting in His timing.

President Ezra Taft Benson taught: "One of the trials of life is that we do not usually receive immediately the full blessing for righteousness or the full cursing for wickedness. That it will come is certain, but ofttimes there is a waiting period that occurs, as was the case with Job and Joseph.

"In the meantime the wicked think they are getting away with something. The Book of Mormon teaches that the wicked 'have joy in their works for a season, [but] by and by the end cometh, and they are hewn down and cast into the fire, from whence there is no return' (3 Nephi 27:11)."[8]

We can help our children discover that bad things happen to good people. We can help them discover this truth in the lives of Nephi,

Abraham, Job, Joseph of Egypt, Joseph Smith, and even Jesus Christ. We can help them see that Abinadi's last words were not "How could you let this happen to me?" But "O God, receive my soul" (Mosiah 17:19). His ultimate consequence was the best possible consequence, to be with the Lord.

We often hear the youth of the Church being praised and encouraged. You are part of that effort. Elder Neal A. Maxwell once remarked, "Just as the rising generation is here, now, by divine design—so are we who have been placed just ahead of them."[9]

A few weeks ago, I had the chance to give a name and a blessing to my new boy, Timothy. I was informed that a young man was attending that day who had decided that he was an agnostic. Anyway, after the sacrament was passed, I asked my older son Andrew if he'd like to bear his testimony. He said that he would, and my four-year-old daughter, Natalie, looked up at me and asked sincerely, "Can I have a testimony?" "You sure can," I said.

When Natalie got up to the stand, she froze—something she never does at home. I whispered in her ear what to say—"I'd like to bear my testimony," and she repeated, "I'd like to *hear* my testimony," which was greeted with a little laughter. Natalie became embarrassed and retreated into my arms. I looked at the congregation and said with a smile, "We'd like to hear your testimony, too."

So, with Natalie in my arms, I decided to direct my testimony to my children (and the agnostic in the congregation who knew better), and to relate it, as Alma did, to a seed (Alma 32:28–43). Alma wanted his listeners to try an experiment—to plant the testimony of Christ in their hearts, and not cast it out, and to see if it would produce evidence. But Alma made it clear that they would have to water the seed and nurture it and take care of it, and if no fruit grew as a result, it was not because the seed was bad, but because their ground was barren. They would have to become participants in the process in order to receive the fruit.

As parents, we would love to be able to give our children our fully grown and fully ripe testimony. But perhaps the best we can do as parents is tell our young people about the seed, let them see how we have enjoyed its fruits, and give them every opportunity to plant it in their hearts. Then we can lead them to as many discovery opportunities as possible, giving the seed sunlight, water, and nourishment. When Alma taught the Zoramites, he asked them to become participants in the spiritual growth process.

When Joseph Smith wrote the Articles of Faith in the Wentworth Letter, he didn't just pick a few principles which sounded good to list as the first principles of the gospel. Joseph was speaking from experience. Just before the young prophet was visited by the Father and the Son, Joseph was overcome by an evil power and was about to "abandon [himself] to destruction" (Joseph Smith—History 1:16). But he was delivered by his faith in Christ, which led him to pray in the first place. Joseph learned by experience the power of faith in the Lord Jesus Christ.

Later, he allowed Martin Harris to take the 116 pages of translation which were eventually lost. Joseph lost the gift of translation, and he went through severe repentance. Later, after Joseph was allowed to translate again, he and Oliver inquired about baptism and were visited and instructed by John the Baptist himself! Peter, James, and John eventually appeared to restore the Melchizedek Priesthood and the power to bestow the gift of the Holy Ghost. Note the sequence—faith, repentance, baptism by immersion, the gift of the Holy Ghost. Joseph didn't just pull those first principles out of thin air—he experienced them. *The Lord made Joseph a participant in his own spiritual growth.*[10] We can help our children, and the rising generation, experience the gospel by allowing them more opportunities to discover, to act in faith, and to receive evidence.

I pray that you will receive evidence in your hearts of the divinity within you and that the Lord will help you to carry on as you impact the lives of the rising generation.

NOTES

1. John L. Lund, "The Art of Parenting Teens and Other Miracles," BYU Family Expo, April 3, 2000, byubroadcasting.org.
2. Joseph Smith, *Lectures on Faith* (Salt Lake City: Deseret Book, 1985), 1.
3. James E. Talmage, *Jesus the Christ* (Salt Lake City: Deseret Book, 1977), 470.
4. Boyd K. Packer, *That All May Be Edified* (Salt Lake City: Bookcraft, 1982), 339–40.
5. George Reynolds, "The Jaredites," *Juvenile Instructor,* 27:282–85.
6. Ronald A. Rasband, "Our Rising Generation," *Ensign,* May 2006, 47–48.

7. Henry Emerson Fosdick, as quoted by Marion D. Hanks, "Changing Channels," *Ensign*, November 1990, 40.

8. Ezra Taft Benson, *The Teachings of Ezra Taft Benson* (Salt Lake City: Bookcraft, 1988), 352.

9. Neal A. Maxwell, "Unto the Rising Generation," *Ensign*, April 1985, 8–9.

10. See Richard E. Bennett, "Carefully Schooled in the First Principles and Ordinances," *Ensign*, March 2001, 50–53.

LOVING AND CARING FOR EACH OTHER

Richard N. Williams

My mother taught me many good things. I count among them how to iron my own clothes, darn my own socks, and how to quilt. She also taught me that the dishes are not finished until the kitchen stove is clean. These have been blessings. She also taught me some important spiritual things. Much of this teaching occurred during what seemed like long days spent with her as a preschooler and later as a child. I remember vividly how my preschool mind whirled a bit and the feeling of "nausea," or existential angst, that swept over me when she taught me that after death we live forever—that time has no end in the eternities. When I think about eternity just right, I can feel that same feeling in my stomach—a nostalgic feeling. One thing my mother taught has had a bit of a haunting feeling to it over the years whenever I remember how cheerfully, after telling me how important it was to behave myself as I should, she recited the words, "Of all sad words of tongue or pen, / The saddest are these: 'It might have been!'"[1]

I could not have been more than six or seven when I had another conversation with my mother that has stayed with me ever since and which bears directly on the topic of loving and caring for each other. I remember the conversation about love and marriage and having a family. I think I must have asked something like, "How do you know when you

---

Richard N. Williams is the associate academic vice president at Brigham Young University. He is currently serving as a stake president.

really love someone?" Her answer was simple and to the point: "When you love someone you care more about them than you do yourself; their happiness is more important to you than your own happiness." Her words might have been slightly more simple, but they found their way indelibly into my memory and into my heart. Suddenly, my own mother's love for me—which I had accepted as fact, but little understood—took on a whole new luster.

I know I took this principle to heart because, not very much later, I was smitten in an unmistakable way by a little girl in my third-grade class, while watching her perform as a dancing Christmas cookie. One might say that I plucked her right out of the third-grade chorus line. But the feeling was not just that she was cute, it was that she was *good*—through and through. In spite of the fact that that relationship did not mature, I have always remembered what it felt like to know that someone was good—through and through—and to know that her happiness and welfare was more important to me than my own.

Within the limits of my own rough edges and imperfections, I can recommend this principle to all as the foundation of a loving and caring marriage. I believe that Sister Williams and I can attest to the benefit of this principle from the perspective of our own relationship. I offer it here as an important foundation for a marriage in which loving and caring for each other can flourish.

President Hinckley declared: "Selfishness is a destructive, gnawing, corrosive element in the lives of most of us. It lies at the root of much of the tension between parents and children."[2]

He also noted: "I am satisfied that a happy marriage is not so much a matter of romance as it is an anxious concern for the comfort and well-being of one's companion. Selfishness so often is the basis of money problems. . . . Selfishness is at the root of adultery, the breaking of solemn and sacred covenants. . . . Selfishness is the antithesis of love."[3]

Among the corrosive elements of selfishness, one of the most common—and perhaps the purest of manifestations—is anger, in all its forms. To become angry, by its very nature, is to accuse another of a wrong—imagined or real.[4] It is the ultimate act of self-assertion in a relationship. By its nature it demands that the other take account of and grant the legitimacy of the angry person's desires and judgments. Anger can turn an act of principled assertiveness into an act of dominance and aggression. In a relationship of loving and caring, one must simply live without anger.

The scriptures warn us against anger and the source of anger: "The devil will grasp them with his everlasting chains, and they be stirred up to anger, and perish; for behold, at that day shall he rage in the hearts of the children of men, and stir them up to anger against that which is good" (2 Nephi 28:19–20).

Notice the interesting contrast Mormon captures in his description of the righteous Nephites after the visit of the Savior: "And it came to pass that there was no contention among all the people, in all the land; but there were mighty miracles wrought among the disciples of Jesus" (4 Nephi 1:13). Mormon also teaches us the reason for the lack of contention: "And it came to pass that there was no contention in the land, because of the love of God which did dwell in the hearts of the people" (4 Nephi 1:15).

It is no wonder, then, that when the Savior appeared to the Nephites at the temple mount in Bountiful, His first proclamation of His gospel was prefaced by a caution about the spirit of contention: "For verily, verily I say unto you, he that hath the spirit of contention is not of me, but is of the devil, who is the father of contention, and he stirreth up the hearts of men to contend with anger, one with another.

"Behold, this is not my doctrine, to stir up the hearts of men with anger one against another; but this is my doctrine that such things should be done away.

"Behold, verily, verily, I say unto you, I will declare unto you my doctrine" (3 Nephi 11:29–31).

By this reading, the spirit of contention—the presence of anger—is inimical to the doctrine Christ came to teach. It prevents our being sensitive to the spirit of the gospel. By extension, a spirit of selfishness will interfere with a gospel-centered marriage and the loving and caring that are inherent to such a relationship.

President David O. McKay spoke of the effect of selfishness on a marriage: "Marriage is a relationship that cannot survive selfishness, impatience, domineering, inequality, and lack of respect."[5]

He was not timid about setting the standard for a marriage very high: "No member of this Church, no husband or father, has the right to utter an oath in his own home, or ever to express a cross word to his wife or to his children. . . . You do what you can to produce peace and harmony, no matter what you suffer."[6]

President McKay also said: "God help us to build homes in which the spirit of heaven on earth may be experienced. You and I know that this is possible, it is not a dream, it is not a theory. . . . We can have homes in which children will *never* hear father and mother wrangle or quarrel."[7]

President Brigham Young articulated a similarly high standard: "In our daily pursuits in life, of whatever nature and kind, Latter-day Saints . . . should maintain a uniform and even temper, both when at home and when abroad. They should not suffer reverses and unpleasant circumstances to sour their natures and render them fretful and unsocial at home, speaking words full of bitterness and biting acrimony to their wives and children, creating gloom and sorrow in their habitations, making themselves feared rather than loved by their families. Anger should *never* be permitted to rise in our bosoms, and words suggested by angry feelings should never be permitted to pass our lips."[8]

And finally, President Young said: "Let us live so that the spirit of our religion will live within us, then we have peace, joy, happiness and contentment, which makes such pleasant fathers, pleasant mothers, pleasant children, pleasant households, neighbors, communities and cities. That is worth living for, and I do think that the Latter-day Saints ought to strive for this."[9]

One might conclude at this point that the foregoing is all well and good. We all know this. But to say it doesn't make it any more realistic, nor any easier to do. It's a pretty easy thing to preach a sermon against anger and its attendant vices—everyone can agree with you and feel good about it. It is quite another thing to offer something that will actually help to put a stop to it. The devil, as they say, is in the details.

In the spirit of offering some insights that might be of practical use, I will share some perspectives that have been helpful to me in trying to live, personally and in my marriage relationship, a life that fosters and supports loving and caring. I offer these as perspectives that can counter the selfishness that so clearly and completely threatens loving and caring relationships. I offer these as perspectives, in a spirit I take to be congenial to what Elder Boyd K. Packer has taught: "True doctrine, understood, changes attitudes and behavior. The study of the doctrines of the gospel will improve behavior quicker than a study of behavior will improve behavior."[10]

While I do not offer these perspectives as doctrine, I hope they might provide some insight capable of moving us toward a clearer understanding of our nature and our relationships. In the end, I hope they might be useful in attaining and maintaining loving and caring marriage relationships.

THE PERSPECTIVE OF CHARITY

I find in Elder Packer's teaching about the beneficial effects of understanding doctrine an echo of the teaching of Alma to the faithful people of Gideon. Near the end of his sermon, he summarizes: "And see that ye have faith, hope, and charity, and then ye will always abound in good works" (Alma 7:24). If I take Alma at his word, the real key to good behavior and righteous living is to have faith, hope, and charity. If we abound in faith, hope, and charity, we will abound in love and caring. When understood from a foundation of charity, certainly most, if not all, interpersonal problems in a marriage will be soluble, and, importantly, we will be able to see them as soluble. People possessed of charity (Moroni 7:47)—which is the pure love of Christ, manifest in the laying down of His life for each of us (Ether 12:32–34)—will certainly be in a position to see their spouses as the children of God and as the redeemed of our Savior. Lesser concerns in a relationship will often fade into obscurity. The same change of heart experienced by the people of King Benjamin when they understood the redeeming love of Jesus Christ (Mosiah 5:2–5), by which they lost all disposition toward evil, has the power to produce marriages characterized by love and caring.

Of course, the mere act of seeing a spouse as a child of God and as redeemed of the Savior may not necessarily result in a change of heart or a change of the behavior of a spouse bent on anger, abuse, and selfishness. But seeing through the lens of charity may bring about greater love and caring in a relationship not already eroded by some "grosser crime" (Jacob 2:22). And even in such deeply eroded relationships, charity can bring an eternal perspective that can provide a measure of peace and understanding, allowing one to make difficult decisions and respond to difficult situations, in love and quiet confidence, rather than acting in ways that might otherwise result from bitterness and reflect revenge.

OPERATING FROM A POSITION OF WEAKNESS—AND GLADLY

One piece of advice, commonly offered in our contemporary culture, is that we should always try to operate in our lives from a position of strength. While in some senses and some settings this is sound advice, I want to suggest here how it might enhance our capacity for loving and caring if we operate from what we might refer to as a position of weakness. Let me suggest two quite fundamental ways of thinking about our basic human condition that can have quite different and quite profound influences on our relationships and our ability to love and care for each other.

One way to think of ourselves in this mortal state is as being born into a world of scarcity with needs. Indeed, some theories of human nature view us as largely, if not entirely, a teeming bundle of needs. In this view the satisfaction of needs becomes the prime directive and the underlying motive of all behavior. If this is our understanding, then other people, deliberately or not, are inevitably understood as among the array of things in life that have the potential for meeting our needs. However else we may relate to them, we can never stray too far from a consideration of the fulfillment of our needs. And, in a world of scarcity, potential for obtaining things that fulfill needs is an important and salient issue.

I believe Korihor, the anti-Christ, reasonably concluded that, in such a world, we all fare "according to the management of the creature . . . [and prosper] according to [our] genius, and . . . [conquer] according to [our] strength; and whatsoever a man [does] is no crime" (Alma 30:17). In such a system, it is quite all right to "look up with boldness, and . . . enjoy [our] rights and privileges" (Alma 30:27). In such a world, however, loving and caring become difficult prospects and hardly escape the attenuating influence of selfishness.

The alternative way of thinking of ourselves is as being born into a world of relative sufficiency (D&C 104:17) and being born with weakness as described in the book of Ether in the Book of Mormon: "If men come unto me I will show unto them their weakness. I give unto men weakness that they may be humble; and my grace is sufficient for all men that humble themselves before me; for if they humble themselves before me, and have faith in me, then will I make weak things become strong unto them" (Ether 12:27).

Putting aside the all too real facts that there are many people in the world in genuine need of the means to sustain life and that there is scarcity in too many parts of the world, I want to concentrate on "needs" and "weakness," "scarcity," and "sufficiency" in their broader metaphorical sense and speak about the implications for our marriages and other relationships of looking at ourselves as fundamentally possessed of needs to be fulfilled, or, alternatively, of looking at ourselves as fundamentally possessed of weakness to be overcome. Which way we understand ourselves will have a profound effect on how we look at others and how we experience our relationships.

If we see ourselves fundamentally as having needs, we will likely evaluate our relationships on the basis of how well they fulfill our needs. We will evaluate other people as relatively satisfactory or unsatisfactory sources of fulfillment of our needs. This orientation is predisposed to produce selfishness. It will view relationships as negotiations and destroy genuine intimacy, because intimacy requires that people be seen as ends in themselves rather than means to other ends, such as the satisfaction of our needs.

If, on the other hand, we see ourselves fundamentally as having weakness and see the concomitant obligation to overcome our weaknesses as a fundamental moral purpose of our mortal experience, then we will likely view our relationships as potential sources of strength—aids to our progress toward moral perfection. We will see other people as sources of help in becoming better people. This orientation will foster humility and selflessness. A crucial purpose for relationships is mutual strengthening, and in a good relationship each party is a better person than he or she would be without the relationship. Genuine intimacy is possible because we do not see each other as means to the satisfaction of our private needs. Rather, we feel gratitude for the other for mutual strength and support. In this kind of relationship, loving and caring can flourish. Loving and caring are understood both as the means of growth and development and the end toward which relationships should take us. Desires (as in Alma 41:3–5) are perfected in loving and caring relationships, while at the same time, loving and caring relationships flow naturally from the perfecting of desire.

Repentance as Loving and Caring

There are two different ways we can think about and understand the process of spiritual progress and the development of virtues. The first way of thinking is that virtues (such as loving and caring) are gained by a process (sometimes long, laborious, and difficult) of acquisition in which virtues are built up through practice and hard work. This is undoubtedly true in some cases and for some purposes, and we all should be anxiously engaged in developing good habits. However, there is also another way of thinking about the process of moral perfection, which perfection is a primary purpose of earth life. Consider the possibility that virtues are acquired and spiritual progress achieved by our ceasing to do those things that interfere with virtue and perfection. In other words, we stop sinning. We can understand virtue and perfection as the core left over when the mantle of sins and falsity, which is an inevitable part of our mortal heritage, is stripped away. In other words, virtue and perfection is what we are left with when we cease to sin.

This possible understanding of the process of acquiring virtue and moving toward perfection makes it clear why repentance occupies such a central position in the gospel of Jesus Christ. At the same time it illustrates for us the consummate importance of the atonement of Jesus Christ. His role as Savior and Redeemer is central and essential to the acquisition of all moral virtue, to our temporal and eternal progress, and to the success of "the great plan of happiness" (Alma 42:8). Seen in this way, then, repentance is a crucial means of perfecting our relationships, allowing us to love and care for each other unrestrained by the bonds of sin and selfishness. According to this way of understanding, love and caring will result when we cease to do those things that interfere with our doing so—in other words, when we cease to sin. Repentance, virtue, atonement, grace, and charity thus come together in loving and caring relationships.

LIVING AND CARING AS FRUIT

Like many of the most important things in life, loving and caring, and a successful ennobling marriage, are in some important ways by-products of a particular way of living—what might be called the living "after the manner of happiness" (2 Nephi 5:27). This is nothing more nor less than living in the way prescribed by the gospel and the example of Jesus Christ. King Benjamin described both the process and the fruits of this way of life:

"As ye have come to the knowledge of the glory of God, or if ye have known of his goodness and have tasted of his love, and have received a remission of your sins, which causeth such exceedingly great joy in your souls, even so I would that ye should remember, and always retain in remembrance, the greatness of God, and your own nothingness, and his goodness and long-suffering towards you, . . . and humble yourselves . . . , calling upon the name of the Lord daily, and standing steadfastly in the faith of that which is to come. . . .

"If ye do this ye shall always rejoice, and be filled with the love of God. . . .

"And ye will not have a mind to injure one another, but to live peaceably. . . .

"And ye will not suffer your children that they . . . transgress the laws of God, and fight and quarrel one with another and serve the devil. . . .

"But ye will teach them [and each other] to walk in the ways of truth and soberness; ye will teach them [and each other] to love one another, and to serve one another" (Mosiah 4:11–15).

Loving and caring for each other are fruits of the Spirit, like the other fruits of the Spirit described in scripture: "But the fruit of the Spirit is love, joy, peace, longsuffering, gentleness, goodness, faith, meekness, temperance" (Galatians 5:22–23).

As fruits of a life lived together under covenant, enlightened and blessed by the principles of the gospel of Jesus Christ, and sanctified by His Atonement, loving and caring marriage relationships will flow quite naturally and "without compulsory means" (D&C 121:46) as we allow the influence of the Holy Ghost into our lives and allow ourselves to become "new creatures" (Mosiah 27:26) and receive "new heart[s]" (Ezekiel 36:26).

May we live so as to enjoy the fruit of the love of God (1 Nephi 11:8–23) in loving and caring relationships so that marriage relationships and family life will be what they are intended to be—now and through eternity.

NOTES

1. John Greenleaf Whittier, "Maul Muller," *The Complete Poetical Works of John Greenleaf Whittier* (Boston: Houghton, Mifflin Company, 1892), 48.
2. Gordon B. Hinckley, "The Environment of Our Homes," *Ensign*, June 1985, 4.
3. Gordon B. Hinckley, "What God Hath Joined Together," *Ensign*, May 1991, 73.
4. See also C. Terry Warner, *Bonds That Make Us Free* (Salt Lake City: Shadow Mountain, 2001).
5. David O. McKay, in Conference Report, April 1956, 9.
6. David O. McKay, in Conference Report, April 1969, 150–51.
7. David O. McKay, in Conference Report, April 1952, 87.
8. Brigham Young, *Discourses of Brigham Young*, ed. John A. Widtsoe (Salt Lake City: Deseret Book, 1954), 203–4.
9. Young, *Discourses of Brigham Young*, 204.
10. Boyd K. Packer, "Little Children," *Ensign*, November 1986, 17.

WE CAN CHOOSE

———◆———

Lyn H. Denna

When I first received my topic, I thought, "'Challenges in Marriage?' I really don't have any challenges in my marriage. If my husband does what I tell him we get along just fine!" After a little more reflection I realized that even in the best of marriages life's journey has twists and turns that are sometimes hard to navigate. The challenges we face are as diverse as we are, but there are some commonalities. We each have experienced or will yet experience blessings that stretch us.

Just hours after our second child was born we sat with a doctor at Primary Children's Medical Center. Our son had a life-threatening heart defect, and the doctor was giving us some counsel. Among other things he told us that many marriages fall apart because of the stress that comes from having a child with chronic illness. Such challenges seem to either solidify a marriage or tear it apart. I was shocked. Could that really be true? If so, I was determined that this would only galvanize our marriage— but I was young and not sure about how to avoid the potholes in the path that lay ahead for us. Many years have passed since that day, and I have studied, prayed, and watched others. Along the way I have learned a few things about heartache, about being stretched beyond what I thought I could bear, about having joy and about feeling peace during the storm.

Lyn H. Denna, a returned missionary and graduate of Brigham Young University, is a professional homemaker and active community volunteer. She and her husband, Eric, have been married twenty-seven years and are the parents of seven children and the grandparents of five.

Our Agency

Most importantly, I have learned that I have a choice. Our agency is key to finding joy in, and peace and strength during, our challenges. Contrary to some thinking, we are not involuntary slaves to what happens to us. Wayward children, a sick family member, natural disasters, abuse, a financial crisis are all challenges we might not have chosen, but we can choose how we react to each challenge. There is a difference between a challenged marriage and challenges in marriage, and how we use our agency is what makes the difference. Placing blame and harboring angry feelings are seldom productive and are usually destructive.

While your marriage can be one of your greatest strengths in a challenge, some of us might feel that our marriage relationship itself is a challenge, despite our best efforts. One good sister who has worn those painful shoes gave me some sage counsel. "I realized that I needed to be my best personal self," she said. "I decided I wouldn't react to unkindness in like manner. I determined to do what a good person would do." She reminded me that dealing with a difficult person or a difficult situation doesn't mean we have to be difficult. The golden rule still holds true. My friend could have chosen to be bitter and angry, but she chose the "higher road" in dealing with her situation.

The Fivesome

When my husband and I were sealed in the Salt Lake Temple, the sealer told us that it would take five to make our marriage a success. While Eric and I were important, if we didn't include our Heavenly Father, our Savior, Jesus Christ, and the Holy Ghost we had little hope of finding eternal joy. If it truly took five, we wanted them to be our constant companions, not sporadic, not just when life got tough. That concept has reminded us to treat each other with the respect we would demonstrate if our Heavenly Father, Jesus Christ, and the Holy Ghost were actually with us all the time. We put on our best selves when we are in the presence of those we respect. Our spouses and families deserve nothing less than our best selves.

In times that we are tempted to be short or unkind, we remember our constant fivesome, and the words that come out are gentler. Even those things we want to share that could be hurtful, when shared in the spirit of the "fivesome" are delivered and received cradled in kindness.

TAKE HIS YOKE UPON US

In essence we have chosen to take His yoke upon us. To be yoked is to be joined securely. When the Godhead is that yoke that binds us together, the load we pull is so much lighter and easier to bear. The secret in a happy marriage is not in two people finding each other, it is in two people finding Christ together—He makes us one! Christ has told us that "my yoke is easy, and my burden is light" (Matthew 11:30). Our burdens are lighter when we wear His yoke. Alma's people chose to take His yoke upon them when they were sorely persecuted by Amulon, and even though the burdens were not taken from them, "the burdens which were laid upon Alma and his brethren were made light; yea, the Lord did strengthen them that they could bear up their burdens with ease, and they did submit cheerfully and with patience to all the will of the Lord" (Mosiah 24:15).

When we choose to take His yoke upon us, we know that we will never truly be alone in our afflictions. As Christ hung upon the cross, the Father withdrew His spirit, and Christ was excruciatingly alone. He paid that price for us and has promised we never need to be alone in our afflictions. But it is our choice.

KEEP OUR COVENANTS

Choosing to take His yoke upon us includes choosing to keep our covenants. To the degree that we take our covenants seriously and keep them meticulously we can bind ourselves to our spouses and to our children. The prophets have told us that even our wayward children will eternally benefit from the covenants that we keep.[1]

Equally Yoked

A yoke helps to evenly distribute the weight of the load, but its effectiveness is negated when one of the partners tries to step out in front of the other, pulls harder, or gets out of step. We must choose to be equally yoked. Progress is unduly cumbersome, and the load we are pulling is so much heavier when we aren't working together in the yoke.

One of the first things I learned after I got married was that men and women are different. My husband doesn't think the way I do. We approach problems and resolve them differently; he pulls in the yoke differently than I do. At first I thought he was always wrong, and if we could do everything my way life would be much better. We got nowhere with that approach. It took some time, but gradually I came to see that he wasn't always wrong, just different and that that difference was good.

We are learning to use our differences as we face challenges together. As he pulls in our yoke using his special strengths and I pull with my uniqueness, but still in step with each other, we have found a comfortable cadence no matter how heavy our burden happens to be. Elder David A. Bednar explains that this is by divine design: "Because of their distinctive temperaments and capacities, males and females each bring to a marriage relationship unique perspectives and experiences. The man and the woman contribute differently but equally to a oneness and a unity that can be achieved in no other way. The man completes and perfects the woman and the woman completes and perfects the man, as they learn from and mutually strengthen and bless each other."[2]

Because of our differences the decisions we make together are far better than any that we attempt to make alone.

Small Things

While he was in the Liberty Jail, Joseph Smith said "that a very large ship is benefited very much by a very small helm in the time of a storm" (D&C 123:16). When my mortal maelstroms rage, it is the "small helms" that steady me. We must choose to do small things every day when the waters are calm. Then when the storm's fury is upon us we are steadied against the temporal *and* spiritual buffetings. One of our greatest "small helms" is our choice to feast upon the word of God every day. It is a well-proven way to steady us when all about us rages. It is a small thing to find time each day to feast upon the word of God—a small investment that yields large dividends.

Our expressions of love shouldn't be saved up and given out on birthdays and Christmas in nicely wrapped boxes. Every day there are small ways to say "I love you." A mother might want nothing more than a phone call, a husband might appreciate his shoes polished, a wife might want someone else, anyone else, to take out the garbage.

Less than a year ago our son passed away. In the months before he died Benjamin found the night hours lonely and his mind too full of thought to be able to sleep, so he would take off his oxygen and come to my bedside. Those solitary hours for me had been my refueling times. I guarded my time alone; thinking of what that day had given me and what I would need to give in the next. At first I gave my precious time to Benjamin begrudgingly, feeling robbed of my solitude. It didn't take long for me to realize that this was a small thing—all he wanted was a little of my time. We talked of nonsense sometimes, of eternal things other times, and there were occasions when no words were exchanged—we were just together. It felt like a sacrifice for me but a gift well worth giving.

It wasn't until after his death that I realized that the true gift had been what he had given me. He knew I was awake and that our time together on earth was running out. He knew that I would want memories to draw on after he was gone. Those talks are in a sacred hollow in my heart. I pull them out sometimes and relive our time together. It was such a small thing but has provided a priceless comfort.

In a day of great materialism we mustn't confuse worldly value with true value. The world would have us believe that the more expensive the gift the greater the love. Our favorite wedding gift that we give is a small vase. The note is actually bigger than the gift box! This is what the note says: "Early in our marriage we found ourselves in student housing at BYU and struggling. It was not uncommon for my sweetheart to pick me a flower on his way home from school and tenderly place it in my hand when he entered the door. Each time, I was filled with such wonder at this kind man and the chance I had to share my life with him. It didn't matter that we had little else.

"In the twenty-seven years since those days we've bought homes, taken trips around the world and accumulated many of the world's goods but nothing has brought more joy than those moments when he placed a small flower in my open hand and encircled me with his love.

"This small gift, wrapped in ribbons and paper is symbolic of what we truly wish to give you, as you begin your lives together. We give you the gift of simplicity. Remember as you frequently put a small flower in this vase that your greatest joys will come from the simple things—the small flower, the tender embrace."

Few people exemplify this better than my friend. Her life has been full to overflowing, raising eight children and supporting her husband in his career and service as stake president and mission president among many other callings. Their resources have never been abundant, but they have been careful and content.

One day, a few years ago, when most of her family had grown and gone, her husband collapsed at work, suffering a sudden and nearly fatal aneurysm that burst in his brain. The months that followed stretched her heartstrings to near breaking point, but she trusted in the Lord. During the tenderness of this time she needed to get something from his wallet. Tucked in there among a few dollar bills was a yellowed, half-chewed piece of paper.

The sight of the note sent her back many years to a time when her days were full of diapers and doing without. She had sent her sweetheart with the usual sandwich, but this day she had found a ruddy little scrap of paper, scrawled a message of endearment on it and tucked it between the lettuce and the leftover meat.

She smiled as she remembered him recounting his surprise as he tried to bite down on the tasteless pulp. She had forgotten all about it, but he hadn't. For decades he had carried that little, half-eaten note around in his wallet. It was a daily reminder of the priceless treasure that his companion was to him. He no longer carries that wallet, but the memory is tucked away in a sacred hollow of his heart. And she had thought it was such a small thing at the time.

"Wherefore, be not weary in well-doing, for ye are laying the foundation of a great work. And out of small things proceedeth that which is great" (D&C 64:33). During our challenges, if we have chosen to do the small things beforehand—the acts of love, the time spent each day in the scriptures—we will be sustained by them. But we must choose now.

Be Grateful

My husband taught me that I can choose to be grateful especially in crisis. After Benjamin was born and the doctors had explained the severity of his heart condition, we found a quiet place and my husband suggested we pray. I was feeling pretty sorry for myself and wondering how we would manage. The thought of prayer hadn't graced my mind, but if it had, it would have been to plead for help and healing. I couldn't see that there was anything in our situation to be thankful for. Eric was voice for our prayer. I wallowed in my self-pity until I listened to his words. He addressed our Heavenly Father and then thanked Him for this son and all that he came with, and all that we would become, thanks to his condition. There were no pleadings for miraculous healings. As I heard these words, I immediately felt the power of His spirit cleanse my heart of the darkness that engulfed it and from that moment began looking forward to the adventure that awaited us.

And the adventure began. For twenty-four years our life has been full of prognoses, prescriptions, procedures, payments and, of course, pain. Amidst it all we have shared lots of love, laughter and learning, and experienced many memories, miracles, and tender mercies.

A few months ago we found ourselves up through the night, trying to do what little we could to help Benjamin in his final hours. The children had all gathered back home. We had laughed and cried and felt the tender mercies of the Spirit with an intensity that comes only at sacred times such as this. The gentlemen from the funeral home had come and gone and Eric and I thought we would try to get a little rest. But before lying down we felt a strong need to go to our Heavenly Father, as we had when we began our life with Benjamin, on bended knee. We, once more, expressed our thanks. As we knelt together, side by side, I realized that the gratitude of an individual is powerfully enabling but when jointly cultivated as a couple its expansion is exponential. When I should have been awash in grief I felt a joy and fulfillment that surpasses the power of words to describe.

I would like to share one last experience. Five years ago I spoke at Women's Conference and shared our experience of when Benjamin nearly died but at the last possible moment he received a heart transplant giving us what Elder Neal A. Maxwell referred to as "a delay in route."[3] At the end of our session a woman approached me with tears in her eyes. She too had had a son with a chronic illness, but she said there had been no miracles for them. Her son had died. I've thought often of her comment— that there had been no miracles for them.

I now stand on the other side of the story. My son, like hers, has died, but that he lived or died has never been the miracle for me. The miracle is to be able to feel the Spirit's calming influence amidst all the cacophony of mortality. To be sustained by His strength when we feel overwhelmingly weak—that's a miracle. I have seen a life extended and I have seen a life extinguished, and each is a miracle to me. To see the hand of the Master Teacher in these majestic moments in the mortal classroom—that's a miracle.

We are not the same people we were when Benjamin was first placed in our arms. While we have been stretched beyond what we thought we would be able to bear, we have become something and learned things we couldn't have without the refiner's fire. Elder Maxwell said, "Righteous sorrow and suffering carve cavities in the soul that will become later reservoirs of joy."[4] We can choose to find joy even during the trial if we follow Paul's counsel to the Thessalonians, "In everything give thanks" (1 Thessalonians 5:18).

CONCLUSION

Marriage can be glorious and enabling even when it isn't easy. I love Elder Jeffrey R. Holland's metaphor of marriage and an airplane ride: "Of course some days are going to be more difficult than others, but if you leave the escape hatch in the airplane open because you think even before takeoff you might want to bail out in midflight, then I can promise you it's going to be a pretty chilly trip. . . . Close the door, strap on those seat belts, and give it full throttle. That's the only way to make a marriage fly."[5]

Do not be discouraged. Elder Bednar has said, "The disparity between the doctrinal ideal of marriage and the reality of daily life may seem at times to be quite large, but you gradually are doing and becoming much better than you probably recognize."[6]

We would all do well to apply President James E. Faust's counsel to women: "May I suggest that you take your challenges one day at a time. Do the best you can. Look at everything through the lens of eternity. If you will do this, life will take on a different perspective."[7]

Our lives will hold challenges, big and small, but the Lord has given us a priceless gift to enable and empower us. It is a gift that we fought for, one that He will never take from us—our agency. We can choose to partake of the bitter cup without becoming bitter. Christ is our exemplar. Elder Maxwell reminds us that "[Christ] partook of the most bitter cup— and did so without becoming bitter!"[8]

I am grateful for the atoning sacrifice of my Savior. He has borne my sorrows and carried my heartaches and done it with grace and dignity. I can thank Him by choosing to take His yoke upon me and choosing to be equally yoked; by doing the small things each day and carrying my burdens with a grateful heart.

NOTES

1. "Four destroying angels holding power over the four quarters of the earth until the servants of God are sealed in their foreheads, which signifies sealing the blessing upon their heads, meaning the everlasting covenant, thereby making their calling and election sure. When a seal is put upon the father and mother, it secures their posterity, so that they cannot be lost, but will be saved by virtue of the covenant of their father and mother." Joseph Smith, *Teachings of the Prophet Joseph Smith* (Salt Lake City: Deseret Book, 1961), 321.

   "The Prophet Joseph Smith declared—and he never taught more comforting doctrine—that the eternal sealings of faithful parents and the divine promises made to them for valiant service in the Cause of Truth, would save not only themselves, but likewise their posterity. Though some of the sheep may wander, the eye of the Shepherd is upon them, and sooner or later they will feel the tentacles of Divine Providence reaching out after them and drawing them back to the fold. Either in this life or the life to come, they will return. They will have to pay their debt to justice; they will suffer for their sins; and may tread a thorny path; but if it leads them at last, like the penitent Prodigal, to a loving and forgiving father's heart and home, the painful experience will not have been in vain. Pray for your careless and disobedient children; hold on to them with your faith. Hope on, trust on, till you see the salvation of God" (Orson F. Whitney, in Conference Report, April 1929, 110).

2. David A. Bednar, "Marriage Is Essential to His Eternal Plan," *Ensign*, June 2006, 83–84.

3. Neal A. Maxwell, "Apply the Atoning Blood of Christ," *Ensign*, November 1997, 22.

4. Neal A. Maxwell, *Meek and Lowly* (Salt Lake City: Deseret Book, 1987), 11.

5. Jeffrey R. Holland, *However Long and Hard the Road* (Salt Lake City: Deseret Book, 1985), 110.

6. Bednar, "Marriage Is Essential to His Eternal Plan," 82.

7. James E. Faust, "Instruments in the Hands of God," *Ensign*, November 2005, 115.

8. Neal A. Maxwell, "In Him All Things Hold Together," March 31, 1991, *Brigham Young University 1990–91 Devotional and Fireside Speeches* (Provo, UT: Brigham Young University Publications, 1991), 109, 111.

Fools Rush in . . .

Kaye Terry Hanson

I teach management communication in the Marriott School at Brigham Young University. Our students study management in a variety of finance, organizational behavior, marketing, accounting, and operations classes. When I joined the faculty twenty-four years ago, there were 116 faculty members, six of whom were women. Today we have 142 faculty members, eleven of whom are women.

My assignments are often in master of business administration classrooms where I average forty-five fine young men with five or six women among them. More often than not I am the only woman teacher my students have had since high school English. Most of my university experience has also coincided with the women's movement and with diversity initiatives in the United States. So I have spent a lot of time over the years thinking about communication between men and women and wondering how to make it work. Here is what I've discovered. I know nothing.

Having said that, and remembering an old song that says "Fools rush in . . . ," let's talk about three things that strike me in this area.

1. Women and men communicate differently.

Kaye Terry Hanson is an assistant professor at the Marriott School of Management at Brigham Young University. She is a former associate director at the Brigham Young University Jerusalem Center. She has also served as a ward Relief Society president and on the Young Women general board.

2. Experience teaches us, if we let it.

3. What can we do?

Women and Men Communicate Differently

Probably that is not news to anyone. Probably you can name a number of generalizations off the top of your head that support that idea.

- Women are intuitive, men less so.
- Women see things clearly, men less so.
- Women talk about things they know nothing about.
- Women talk too much.
- If only he would see things my way our world would run much better.

We all have experienced examples of miscommunication between men and women for any number of reasons. But what we are after here is *communication,* not *mis.* We search for understanding between us.

As we examine understanding more closely, I encourage one more thing. We don't need to worry about any of this information applying to our husband, or boss, or brother-in-law, or son that we are trying to communicate with. We can't do anything about them. The only person in this whole world we have any influence over is right here. Ourselves. Remember, we are not responsible for how the other person understands. We are not responsible for how the other person responds. But we are each responsible for how we respond. And that is a great deal to be responsible for.

Studying communication between men and women is fascinating. A quick search of Amazon.com will find a number of volumes exploring how to help the world run more smoothly by understanding gender communication. There are two general ideas that we talk about in my classes that seem to be effective in helping us understand one another better. And isn't that what we're really after? Understanding?

The first idea is that difference is apparent from very young ages. Deborah Tannen, in a video exploring her research on gender communication,[1] discovers that little boys communicate with each other in a "one-upmanship" way, while little girls communicate by trying to make connections. An eavesdropping camera, for example, listened to a group of little boys on the playground. One boy said he could hit a ball "up high." The next boy said he could "hit it higher than the school." A third boy said he could hit a ball "all the way up to the sky." The first boy responded that he "could hit it all the way up to God." When I show that video, the young men in my classes laugh uproariously as they recognize familiar patterns. Let me make it perfectly clear here that I am not saying one way of communicating is right and one is wrong. They are just different.

The camera then eavesdrops on two little girls. Instead of talking one-upmanship, the little girls try to make connections. For example, one says her mother and her father wear contact lenses. The other excitedly says her baby-sitter named Amber also wears contact lenses. Then they both giggle at finding something in common.

The second idea Professor Tannen explores with children involves putting two chairs in a room with a camera. In the room we see pairs of children get involved in conversation. First, we see 2 five-year-old girls, then 2 five-year-old boys. Next, 2 ten-year-old girls, then 2 ten-year-old boys. Then 2 fifteen-year-old girls, then 2 fifteen-year-old boys. In each case the same thing happens. Within minutes the five-year-old girls have scooted the chairs around so they face each other and they talk animatedly, looking at each other. Within minutes the five-year-old boys have aligned their chairs side by side. They also engage in conversation, but they speak out toward the room, not toward each other. The same thing happens with the ten-year-olds and the fifteen-year-olds. The girls prefer looking at each other as they speak, and the boys prefer speaking out toward the rest of the room.

Next, our researcher takes her cameras into the workplace and shows situation after situation where the same patterns are apparent. Women work at making connections while looking at each other, and men work at one-upmanship while looking anywhere but at the colleague. You can see the problem here. Communication seems to progress nicely until, oh dear, a woman and a man have to talk to each other. She tries to connect, he tries to one-up. No wonder we misunderstand each other.

Many of my students—both men and women—have commented that just knowing that men and women communicate differently from the beginning has made them see more humor in our differences, be more patient, more understanding, and more aware of what is happening in a conversation with the other gender.

One more thing. Probably because little girls prefer looking at each other when they talk, it seems we grow adept at listening with our eyes as well as our ears. Is that what we call intuition?

I think about Sariah and Lehi. I think about communication between them as Lehi tells Sariah his most remarkable dream where he learns that they have to take their family away from Jerusalem. I think about her concerns in feeding and clothing a family in the wilderness for who knows how long and her understanding of what this promised land might be like. I think of her caring for almost grown sons as well as younger children in the harsh climate of the Middle East. I wonder at her own communication with our Father in Heaven and what answers might come to her own prayers as she matriarchs her family.

Mostly I think about the weeks her four big sons are gone back to Jerusalem to get the plates of brass when she becomes so worried. So worried that she complains against Lehi, calling him a visionary man. Sure that they have perished, her heart breaks at the eventuality of the loss of her sons. That strong prophet Lehi, surely dismayed by her worries, bears witness to his faithful wife that her sons will be all right, delivered from the hands of Laban, his kinsman. Sariah is "comforted." When the boys return, Sariah is "exceedingly glad," "comforted" again, and knows "of a surety that the Lord hath protected [her] sons, . . . and given them power whereby they could accomplish the thing which the Lord hath commanded them." Then "they did rejoice exceedingly, and did offer sacrifice and burnt offerings unto the Lord; and they gave thanks unto the God of Israel" (1 Nephi 5:1–9).

It's easy to say that times were different then, but was understanding different between men and women? I don't think so. I think our human experience is strikingly familiar whether we live in Sariah's wilderness or now, in our own.

Experience Teaches Us, If We Let It

If we could interact on this subject we could make a list of things we have learned by experience that might include these concepts:

- Don't assume people know what you're thinking.
- Remember, there are many ways to communicate without words.
- Revel in the feeling that comes when you are listened to and no one interrupts.
- Learn to guard sacred experiences and not to bare your soul to everyone.

The Doctrine and Covenants tells us, "Remember that that which cometh from above is sacred, and must be spoken with care, and by constraint of the Spirit" (D&C 63:64).

Remember, Mary didn't shout out to the neighbors what the angel had told her. Instead, she "kept all these things, and pondered them in her heart" (Luke 2:19).

In my early years at BYU, I approached my work with a grateful heart and much trepidation. My first assignment on finishing my PhD in theater and directing was to help develop an oral communication course for MBA students using performance skills. Soon I was assigned to a committee working on the vision of the Marriott School. Then they asked me to work with an expanded committee to redesign the entire MBA program. All these committees were peopled with various male colleagues—and me. You remember me, don't you? I'm the one who knows nothing.

I remember several glitches of miscommunication during those times, but let me illustrate something I learned from experience with this one example. Just at lunchtime one day we wrapped up a meeting about future Marriott School plans in our beautiful boardroom on the seventh floor of the Tanner Building. As I recall there were four men on the committee—and me. As we finished, an associate dean came into the room, pointed to each one of the men in turn and asked, "Wanna go to lunch? Wanna go to lunch? Wanna go to lunch? Wanna go to lunch?" He skipped right over me. Now, when I was growing up, my mother taught me that it was rude to invite someone to do something in the presence of others you were not inviting. I remember leaving that room disappointed that day. I went to my secretary—by now I was the associate director of the MBA program—and said to her, "I'll know I've arrived when they invite me to lunch." Then I ate alone in my office, wondering if I was ever going to fit in.

A few weeks later I traveled with several of my male colleagues and an entire class of executive MBA students to Europe for our foreign business excursion. Our purpose was to visit businesses and learn applications from our classroom studies that explained how and why they manufactured goods or provided services the way they did. As I recall, the faculty group consisted of five men—and me.

On a late afternoon the six of us found ourselves in Gothenburg, Sweden, several blocks from our hotel and apparently hopelessly lost. We huddled in a circle and deliberated a bit while the men disagreed on which direction we should go. Eventually, pointing, I said, "If we go to that street, cross the bridge, and take a left, we'll see our hotel." They went on discussing as though I had said nothing, finally agreeing that they would stop someone and ask. The man they stopped proved unable to be helpful because he was clearly drunk. So I tried again, "If we go to that street, cross the bridge, and take a left, we'll see our hotel." This time they decided to go into a store and buy a map, which they did. It turned out that the Swedish written on the map was of no help to them, so I tried the third time, "If we go to that street, cross the bridge, and take a left, we'll be there."

All these colleagues of mine were in my age group, except one. In fact, he had been a former student of mine who had completed his doctoral studies and now had joined our faculty. This time he said, "I'm willing to follow Kaye's suggestion." I could have hugged him. I responded with, "Well, I'm going that way, if anyone wants to come." And I started down the street. They followed. I was right.

Back on campus a few days later, I was working in my office at lunchtime when a knock came at the door and one of my colleagues from the street in Gothenburg leaned his head in to ask, "Wanna go to lunch with us?" I had arrived.

As I look back I realize my friends and colleagues probably never even heard me make my suggestions. In their problem-solving ways they were one-upmanshipping each other to find our hotel. Ultimately, the whole experience has become one of my favorite stories because it broke down the barrier that made us so conscious of being men and women and built a bridge of collegiality between us that has developed into delightful working relationships over the years. I do, however, continue to give them all a bad time about consulting a drunk for directions.

I began to learn to get over what I perceived as miscommunication and worked at not being bitter over perceived slights. I tried to look for intentions and motives instead of the words on the surface. I have long been convinced that my colleagues in the Marriott School meant no harm by their miscommunication. One big thing that softened my heart over the years was the practice we have of opening every committee meeting with prayer. I heard my colleagues pray. By listening to them plead with our Father in Heaven, I learned of their love of the Savior and of the desires of their hearts.

I wonder about Ruth and Boaz in Bethlehem. Think of it. The foreign young widow arrives with her mother-in-law, Naomi. Two women who come to Bethlehem with nothing left but a bit of land that belonged to Naomi's husband. As women they are not allowed to own it, so must sell it. Ruth gleans in the fields and happens on the land belonging to Boaz. I love the communication between them the first time they meet.

Boaz says to Ruth, "Hearest thou not, my daughter? Go not to glean in another field, neither go from hence, but abide here fast by my maidens:

"Let thine eyes be on the field that they do reap, and go thou after them: have I not charged the young men that they shall not touch thee? and when thou art athirst, go unto the vessels, and drink of that which the young men have drawn.

"Then she fell on her face, and bowed herself to the ground, and said unto him, Why have I found grace in thine eyes, that thou shouldest take knowledge of me, seeing I am a stranger?

"And Boaz answered and said unto her, It hath fully been shewed me, all that thou hast done unto thy mother in law since the death of thine husband: and how thou has left thy father and thy mother, and the land of thy nativity, and art come unto a people which thou knewest not heretofore.

"The Lord recompense thy work, and a full reward be given thee of the Lord God of Israel, under whose wings thou art come to trust.

"Then she said, Let me find favour in thy sight, my lord; for that thou hast comforted me, and for that thou hast spoken friendly unto thine handmaid, though I be not like unto one of thine handmaidens" (Ruth 2:8–13).

Does it seem to you that Boaz and Ruth understand each other? They seem to truly listen to one another. I see great kindness on both sides. Gratitude and graciousness. Ruth, the foreigner, has every reason to be uncomfortable. In fact, the very God she has come to worship is new to her. A convert, a foreigner, a woman in a world where men are most important, and Boaz is kind to her. We know they eventually marry and raise up a son named Obed, the father of Jesse, the father of David. From that line almost a thousand years later, the Savior Himself is born.

Will experience teach us if we let it? Will the experiences of others teach us? It's easy to say that times were different then, but was learning from experience different as women and men struggled to communicate with each other? I don't think so. I think our human learning is strikingly familiar whether we glean by Ruth in Boaz's field, or now, in our own.

What Can We Do?

So, what can we do? How can we let go of frustration and exasperation and, yes, pain as we work at understanding one another? Here are some ideas:

- Be kind.
- As we communicate about a subject, let's remember it long enough to take care of it, then forget it.
- Realize we are all sojourners in this telestial world, and, as a result, we need to change, or we will never be celestial.
- Recognize that we need to change. That is an indication that we know we are not as close to the Savior as we need to be. Are we willing to be closer?
- Love the Savior first. Love for our fellow sojourners will follow.

Section 121 of the Doctrine and Covenants gives us the perfect formula for communication: "No power or influence can or ought to be maintained by virtue of the priesthood [and I submit, by the women who share in all those priesthood blessings], only by persuasion, by long-suffering, by gentleness and meekness, and by love unfeigned;

"By kindness, and pure knowledge, which shall greatly enlarge the soul without hypocrisy, and without guile—

"Reproving betimes with sharpness [which means clarity], when moved upon by the Holy Ghost; and then showing forth afterwards an increase of love toward him whom thou hast reproved, lest he esteem thee to be his enemy" (D&C 121:41–43).

I think of this pattern of communication in relationship to the Savior, especially in the Bible. I am moved in reading in Exodus again in the Old Testament that as Jehovah gives instructions on how to build a tabernacle in the wilderness—a portable small temple—that He clearly asks for the law—the testimony—to be placed within the Ark of the Covenant. Then, on the top of the Ark—between the cherubim—he tells Moses to put the "mercy seat." "And there I will meet with thee, and I will commune with thee from above the mercy seat . . . of all things which I will give thee in commandment unto the children of Israel" (Exodus 25:22). By the way, Jewish tradition has it that one cherub is male and one is female.

I am intrigued that the law is enclosed and within the mercy seat. Somehow mercy is not tucked inside to be enclosed by the law. No, the law is surrounded by the mercy seat that the prophet is to use as he pleads with the Lord for us. What a type of Jesus Christ is that? He places His atonement before His father and pleads for us because He has paid the necessary price for our sins, and our sorrows. He understands us whether we are His daughter or His son.

Is such understanding a pattern of communication for us? Can we give mercy to those we misunderstand and to those who misunderstand us? Is not the ultimate communication between men and women between each of us and our Father in Heaven, availing ourselves of the offer tendered by Jesus Christ Himself?

I know a young mother who understands this principle. As her husband began to make choices that were destined to break her heart, she worked her hardest to be loyal to him. She found there was no relief for her agony and disappointment—except at her bedside alone, kneeling in prayer. She couldn't confide in anyone else what her fears and pain might be. For weeks her only courage came from the strength gained in that most sacred of communications, prayer. Still, now, long after the divorce and the publicness of her sorrow, she weeps openly and gratefully at the mercy extended to her when she felt so alone.

Patricia Holland, in a speech to BYU students in 1987 when her husband, Jeffrey Holland, was still president of Brigham Young University, explained her understanding of this principle this way:

"He has promised that *the very hairs of your head are all numbered to Him.* 'The very hairs of your head'—that proclaims a *lot* of fatherly interest. He has also declared that not even one sparrow will fall to the ground unnoticed. 'Fear ye not therefore, ye are of more value . . . than sparrows' (Matthew 10:30–31)."

Sister Holland continues, "He knows that all people struggle with fears and anxieties and problems. . . . If we will but come to him, he will comfort and reassure us. And he will carry us in his arms until we are able to walk by ourselves.

"'For I the Lord thy God will hold thy right hand, saying unto thee, Fear not; I will help thee.*

"'*Fear thou not; for I am with thee: be not dismayed; for I am thy God: I will strengthen thee; yea, I will help thee; yea, I will uphold thee with the right hand of my righteousness'* [Isaiah 41:13, 10]."

Here's the communication part: "Take your fears to the Lord. Talk to him, and listen to him. . . . Let his influence work upon you. The Lord wants you to succeed even more than you want to yourself. Have faith in a perfect Father's love, fearing nothing."

Sister Holland explains further by drawing on an analogy that we women might understand. She says, "I think I have a glimpse of that kind of love because of my own experience of giving birth to three beautiful children. I have discovered that the child who is at the moment content and happy often has little need of me. That gladsome child usually runs away to play. But the child who has made a mistake, has faltered, or is wounded or frightened turns quickly to come back home for reassurance. As that child draws near unto me, nothing—I repeat nothing—can stop the opening of my heart or the reaching out of my arms to enfold him or her into my protection.

"Is anything more powerful than a mother's love? The scriptures say *one thing* is more powerful.

"'But, behold, Zion hath said: The Lord hath forsaken me, and my Lord hath forgotten me*—but he will show that he hath not.

"'For can a woman forget her sucking child, that she should not have compassion on the son of her womb? Yea, they may forget* [As unwilling as I am to believe it, Pat Holland may forget her children. Yea, earthly mothers may forget], *yet I will not forget thee, O house of Israel.*

"'Behold, I have graven thee upon the palms of my hands'* [1 Nephi 21:14–16; emphasis added].

"Christ's compassionate atonement is more powerful than even a mother's love. He has engraven us upon the palms of his hands and those marks make certain that he will never forget us."[1]

Gradually, through this ultimate communication with our Father in Heaven, we may learn to become more like His Son, Jesus Christ. Then, as the Atonement works upon us, we begin to love more wholly, more completely, not only the people closest to us but ultimately all our Father in Heaven's children.

We can learn to communicate more clearly with all the men—and women—in our lives by striving to be more like the Savior, who loves us and intercedes for us at the mercy seat with a surety that is astounding. So, whether we struggle in the wilderness like Sariah, or glean in Bethlehem like Ruth, or find that the gardens we kneel in seem as familiar as Gethsemane, He gives us the privilege of learning to be more like Him, which will make all the difference.

NOTES

1. *Talking 9 to 5: Women and Men in the Workplace* (Burnsville, MN: Charthouse International Learning Corp., 1995), video recording.
2. Patricia Holland, "Fear Not," *Brigham Young University 1987–88 Devotional and Fireside Speeches* (Provo, UT: Brigham Young University Publications, 1988), 11–15.

HEART TO HEART: ENGAGING THE SCRIPTURES IN THE SERVICE OF THE LORD

Kim B. Clark

Early one morning in the fall of 1968, I knelt in prayer in a small basement apartment in Boeblingen, Germany. I had been a missionary in southern Germany for less than two months, and I was confused, worried, and discouraged. The work was hard; few people wanted to talk to us; and some heaped on us anger, scorn, and ridicule. I felt under attack on all sides, and I did not have all the answers. I had searched and pondered and had tried to find understanding and greater faith, but I had made little progress. And so, there I was on my knees pleading with the Lord for help.

As I prayed, I heard in my mind, as though someone had spoken to me, these three words: "Believe in God." I looked up and looked around. My companion was fixing breakfast. I asked him if there was a scripture that said, "Believe in God." He said, matter-of-factly, "Yeah, Mosiah 4:9." I opened the Book of Mormon and read these words:

"Believe in God; believe that he is, and that he created all things, both in heaven and in earth; believe that he has all wisdom, and all power, both in heaven and in earth; believe that man doth not comprehend all the things which the Lord can comprehend."

As I read those words, the message from the Lord—have faith and trust in me—sank deep into my heart. Hearing those words and reading

---

Former dean of Harvard Business School, Kim B. Clark currently serves as the president of BYU–Idaho. He and his wife are the parents of seven children and the grandparents of nine grandchildren.

that scripture was a defining experience. I learned to trust the Lord, to hear His voice, and to see the scriptures as a source of inspiration and power.

I love the scriptures. They are one of the greatest of all the blessings the Lord has given us. Each of us has the opportunity to read and search them and to *engage* them in our service in the kingdom. I know the scriptures are important to you, and I pray that the Holy Ghost will teach us how the scriptures might become an even greater source of truth, knowledge, and power in our lives.

There is no better statement of that power, and how one obtains it, than Mormon's description of the sons of Mosiah in Alma 17:2–3:

"Now these sons of Mosiah were with Alma at the time the angel first appeared unto him; therefore Alma did rejoice exceedingly to see his brethren; and what added more to his joy, they were still his brethren in the Lord; yea, and they had waxed strong in the knowledge of the truth; for they were men of a sound understanding and they had searched the scriptures diligently, that they might know the word of God.

"But this is not all; they had given themselves to much prayer, and fasting; therefore they had the spirit of prophecy, and the spirit of revelation, and when they taught, they taught with power and authority of God."

The sons of Mosiah engaged the scriptures through the observance of four principles:

- Make and keep sacred covenants with the Lord.
- Search diligently to know the truth.
- Fast and pray to have the guidance of the Spirit.
- Teach with power and authority.

I call these principles the "framework of engagement." As we consider them, please pay close attention to the way each principle deals with our hearts. Engaging the scriptures is not primarily a matter of cognition or intellect. It is primarily about our hearts. The framework, therefore, is an engagement of the heart.

PRINCIPLE 1:
MAKE AND KEEP SACRED COVENANTS WITH THE LORD

The connection between making covenants and engaging the scriptures lies in our hearts. Throughout the scriptures the prophets have used the image of the heart to capture what is at the very core of our emotional and spiritual life—our innermost desires, our central drives, our deepest emotional commitments, and our capacity for love. This is what we give to the Lord when we make and keep sacred covenants with Him. Our hearts become His, and He writes the promises in our hearts. The promises of the covenant shape our desires and become our defining commitments. Through the power of the Atonement He gives us a new heart, with desires and commitments that are pure before Him.

This is not something that happens all at once. But if we are true and faithful, if we "[yield] to the enticings of the Holy Spirit" (Mosiah 3:19), the Lord works a mighty change in our hearts. Hearts that are turned to the Lord with desires and commitments defined by sacred covenants are open to His word and His light. Here is the promise:

"And if your eye be single to my glory, your whole bodies shall be filled with light, and there shall be no darkness in you; and that body which is filled with light comprehendeth all things" (D&C 88:67).

PRINCIPLE 2:
SEARCH DILIGENTLY TO KNOW THE TRUTH

To engage the scriptures we must read them and search them. Since the days of my mission I have read the scriptures every day. But there came a time a few years ago when I realized that I needed to do much more than I was doing. I made a commitment to the Lord that I would get up earlier and really dig into the scriptures with intensity and focus. It has been a wonderful experience. Let me share with you what I have learned.

First, if you do not have a copy of *Preach My Gospel,* please go and get one and use it. It is inspired and powerful. You might also find Elder Gene R. Cook's wonderful book *Searching the Scriptures* useful in your search.

Second, here are my practical ideas for searching the scriptures:

- Set aside time—the same time—*every* day.
- Begin with prayer.
- Use whatever approach feels best—read, cross-reference, mark.
- Listen for the Lord's voice, His message to you.
- Write down impressions and ideas.
- Pray about the impressions that come.
- Act on the impressions you receive.

I have had some wonderful experiences searching the scriptures. But of all that I have learned, the one thing that has deeply changed how I think about and use the scriptures is this: When I am really searching, no matter what the topic, the search leads me to Christ.

Jesus said, "I am the way, the truth, and the life" (John 14:6). When we search the scriptures to find the truth, we are searching for the Savior. In that search we use our minds, but we will only find the Savior and His truth if we also listen and feel with our hearts. Nephi taught Laman and Lemuel this principle when he said, "Ye were past feeling, that ye could not feel his words. . . . Why is it, that ye can be so hard in your hearts?" (1 Nephi 17:45–46).

With a heart and mind open to the Spirit, we search to understand and feel His words and hear His voice. I know the Savior speaks to us through the scriptures. When we read and ponder under the direction of the Spirit, we receive very personal guidance and instruction from the Lord. Like the disciples on the road to Emmaus, our hearts may "burn within us" as He speaks to us and "[opens] to us the scriptures" (Luke 24:32).

Herein lies the power of writing down what we learn in our searching and pondering. Indeed, the Lord has commanded us to obtain His word and to treasure it up in our hearts (D&C 11:21, 26). When we write down what we receive and review it and pray about it, we make it our own. When we truly hear and feel the voice of the Lord and treasure it in our hearts, we reinforce our covenants, deepen our desire to do His will, and strengthen our commitment to serve Him.

Principle 3:
Fast and Pray to Have the Guidance of the Spirit

Fasting is an ancient practice in which we humble ourselves, set our face to the Lord (Daniel 9:3), and yield our hearts to God (Helaman 3:35). In Joel 2:12–13 the Lord powerfully underscores this connection between fasting and our hearts:

"Therefore also now, saith the Lord, turn ye even to me with all your heart, and with fasting, and with weeping, and with mourning:

"And rend your heart, and not your garments, and turn unto the Lord your God: for he is gracious and merciful, slow to anger, and of great kindness."

Fasting, with prayer, is thus much more than going without food. It is a small sacrifice; but if it comes with purpose and commitment, it is acceptable of the Lord. When we fast with a purpose in Him—or turn our faces to the Lord and yield our hearts to Him—there is a cleansing power in that sacrifice that engages and shapes the desires and commitments of the heart.

Here is an analogy: Imagine an automatic garage door that will not open. You look and find that the infrared light receptor is dirty and misaligned. The light signal, and thus the circuit, has been interrupted, so the door will not open. You clean the receptor, align it with the source of light, and the door works. Fasting and prayer are like cleaning and aligning our spiritual light receptors. Through fasting and prayer we open ourselves more fully to the ministry of the Holy Ghost and, thus, to receive light and truth in our search of the scriptures. If we keep those receptors clean and aligned, we may then say of our search for the things of heaven, as Alma said, "For the Lord God hath made them manifest unto me by his Holy Spirit; and this is the spirit of revelation which is in me" (Alma 5:46).

As we fast and pray and invite the Holy Ghost into our search for truth, the Spirit will teach us what we need to know and do. We will receive guidance for our families and our callings in the work of the Lord. If we are consistent in our fasting and prayer, and if we always remember Him, the Holy Ghost may be our constant companion.

PRINCIPLE 4:
TEACH WITH POWER AND AUTHORITY

Every call in the Church is a call to teach. When we serve in the Lord's kingdom, we teach. It is true in our families, in the Relief Society, in every part of the Church. This is the sacred purpose for engaging the scriptures: We search to know the truth so that we might serve and teach more effectively in the kingdom. And it is our privilege to teach with power and authority of God.

Listen to these words of the Lord to Hyrum Smith in Doctrine and Covenants 11:20–21:

"Behold, this is your work, to keep my commandments, yea, with all your might, mind and strength.

"Seek not to declare my word, but first seek to obtain my word, and then shall your tongue be loosed; then, if you desire, you shall have my Spirit and my word, yea, the power of God unto the convincing of men."

Here the Lord teaches us that there are two sources of "the power of God unto the convincing of men." The first is the Spirit. The Lord promised Hyrum, and promises us, that if we are obedient and work hard to obtain the words of Christ, "then shall your tongue be loosed; [and] then . . . you shall have my Spirit." With the power of the Holy Ghost, we may speak the words of Christ "with the tongue of angels" (2 Nephi 31:13). Indeed, the Spirit carries those words unto the hearts of those who hear (2 Nephi 33:1) and bears witness that the words are true (D&C 100:7–8). What is taught is powerful because it is taught by the Spirit.

The second source of power is the word itself. Paul taught in Hebrews:

"For the word of God is quick, and powerful, and sharper than any two-edged sword, piercing even to the dividing asunder of soul and spirit, and of the joints and marrow, and is a discerner of the thoughts and intents of the heart" (Hebrews 4:12).

The words of Christ penetrate into the mind and heart with force and depth. Paul describes them as sharp, powerful, and quick—or living. When the Lord speaks, His words are perfectly adapted to the needs of those who hear. They strike at the very heart of the issues and concerns and hopes and dreams that people have. Thus, the word of God discerns the thoughts and intents of the hearts of those who hear.

Teaching with power and authority of God is all about the heart. If there is a desire in our hearts and if we have treasured the word in our hearts, the Lord will give us "in the very hour, yea, in the very moment, what [we] shall say" (D&C 100:6). Thus, what we teach touches the hearts of those who are prepared because we speak His words with His power. We teach with power and authority when we teach heart to heart.

THE FRAMEWORK OF ENGAGEMENT: TWO STORIES

Engaging the scriptures with these four principles brings marvelous promises: hearts that are His; hearts that know and treasure His voice; pure hearts filled with the Spirit; the capacity to serve and teach heart to heart. This is the framework of engagement. But it is also the cycle of engagement. As we search and teach, we learn. When we receive "in the very hour" what we should say, we gain insights that reinforce our desires and commitments and that send us back to the scriptures to seek deeper understanding.

I know these principles and promises are true. I have seen them in action in the lives of people close to me, and I have experienced them in my life. In the last nine months, Sue and I have had the great privilege of serving at BYU–Idaho. On that campus we have many opportunities to teach, and we have put the framework of engagement into practice. I would like to close today with two stories from our experience.

The first story is about a talk Sue gave in January for the first devotional of the winter semester. As she always does, she poured her heart and soul into that talk. She felt impressed to talk about the Christmas star. She fasted and prayed and searched the scriptures. In that search she connected the star to the Savior through a verse in 2 Peter and one in Revelation:

"We have also a more sure word of prophecy; whereunto ye do well that ye take heed, as unto a light that shineth in a dark place, until the day dawn, and the day star arise in your hearts" (2 Peter 1:19).

"I Jesus have sent mine angel to testify unto you these things. . . . I am the root and the offspring of David, and the bright and morning star" (Revelation 22:16).

These passages connect the dawn with the morning and the Savior with the daystar, the bright and morning star, that can arise in our hearts. These are beautiful passages, but the Lord had something more for Sue. Early one morning she woke up with two phrases going through her mind. I know this because she woke me up to tell me about them. Here are the phrases she received: "The daystar will only rise in hearts that are pure," and "Our hearts are purified only through the atonement of the Savior." Those were the insights that completed the talk the Lord wanted her to give about the star, the Savior, and our hearts.

On the day of the devotional, just before she stood to speak, one of the members of the faculty sang a special musical number. Without any consultation with us, he chose to sing *The Light Divine*. As he sang so beautifully, Sue and I looked at each other. We knew the Lord had blessed her with one of His tender mercies. She had a witness that He was aware of her talk and wanted her to know of His love and His blessing upon her words. She stood and taught heart to heart.

The second story is about an experience I had in a memorial service in February for a young student from Albania who was killed in a terrible car accident. As I prepared for the service, I read the fifty-seventh verse of section 138 in the Doctrine and Covenants in which the prophet says that faithful elders who depart this life continue to preach the gospel in the spirit world. I knew that scripture described that young man. He had returned from his mission just a few weeks before he died, and he was a great missionary. I decided to talk about that scripture in my remarks.

I was the last speaker. Each of the four speakers before me talked about what I had planned to say. We had all had the same spiritual impression. I leaned over to Sue and whispered, "What am I going to talk about?" Meanwhile, a young sister in the front of the chapel had been overcome with a great spirit of sadness and wept almost uncontrollably. She was one of the last people to see this young man alive. There was a strong sense of sadness and grief in the chapel.

Just before I stood to speak, two thoughts came into my mind: Doctrine and Covenants section 42 and the early part of section 138 where the spirits of the just rejoice together in the hope of the Savior's resurrection. So I stood and read these verses in section 42:

"Thou shalt live together in love, insomuch that thou shalt weep for the loss of them that die, and more especially for those that have not hope of a glorious resurrection.

"And it shall come to pass that those that die in me shall not taste of death, for it shall be sweet unto them" (vv. 45–46).

As I read those words, I saw for the first time that we are commanded to weep—but not for those who die; death is sweet to them. We are commanded to grieve so that we may learn to live together in love, so that we may learn to support and comfort one another in the loss of those we love.

I then read these words from section 138:

"All these had departed the mortal life, firm in the hope of a glorious resurrection, through the grace of God the Father and his Only Begotten Son, Jesus Christ.

"I beheld that they were filled with joy and gladness, and were rejoicing together because the day of their deliverance was at hand" (vv. 14–15).

In that very moment, the Lord taught me this principle: We have the same hope on this side of the veil as they had then on their side. The glorious message to all who grieve, to all who weep for the loss of a loved one, is that He lives! And because of Him, we too may look forward and rejoice in the hope of a glorious resurrection—just as they did.

The young woman who wept so sadly grew quiet just a few seconds after I began to speak. As the Holy Ghost taught us that evening, there came into that chapel a sweet spirit of peace and hope. It was a wonderful experience, a gift from a loving Heavenly Father. I know that in those moments the Spirit taught heart to heart.

I would like to share my testimony about you and about the promises the Lord has given us if we will engage the scriptures in our lives.

One day not long ago I sat in the Idaho Falls Temple pondering my talk for Women's Conference. There came into my mind a clear impression of the power in the sisters who would be sitting in my class. I know that power. I have seen it in Sue, the love of my life; in my daughters; in the wives of my sons; in my sister, my grandmothers, my sweet mother. I have known them and seen them, and I have seen you.

I have seen you in your homes nurturing and teaching children, grandchildren, nieces, and nephews. I have seen you in Relief Society, Primary, and Young Women—teaching, serving, saving lives. I have seen you share the gospel in word and deed in your neighborhoods and at work. I have seen you visiting sisters and families, healing body and soul. I have seen you in the temple, serving in the presence of the Lord. I have seen you nurture and love, teach and inspire, organize and lead. I have seen you do all these things clothed in power and glory, filled with the Spirit.

There is a marvelous work before you. It is His work. This is His Church and kingdom. I bear witness that Jesus is the Christ, the Savior and Redeemer. His light and His voice are in the scriptures. His invitation is to all: "Come. And let him that heareth say, Come. And let him that is athirst come. And whosoever will, let him take the water of life freely" (Revelation 22:17).

May God bless us all to engage the scriptures with full purpose of heart that, like the sons of Mosiah, we might serve and teach in the kingdom of God with power and authority, heart to heart.

"SPIRITUAL POISE"

Sally Wyne

Years ago, my friend had a traumatic experience. After tucking her two-year-old into bed for an afternoon nap, Rhonda took advantage of this rare quiet time to indulge in a bubble bath. As she relaxed in the warm water, she was alarmed to hear heavy footsteps downstairs in her kitchen. Then those noisy footfalls began to come up the flight of stairs that ended on a landing right outside her bathroom door. She knew that her toddler was in the next room and that she should jump out of the tub and run to protect her child, but she was frozen with fear. She simply could not move; she could only barely breathe. Her paralysis became complete as she watched the doorknob of the bathroom turn ever so slowly—and in walked her supposedly sleeping two-year-old, clomping around in her daddy's Sunday shoes! She felt enormous relief and, at the same time, overwhelming disappointment in her failure to be brave under that intense moment's pressure.

I have thought of her experience many times as I have prepared for this day with you. On the matter of personal spiritual preparation Elder Eyring has said: "It is not to endure storms, but to choose the right while they rage."[1]

Sally Wyne has her MS in communication from Idaho State University. She is a part-time religious education instructor at Brigham Young University. She has also served as a stake Relief Society president and currently serves as stake Institute teacher. She and her husband are the parents of ten and the grandparents of thirty-seven.

With all the changes that have come to our world since September 11, 2001, I wonder if I will be brave under intense pressure? Have I prepared adequately? How will I know what the Lord expects of me when decisions must be made in an instant? Am I spiritually prepared as the Brethren have so often counseled? Can I rise to the selflessness that the divinity within me requires?

Poise under pressure is my favorite definition of courage. Remembering five principles will help us to develop that kind of courage.

1. Follow the Savior's example.
2. One commandment is a springboard to others.
3. Count on immediate blessings.
4. Being obedient may be the most important part of our message to our posterity.
5. The challenges we face today may be preparing us for future joys.

First principle: We follow the Savior's example willingly. Listen to these statements from the book of John as the Savior tells us of His motivation.

"Then answered Jesus and said unto them, Verily, verily, I say unto you, The Son can do nothing of himself, but what he seeth the Father do: for what things soever he doeth these also doeth the Son likewise.

"For the Father loveth the Son, and sheweth him all things that himself doeth: and he will shew him greater works than these, that ye may marvel" (John 5:19–20).

"I can of mine own self do nothing: as I hear, I judge: and my judgment is just; because I seek not mine own will, but the will of the Father which hath sent me" (John 5:30).

"Jesus answered them, and said, My doctrine is not mine, but his that sent me.

"If any man will do his will, he shall know of the doctrine, whether it be of God, or whether I speak of myself.

"He that speaketh of himself seeketh his own glory: but he that seeketh his glory that sent him, the same is true, and no unrighteousness is in him" (John 7:16–18).

"For I have not spoken of myself; but the Father which sent me, he gave me commandment, what I should say, what I should speak.

"And I know that his commandment is life everlasting: whatsoever I speak therefore, even as the Father said unto me, so I speak" (John 12:49–50).

As we live lives of steady obedience, we become like the Savior. If His submission of will was a necessity, how much more critical is our own? With each choice to be immediately obedient, our faith is increased and our obedience becomes more childlike, more trusting, more eternity-oriented. We are childlike in our obedience as the Savior was childlike in His. His trust in the Father and His love for us made His obedience sacred. Our own responses become consecrated when poise under pressure becomes a personality trait, and not a one-time event.

When we know the Father's will and choose to do otherwise, we are going "our own way." President Kimball has said: "Whatever thing a man sets his heart and his trust in most is his god; and if his god doesn't also happen to be the true and living God of Israel, that man is laboring in idolatry."[2]

Surely, idolatry would not be the choice of a woman who seeks to create a Zion society in her home, her ward, or her community!

I have loved reading Sister Camille Fronk Olson's new book *Mary, Martha, and Me.* In it she shares this insight:

"A national Gallup survey . . . considered beliefs of college-educated Christians. . . . The results showed that 'college graduates are about three times more likely than persons without college education to put the Second Commandment (loving your neighbor) ahead of the First Commandment (loving God).' Notice what naturally follows those who take God out of first place, according to the same survey. 'The better educated are also about three times as likely to think it possible to be a true Christian without believing in the divinity of Christ.'"[3]

Lest we think that the order is not all that important, listen to these thoughts from Elder Neal A. Maxwell: "By choosing the Lord *first,* choosing one's friends becomes easier and much safer. Consider the contrasting friendships in the city of Enoch compared to peers in the cities of Sodom and Gomorrah! The citizens of the city of Enoch chose Jesus and a way of life, then became everlasting friends. So much depends on whom and what we seek *first.*"[4]

Second principle: Sometimes obedience to one commandment becomes a springboard to others.

Again, quoting from Elder Eyring: "You can gain confidence that God keeps his promises by trying them. That's why I so appreciate those commandments to which God has attached an explicit promise. I see those commandments as schoolmasters."[5]

My husband and I are converts to the Church. We were students at the University of Illinois in Champaign when Elder Beers and Elder Jensen came tracting in our student housing complex. (Perhaps you have heard our conversion story. We are the Wynes, who were tracted out in Champaign by Elder Beers.) After challenging us to come to church several times, the next pair of missionaries offered to arrange a ride for us. We traveled to our first sacrament meeting in a VW hatchback with a graduate student couple who lived nearby. Both of the women in that tiny car were pregnant, and there were two toddlers who were also along for the ride. We will be forever grateful for this family's caring, their willingness to reach out to us, and for their tiny but serviceable car.

After that first church meeting the elders asked if we had any questions. One of our questions concerned the payment of tithing. Why had we not seen an offering plate pass by? Our families had taught us that when you visit someone else's church, you should try to be as inconspicuous as possible. If they knelt, you knelt. If they chanted, you joined in. If an offering was taken, you contributed something. That, we were taught, was only polite. Since that week's fourth discussion had been on tithing, we had written a tithing check to take with us to the Sunday sacrament meeting. Why didn't we see a basket to put it in?

The elders explained that tithing monies are taken directly to a member of the bishopric, and then they walked us through that exercise by introducing us to a man who would become our lifelong mentor, Bishop Joseph R. Larsen. We handed him our envelope, and he had the grace to accept it. The next morning my husband arrived at his campus workplace and was invited in to the dean's office. The dean announced, "Ed, you have been doing such fine work here in the department that we have decided to give you a ten percent raise." Ed called me from campus and said, "You'll never guess what just happened!"

That experience became a touchstone for us in our further investigation of the Church. Not only did we receive an immediate testimony of the principle of tithing, but we saw in a very real way that the Lord was mindful of us and our spiritual development. Tithing became a school-master commandment for us.

When a young shepherd named David was chosen to fight the mighty Goliath, King Saul's reaction was less than enthusiastic. He said "Thou art not able to go against this Philistine to fight with him: for thou art but a youth, and he a man of war from his youth" (1 Samuel 17:33). David's response is indicative of his previous preparation. "Thy servant kept his father's sheep, and there came a lion, and a bear, and took a lamb out of the flock:

"And I went out after him, and smote him, and delivered it out of his mouth: and when he arose against me, I caught him by his beard, and smote him, and slew him" (1 Samuel 17:34–35).

Like young David, perhaps it is in our obedience to early commands that we gain the spiritual maturity to make later, more eternally signifi-cant choices. Are our youth fighting lions and bears when they refrain from dating until sixteen, choose modest clothing, or make an effort to befriend someone who isn't on the most popular list? What lions and bears are LDS women smoting and slaying in a world that consistently under-values a woman's contribution? Each lion and bear we dispatch adds to our spiritual poise.

Third principle: When we are immediately obedient, the blessings can begin immediately, too.

I have a dear friend who learned this lesson as a young mother. She was happily doing the morning dishes while her children played outside in the yard. A prompting came. Go get the mail! Her husband always brought the mail in when he came home for lunch—what a silly thought! When the impression came forcefully a second and a third time, she dried her hands and walked outside to the mailbox. As she headed back for the house, just a few steps from the mailbox and her little ones, she saw, coiled in the grass, a rattlesnake. Now the prompting made sense. So did her need for immediate obedience.

We do ourselves a disservice if we insist on knowing why before we act on such a prompting. Elder Oaks has taught that "if you read the scrip-tures with this question in mind: Why did the Lord command this or why did he command that, you find that in less than 1 in 100 commands was any reason given. It's not the pattern of the Lord to give reasons."[6]

Another friend tells this story. He and his four-year-old son were in the pasture outside their rural home. As Jim watched in horror, a temperamental ram began to charge his little boy. David saw the animal too and began to run toward the gate. His father knew that those little legs would never make it to safety outside the fence, and he called to his son "David! Drop!" There was no time for explanation. David needed to hear his father's voice, recognize it, trust it, and be immediately obedient. He dropped face down into the grass. The ram nosed around the now unthreatening form of the little boy and walked away, disinterested. The parallels are obvious. We must learn to recognize our Father's voice, trust it, and respond without delay to be safe. Sometimes there simply is no time for an explanation. It's learning to respond to His familiar voice that is critical.

Elder Bednar says it this way: "The scriptures, in essence, are a written 'recording' of the voice of the Lord—a voice we feel in our hearts more than we hear with our ears. And as we study the content and feel the spirit of the written word of God, we learn to hear His voice in the words we read and to understand the means whereby the words are given to us by the Holy Ghost."[7]

It takes practice to develop a new skill. Reading the scriptures becomes practice for recognizing our Father's still, small voice.

My stake was created a little over nine years ago. On the Thursday before our very first stake conference, someone from President Hinckley's office called to tell our brand-new stake president that the prophet would like to attend our Sunday morning stake conference session. President Jorgensen was to tell absolutely no one. The day arrived and as I glanced toward the door of our chapel from my opposite corner seat, I saw people begin to stand as President Jorgensen entered the chapel. I thought this was odd, but assumed that people were trying to be ultra-respectful of our new leader.

Then I saw, walking behind him, both President and Sister Hinckley. Immediately, thirty-five people rushed to use the phone to announce the prophet's presence to those who had chosen not to come to stake conference that day. When your local leader asks for your obedience, he may be telling you all he's allowed to say! Complying with the invitations of bishops and stake presidents will also add to our storehouse of spiritual poise.

Fourth principle: When we are steadily obedient over time, our message may be more in the *observation* of the law than in the content of our teaching.

I do not know that any of our ten children could recount a single lesson that was taught in our family home evenings, but they do remember that we did it week after week.

When the world tries to copy our programs, their results are not the same. Elder Eyring offers this thought: "[If a person should say], 'Could I borrow your family home evening manual? I want to have a family like yours.' And the answer is, 'It ain't in the manual.' The manual is a reflection of what it is that happens in those family home evenings."[8]

Steady obedience, even without immediately visible rewards, also helps us toward our goal of spiritual poise.

Fifth principle: A call today may be a survival skill for tomorrow.

One of my BYU students explained that when he was thirteen his father was called as a branch president. There were few priesthood holders available, and my student, then only a deacon, was called to act as the branch executive secretary. He reacted with typical teenage enthusiasm for early-morning meetings but fulfilled this unusual calling.

When my student entered the mission field, the leadership of a branch became his almost immediate assignment. He was prepared for this otherwise daunting task by his earlier obedience. What nearly impossible thing have you been asked to do that is preparing you for all that you need to be in some future assignment?

Another student shared this insight. All foreign missionaries have been withdrawn from Venezuela because of intense political unrest. The very young men who were converted so recently are now serving as bishops and mission presidents. What will their lives hold with this kind of leadership experience behind them?

The Prophet Joseph Smith said: "Go in all meekness, in sobriety, and preach Jesus Christ and Him crucified; not to contend with others on account of their faith, or systems of religion, but pursue a steady course."[9]

In Venezuela, steady obedience over time is keeping the gospel alive. Members with little experience are listening to the voice of a loving Father, and under His humble direction, the work is succeeding.

How did your family respond to the prophet's challenge to read the

Book of Mormon last year? We were given powerful promises that if we would be faithful, great blessings would come to us and to our families. At a recent fast and testimony meeting, one young woman shared this thought: "I got behind but I really wanted to finish, so I read 112 pages on New Year's Eve!" I rejoice at her commitment but wonder if blessings that might have come more frequently were forfeited by a decision to forego reading on all of those intervening days.

Perhaps it is the repetitive nature of our womanly tasks that wears us down. Virginia H. Pearce suggests that "most of our lives, rather, consist of daily routines, even monotonous tasks, that wear us down and leave us vulnerable to discouragement. Sure, we know where we're going, and if it were possible we would choose to jump out of bed, work like crazy, and be there by nightfall. But our goal, our journey's end, our Zion is life in the presence of our Heavenly Father. And to get there we are expected to walk and walk and walk."[10]

How many pioneers would have arrived in the Salt Lake Valley alive if President Brigham Young had insisted that they take off from Nauvoo on a dead run and that no one should stop along the way! Perhaps our frenzied attempts to be sporadically obedient are just as nonsensical. In an effort to drum up enthusiasm for our yearly family reunion, my husband and I have begun to write a monthly family newsletter that always includes an age-appropriate challenge for the grandchildren. If the children accomplish the challenge for that month, they get points to spend at the Reunion Store. Some of the challenges have included drawing a picture of one of their cousins, a baby's handprint traced in marker, or a short essay requesting our eldest grandson's thoughts about his recent ordination to the Aaronic Priesthood.

One of the sweetest of those responses was a phone call from seven-year-old Rian. That month her assignment was to call Grandma and Grandpa and sing her favorite Primary song. Because I have not worked in Primary in a very long time, the words to this song were new and especially touching to me.

> I lived in heaven a long time ago, it is true;
> Lived there and loved there with people I know. So did you.
> Then Heav'nly Father presented a beautiful plan,
> All about earth and eternal salvation for man.[11]

Can you imagine my joy as I realized that this sweet young girl knew the whole plan? I knew that her parents had been teaching her and had been providing growth experiences for her in a steady and obedient fashion. Through tears, I tried to explain how proud I was of this granddaughter and her grand understanding of that grand and beautiful plan.

One more story from a friend. Janet was cajoled into running a marathon by a group of Laurels she was teaching. She was forty-two. She trained physically and prepared mentally and ran that first 26.2-mile race in five hours. She was inspired to try again and this time to run faster. Her ultimate goal? To qualify for the Boston Marathon. At age forty-two her finishing time had to be three hours and fifty minutes or less. If she waited until she was forty-five, she could qualify with a time of four hours. That magic forty-fifth birthday came, and by now she had seven marathons under her worn-out running shoes.

She committed herself to the four-hour time and gave up chocolate, cookies, cakes, and candy, all the while reading every training tip she could get her hands on. She ran hills to the point of nausea and then walked down and ran up again. During that summer she ran eleven races of varying lengths. She was hopeful, prepared, and she had done all that she could do.

The St. George Marathon took place that year on October's general conference weekend. The night before the race her husband gave her a priesthood blessing. The next morning the two of them reviewed the pacing that would be necessary to meet her goal for each portion of the race. The starting gun was fired, and she was off.

Along the way there were some discouraging discussions overheard as she passed other runners. Some claimed that her present pace was too slow to make a four-hour time. Then she would remember that she had worked it all out. If she stayed steady within the plan, she would realize her goal.

At the twenty-mile marker she knew that she could actually do it! She was so excited that she nearly lost her focus. She had to remind herself to stay steady and be consistent. When she crossed the finish line the overhead clock read exactly three hours and fifty minutes. She had done it! She even qualified for that younger age group!

Back at the hotel, after a quick shower, she flipped on the TV to watch general conference. Elder Eyring was speaking about the importance of being immediately and steadily obedient, and she experienced one of those tender mercies that Elder Bednar has taught us to watch for. She listened and understood the parallels.

We can't spend a solid month of diligent scripture study and then do nothing for years, hoping to call up those long-past insights when times are tough. "Great faith has a short shelf life," according to Elder Eyring.[12]

In life, as in preparing for a marathon, it's steady obedience that helps us toward the poise under pressure that we so desire.

President Faust has shared this thought: "Living a Christ-like life every day may for many be even more difficult than laying down one's life. We learned during wartime that many men were capable of great acts of selflessness, heroism, and nobility with regard to life. But when the war was over and they came home, they could not bear up under the burdens of living the eternal every day and became enslaved by tobacco, alcohol, drugs, and debauchery."[13]

One last grandchild story. We spent a general conference weekend at our daughter's home in Idaho. During the last session on Sunday afternoon, one of our older grandchildren made some popcorn. Joshua, who is two, went immediately to the bowl and helped himself. He assumed that the blessings of that snack were for him, and he did not hesitate to partake. I thought how being childlike might also include the assumption that every good gift was meant for us, just as Joshua did. I believe it would please our Heavenly Father to know of our trust in Him and in His glorious plan.

As Rian taught me of that grand plan in the last verse of her favorite Primary song,

> Jesus was chosen, and as the Messiah he came,
> Conquering evil and death through his glorious name,
> Giving us hope of a wonderful life yet to be—
> Home in that heaven where Father is waiting for me.[14]

I testify that the words of that song are true. There is a patient, yet eager Father waiting for us in that lovely place. When we have been steadily obedient through the choices of a lifetime, we will be like the Savior who was sent to teach us all that the Father commanded. We will have learned to use one commandment as a stepping-stone to another. We will know that immediate blessings can be counted upon. We will understand that the faithful observance of the law may be the most permanent message we leave for our posterity. We will watch for opportunities to serve that will prepare us for still greater joys. Our spiritual poise will prevent our being paralyzed by fear, even as the heavy footsteps of the adversary pound threateningly up the stairs.

In short, we will rise to the divinity within us and find in the rising, our Father's outstretched hand.

NOTES

1. Henry B. Eyring, "Spiritual Preparedness: Start Early and Be Steady," *Ensign*, November 2005, 37.
2. Spencer W. Kimball, "The False Gods We Worship," *Ensign*, June 1976, 4.
3. As quoted in Camille Fronk Olson, *Mary, Martha and Me* (Salt Lake City: Deseret Book, 2006), 99.
4. Neal A. Maxwell, "The Tugs and Pulls of the World," *Ensign*, November 2000, 35; emphasis in original.
5. Henry B. Eyring, "Child of Promise," in *Brigham Young University 1985–86 Devotional and Fireside Speeches* (Provo, UT: Brigham Young University, 1986), 126.
6. Dallin H. Oaks, *Provo Daily Herald*, June 5, 1988, 21.
7. David A. Bednar, "Because We Have Them before Our Eyes," *New Era*, April 2006, 5.
8. Henry B. Eyring, "A Steady, Upward Course," BYU–Idaho Devotional, September 18, 2001.
9. Joseph Smith, *History of The Church of Jesus Christ of Latter-day Saints*, ed. B. H. Roberts, 2d. ed., 7 vols. (Salt Lake City: The Church of Jesus Christ of Latter-day Saints, 1932–51), 2:431.
10. Virginia H. Pearce, "Keep Walking, and Give Time a Chance," *Ensign*, May 1997, 86.
11. Janeen Jacobs Brady, "I Lived in Heaven," *Children's Songbook of The Church of Jesus Christ of Latter-day Saints* (Salt Lake City: The Church of Jesus Christ of Latter-day Saints, 1989), 4.
12. Eyring, "Spiritual Preparedness: Start Early and Be Steady," 37.
13. James E. Faust, "The Price of Discipleship," *Ensign*, April 1999, 2.
14. Brady, "I Lived in Heaven."

"My Mind Was Called Up to Serious Reflection"

Randy L. Bott

As a young boy, Joseph Smith attempted to make sense out of the senseless confusion so prevalent in the teachings of the churches of his day and their conflicting doctrines. How could a person so young make sense out of the happenings of life? His method for attacking the problem gives us an effective way of getting a clearer vision of the big picture of eternity.

With the permission of the family, I would like to share an incident that changed forever the lives of all who participated. Five-year-old Andrew York, whose family lives in our stake, was with his family on a well-deserved family vacation. While his parents were setting up camp near the banks of the Colorado River just outside Moab, Utah, little Andrew and his older sister went exploring, as children always do. Soon they were standing on the bank of what appeared to be a placid bend in a deceptively calm river. After throwing a few rock and sticks into the river, Andrew innocently took just one step into the water. Hidden beneath the surface was a swirling, raging undercurrent. In a heartbeat, Andrew disappeared. Frantically, Andrew's sister ran to her parents for help. Without regard for his own safety, Andrew's father dove into the frigid water. Time

---

Randy L. Bott is a professor of Church history and doctrine at Brigham Young University. He has an EdD in educational leadership and serves as a counselor in a branch presidency at the Missionary Training Center.

and again diving, searching, frantically trying to find his beloved son. But it was not to be.

That evening the stake presidency received a call from Andrew's bishop informing us of the tragedy. At four o'clock the next morning the bishop and the three of us in the stake presidency were traveling to Moab. We arrived and went directly to the site where Andrew was last seen. For the next seemingly endless hours we combed every square inch of the river's banks. We prayed, we plead with Heavenly Father that somehow Andrew had miraculously floated downstream and would be found huddling on the bank of the river, cold but safe. However, his little body would not surface for another five days, four-and-a-half miles from where he entered the water.

Finally, after many hours of fruitless searching, we visited the family who were holed up in their motel room. Words cannot adequately explain the feelings we had when we entered the room and found an emotionally spent mother being comforted by a physically exhausted father as she tried to console her other children. As her pleading, tear-stained face turned towards us, she said, "I just want to know one thing. Is it all true? It is really true what we have been taught about families being together for-ever? About parents being able to have their children again? Is it really all true?"

At that moment a superficial answer would not have been appropri-ate. Our minds were called up to serious reflection. How secure were we, four seasoned priesthood leaders, in our knowledge of what we had been taught and had been teaching for many years? A scripture came to mind that took on more significance in that single instant than in all the years I had taught it.

In Doctrine and Covenants 101:16 the Lord said, "Therefore, let your hearts be comforted concerning Zion [Andrew]; for all flesh is in mine hands; be still and know that I am God."

Blessings were given, reassuring counsel offered, and then we left for home, never to be the same again.

It really shouldn't require such an incident to cause us to seriously reflect on what is really important. But life seems to be so insanely busy. It is like we are on a treadmill where some evil being is turning up the speed, faster and faster, to where we can hardly keep up, let alone find time to seriously reflect on anything, let alone life's essential lessons.

So much of what happens to us seems senseless. Many years ago, when I was but four-and-a-half years old, my father died of a heart attack at age thirty-three. For the next fourteen-and-a-half years, I engaged in occasional pity parties. Why would God do such a thing to me? Was I somehow being punished for being bad? Why couldn't I enjoy the same father/son relationship that so many of my friends had? The questions were many, but in the rush of being a teenager, I really didn't take much time to try to make sense of the senseless.

As a young missionary, sitting alone on a beach in the South Pacific, watching the breakers crash across the reef, I finally stepped off the treadmill and pleadingly asked my Heavenly Father to help me understand why I had been dealt such a cruel hand in life. I didn't see a vision or hear a voice, but in a nanosecond, understanding was communicated to me. I began to see the many lessons I had learned, lessons that likely I wouldn't have learned if my father had lived. I was so overwhelmed with the insights being communicated to me that I got down on my knees right there on that sandy beach and thanked Heavenly Father for what had been, to that point in my life, a senseless tragedy.

I am confident, in retrospect, that Heavenly Father had tried many times before to communicate to me His love and the reassurance I was seeking that although I wasn't mature enough to see the wisdom in what was happening to me, He did.

To the Saints who experienced so much senseless persecution in the early days of this dispensation, the Lord said, "For verily I say unto you, blessed is he that keepeth my commandments, whether in life or in death; and he that is faithful in tribulation, the reward of the same is greater in the kingdom of heaven.

"Ye cannot behold with your natural eyes, for the present time, the design of your God concerning those things which shall come hereafter, and the glory which shall follow after much tribulation.

"For after much tribulation come the blessings. Wherefore the day cometh that ye shall be crowned with much glory; the hour is not yet, but is nigh at hand.

"Remember this, which I tell you before, that you may lay it to heart, and receive that which is to follow" (D&C 58:2–5).

After a painful separation from his beloved wife, Elder Richard G. Scott of the Quorum of the Twelve Apostles gave us these words of counsel from his own personal heartbreaking experience:

"Just when all seems to be going right, challenges often come in multiple doses applied simultaneously. When those trials are not consequences of your disobedience, they are evidence that the Lord feels you are prepared to grow more (see Prov. 3:11–12). He therefore gives you experiences that stimulate growth, understanding, and compassion which polish you for your everlasting benefit. To get you from where you are to where He wants you to be requires a lot of stretching, and that generally entails discomfort and pain."[1]

However, too many people, when faced with these apparently senseless trials, become bitter, some abandoning their faith, some turning away from God. Without being called up to serious reflection, as in my case, the learning of the profound lessons of life may be postponed, or as with so many who abandon their faith, missed altogether.

So how do you find the time in this busy world to call up your mind to serious reflection? With children to care for, a husband, a household to run, several callings in the Church to magnify, and, for many, a job to hold down, just when are you supposed to find time for serious reflection?

Perhaps you won't have a sandy beach in the South Pacific or a Sacred Grove in upstate New York. But how about a precious moment or two while standing over the gaping mouth of an insatiable washing machine awaiting the tenth load of wash? How about pausing for a few moments over the sleeping body of your sick child before racing off to attend to the needs of the rest of the family? How about sitting for a few minutes with the engine and radio turned off before going into the supermarket to purchase this week's groceries? There are islands of time—maybe not in the South Pacific, but just as necessary and just as real.

Sometimes we get the idea we must "go it alone." Many years ago when I finally realized that my brave, young sweetheart was going under trying to keep up with three little girls while I tried to be everything to everybody as the CES representative in eastern North Carolina, we sat down to counsel. We didn't have the money to hire a baby-sitter or a maid. The answer to our prayers came in the person of Joan. She was equally as stressed with her three little boys. However, trading off baby-sitting not only provided the relief necessary for each young mother but gave the children something to look forward to each week. Are you think-ing outside the box in trying to find solutions to your time crunch? If you do, I promise that Heavenly Father will enlighten your mind and help you find a solution to your problems. Finding time for serious reflection isn't easy, but it is essential.

Even the Savior saw the necessity of His disciples taking a break from the demands of their apostolic calling: "And he said unto them, Come ye yourselves apart into a desert place, and rest a while: for there were many coming and going, and they had no leisure so much as to eat" (Mark 6:31). At times we think we ought to be tough enough to handle the stress of life without having to take a time-out. Note this scripture which holds more thought-provoking principles than we have time to discuss: "When Jesus therefore perceived that they would come and take him by force, to make him a king, he departed again into a mountain himself alone" (John 6:15). Sometimes we think we ought to be able to be everything to every-body. Even the Savior, who had the power to be exactly that, didn't. Are you trying to take on too much without the rejuvenation which comes when you take the time for serious reflection?

What are you to call up your mind to serious reflection about? After Joseph Smith, who was then in Kirtland, Ohio, learned by revelation that the Saints in Missouri were suffering terrible persecutions, he asked for enlightenment from our Heavenly Father. The Lord said, "Verily I say unto you my friends, fear not, let your hearts be comforted; yea, rejoice evermore, and in everything give thanks;

"Waiting patiently on the Lord, for your prayers have entered into the ears of the Lord of Sabaoth, and are recorded with this seal and testament—the Lord hath sworn and decreed that they shall be granted.

"Therefore, he giveth this promise unto you, with an immutable covenant that they shall be fulfilled; and all things wherewith you have been afflicted shall work together for your good, and to my name's glory, saith the Lord" (D&C 98:1–3).

Several quick observations: First, the Lord calls them His "friends"— He says the same about you. Sometimes we wonder if we have offended

God when such trying circumstances come upon us. Instead of complaining and becoming depressed over the seemingly senseless trials, the Lord tells us to let our hearts be comforted and rejoice. That may take some doing to accomplish. Know for sure, if it wasn't possible, He wouldn't have instructed us to do it.

Now for the hard part: "And in everything give thanks." Even the bad things? It will take some time of serious reflection where you look deeply into your heart and see that the blessings you received, the lessons you learned, the growth you have experienced far, far outweighs the pain and discomfort of the trial you received. It may not happen immediately. It may actually, as in my case, take many years. But if you are persistent in looking for the blessings, you will find them. To give thanks before you can see the outweighing, counterbalancing blessings would be disingenuous at best and totally hypocritical at worst.

At the end of the third verse, the Lord makes another statement that only an omnipotent God could make: "All things wherewith you have been afflicted shall work together for your good, and to my name's glory"—your good is here in mortality; His name's glory is to exalt you. Knowing that Heavenly Father is a very efficient being, I have come to know for myself that He will not require that I suffer one iota more nor one moment longer than is absolutely necessary for my eternal benefit— and neither will He require it of you.

I cannot, with my limited vision and experience, see how some of the terrible things that have happened to so many of you can possibly be turned around for your benefit. But the Lord didn't say "some things you have been afflicted with." He said *all things* would work together for your good. Trust Him.

Sometimes life seems so difficult that we lose our zest for living. If we dwell too much or too long on what, at the moment, seems to be the negatives, it is easy to miss the joy and blessings which come our way daily. President Lorenzo Snow gave the following insightful comment:

"Brethren and sisters, the thing you should have in your mind, and which you should make a motto in your life, is this: Serve God faithfully, and be cheerful. I dislike very much, and I believe people generally do, to see a person with a woe begone countenance, and to see him mourning as though his circumstances were of the most unpleasant character. There is no pleasure in association with such persons. In the family it is always a good thing for the parent to be cheerful in the presence of his wife and children. And out of that cheerfulness may arise many good gifts. The Lord has not given us the gospel that we may go around mourning all the days of our lives. He has not introduced this religion for this purpose at all. We came into the world for certain purposes, and those purposes are not of a nature that require much mourning or complaint. Where a person is always complaining and feeling to find fault, the Spirit of the Lord is not very abundant in his heart. If a person wants to enjoy the Spirit of the Lord, let him, when something of a very disagreeable nature comes along, think how worse the circumstance might be, or think of something worse that he has experienced in the past. Always cultivate a spirit of gratitude. It is actually the duty of every Latter-day Saint to cultivate a spirit of gratitude."[2]

As I read and ponder the scriptures, there are far more stories and examples of difficult times than there are of good times. Yet in the scriptures the Lord consistently tells us to "be of good cheer" (Matthew 9:2) or to "rejoice ever more."

President Ezra Taft Benson quoted an experience that demonstrates the indomitable attitude of the Prophet Joseph Smith:

"When George A. Smith was very ill, he was visited by his cousin, the Prophet Joseph Smith. The afflicted man reported: 'He told me I should never get discouraged, whatever difficulties might surround me. If I were sunk into the lowest pit of Nova Scotia and all the Rocky Mountains piled on top of me, I ought not to be discouraged, but hang on, exercise faith, and keep up good courage, and I should come out on the top of the heap.' (George A. Smith Family, comp. Zora Smith Jarvis, p. 54).

"There are times when you simply have to righteously hang on and outlast the devil until his depressive spirit leaves you. As the Lord told the Prophet Joseph Smith: 'Thine adversity and thine afflictions shall be but a small moment; And then, if thou endure it well, God shall exalt thee on high' (D&C 121:7–8)."[3]

I see people every day who feel they must have large blocks of uninterrupted time before they can undertake a project. That rarely happens. I see others who insist that as soon as this or that or the other event is over, they will begin in seriousness their quest to get their lives organized and in order. I have grown very fond of a statement made by Elder John Longden, formerly an Assistant to the Twelve, now of the spirit world:

"*Today* is here. I will start with a smile, and resolve to be agreeable. I will not criticize. I refuse to waste my valuable time.

"*Today* has one thing in which I know I am equal with others—Time. All of us draw the same salary in seconds, minutes, hours—*24 Golden Hours each day.*

"*Today* I will not waste my time, because the minutes I wasted yesterday are as lost as a vanished thought.

"*Today* I refuse to spend time worrying about what might happen. I am going to spend my time making things happen.

"*Today* I am determined to study to improve myself, for tomorrow I may be wanted, and I must not be found lacking.

"*Today* I am determined to do things I should do. I firmly resolve to stop doing the things I should *not* do.

"*Today* I begin by doing and not wasting my time. In one week I will be miles beyond the person I am today.

"*Today* I will not imagine what I would do if things were different. They are not different. I will make a success with what material I have.

"*Today* I will stop saying, 'If I had time,' for I never will 'find time' for anything—if I want time I must take it.

"*Today* I will act toward other people as though this might be my last day on earth. I will not wait for tomorrow. Tomorrow never comes."[4]

Taking time for serious reflection is essential; it is not a wasting of your precious time.

I am frequently asked if I have a favorite scripture. I have many of them, but this one is especially appropriate. In Doctrine and Covenants 78:17–19 the Lord says:

"Verily, verily, I say unto you, ye are little children, and ye have not as yet understood how great blessings the Father hath in his own hands and prepared for you;

"And ye cannot bear all things now; nevertheless, be of good cheer, for I will lead you along. The kingdom is yours and the blessings thereof are yours, and the riches of eternity are yours.

"And he who receiveth all things with thankfulness shall be made glorious; and the things of this earth shall be added unto him, even an hundred fold, yea, more."

I suppose those of us who are older might be tempted to take offense at someone calling us little children in our understanding; however, when that someone is the Lord, we seem to know that He is telling it the way it really is. He emphatically tells us that we "cannot bear all things now"— we aren't going to be perfect in this life. However, we are commanded to "be of good cheer"—don't get discouraged because you are human. Don't become depressed because you can't do everything or be everything to everybody. His promise is sure: "I will lead you along." Then the glorious promise is that if we will take enough time and put in enough effort to call our minds to serious reflection, the kingdom is ours—both the Church and the celestial kingdom, the blessings promised to the faithful are yours, the riches of eternity will be yours. If we can just learn to receive all things with thankfulness, you will increase your joy and happiness by over a hundred times. I believe Him. I know it is true.

So in answer to Sister York's soul-piercing question, "Is it all true?" My solemn testimony is a resounding yes! My testimony is not based on the ease and luxury of my life. It has not resulted from the lack of trials, sorrows, and challenges. That sure testimony has come through and because of the afflictions, the trials, the experiences, and finally by the revelations which God has promised and fulfilled. I am confident that many of you share the same testimony. For those who are still struggling, take time to call up your mind to serious reflection and, as God lives, you will know for yourself, as I testify, that Jesus is the Christ, that Joseph Smith was and is the Prophet of the Restoration, that we are lead by living prophets today, that the gospel has been restored in its fulness, that the Book of Mormon really is the word of God, and that personal revelation is a reality available to each and every sincere son or daughter of God who will pay the price. I testify that sooner or later, according to the Lord's will for you, that every jig and jog in the pathway of your life, every bump and pothole in the pathway to perfection will make perfect sense when seen through eternal eyes. And lastly, that God our Eternal Father is not an absentee Father but knows you by your first name, is aware when a hair of your head falls to the ground, and is doing all in His omnipotent power to prepare you for the exaltation which lies ahead.

NOTES

1. Richard G. Scott, "Trust in the Lord," *Ensign*, November 1995, 16.
2. Lorenzo Snow, *The Teachings of Lorenzo Snow*, ed. Clyde J. Williams (Salt Lake City: Bookcraft, 1996), 61–62.
3. Ezra Taft Benson, *The Teachings of Ezra Taft Benson* (Salt Lake City: Bookcraft, 1988), 395–96.
4. John Longden, in Conference Report, April 1966, 39.

THE PRECIOUS GIFT OF TIME

Claudia Eliason

Robert Fulghum, author of *All I Really Need to Know I Learned in Kindergarten,* described a seminar he attended on the island of Crete in one of the essays in his book, *It Was On Fire When I Lay Down On It.* The seminar leader was Alexander Papaderos, renowned philosopher. After a two-week study of Greek culture and history, the class was preparing to leave when Papaderos asked the usual: "Are there any questions?" Fulghum asked, "What is the meaning of life?" Papaderos looked carefully into Fulghum's eyes to see if he was serious. When he determined his question was sincere, he pulled from his wallet a "very small round mirror, about the size of a quarter."

Papaderos said: "When I was a small child, during the war, we were very poor and we lived in a remote village. One day, on the road, I found the broken pieces of a mirror. A German motorcycle had been wrecked in that place.

"I tried to find all the pieces and put them together, but it was not possible, so I kept only the largest piece. This one. And by scratching it on a stone I made it round. I began to play with it as a toy and became fascinated by the fact that I could reflect light into dark places where the

---

Claudia Eliason has served on the Primary general board and has been a ward Relief Society instructor and stake single adult advisor. A university professor and author, she is also a wife and mother.

sun would never shine. . . . It became a game for me to get light into the most inaccessible places I could find.

"I kept the little mirror, and as I went about my growing up, I would take it out in idle moments and continue the challenge of the game. As I became a man, I grew to understand that this was not just a child's game but a metaphor for what I might do with my life. I came to understand that I am not the light or the source of light. But light . . . is there, and it will only shine in many dark places if I reflect it.

"I am a fragment of a mirror whose whole design and shape I do not know. Nevertheless, with what I have I can reflect light into the dark places of this world . . . and change some things in some people. Perhaps others may see and do likewise. This is what I am about. This is the meaning of my life."[1]

Much of what Fulghum learned about Greek culture and history that summer are gone, but in the wallet of his mind he still carries that small round mirror.

My topic is "Today, While the Sun Shines."[2] Our desire is to focus on what we can do *today,* and I would like to suggest that even when the sun does not shine, when we face clouds and darkness, we can cast the gospel light into first our own life and then into the lives of others—we *can* brighten the world around us. However, to cast "light" into our own life and the lives of others requires time.

To use time effectively each day is a true test of discipleship. We talk about saving time, making time, losing time, as if time were flexible or relative. In truth, each of us has only twenty-four hours a day, and we must learn to manage ourselves within the limited time. Elder Neal A. Maxwell reminded us, "Time, unlike some material things, cannot be recycled."[3]

Elder William H. Bennett, former Assistant to the Council of the Twelve, said, "We live our lives . . . in the present—one moment at a time. But with each tick of the clock the present becomes the past, and the past cannot be changed. It is also true, however, that with each tick of the clock a part of the future becomes the present. Thus, the key to a successful and happy life is to strive diligently always to make the most of the present—to make the most of each moment as it arrives."[4]

President Gordon B. Hinckley has reminded us to avoid wasting time and being idle. He said, "One of the great tragedies we witness almost daily is the tragedy of men of high aim and low achievement. Their motives are noble. Their proclaimed ambition is praiseworthy. Their capacity is great. But their discipline is weak. They succumb to indolence. Appetite robs them of will."[5]

On this same note Elder Neal A. Maxwell said, "There are no idle hours; there are only idle people. In true righteousness there is serenity, but there is an array of reminders that the 'sacred present' is packed with possibilities which are slipping by us, which are going away from us each moment."[6]

President Brigham Young said that the gift of life is time and our power and agency to use it well.[7] It is such a great inheritance that we should look on it as our capital. How do we invest our time each day? How might we use it in such a way that we will cast light into dark places? I propose to you that if we spend our time well, it will be invested, even compounded, and will echo in eternity. Let me suggest six reminders to help us wisely expend our precious daily time.

1. Take time daily to draw closer to our Savior, strengthen testimony, and assure that the Holy Ghost will be our constant companion. Today, kneel to pray; stop to feast on the scriptures; attend the temple; pause to read, reflect, and think of how you might apply a conference talk; and, prepare well for your callings in the Church.

While serving as a Primary leader, I challenged leaders and teachers to prepare their lessons at least one week in advance so they might practice the principle found in the lesson. Later as I was called as a Primary teacher of eight-year-old children, I tried to practice what I preached, so I studied the lesson on Sunday afternoon in preparation for the next Sunday.

I recall one Sunday afternoon that the lesson was on the blessings we receive when we attend the temple. I decided that a trip to the temple that week would better prepare me to teach the young children about the temple and also help me to bear a stronger testimony about temple blessings. Attending the temple that week with a special purpose in mind was a spiritual experience. Years later I remember the spirit I felt as I taught those eight-year-old Primary children that particular temple lesson.

In today's world there are so many distractions that literally grab our time. The Internet, TV, and other forms of media all draw on our capital of time and often rob us of more precious use of the daily 24 hours. It is important that we not procrastinate doing today those activities that we know will strengthen our testimonies and bring us closer to living an obedient life. President Ezra Taft Benson said, "When we put God first, all other things fall into their proper place or drop out of our lives. Our love of the Lord will govern the claims for our affection, the demands on our time, the interests we pursue, and the order of our priorities."[8]

2. Take time to build faith to be ready to face the trials life brings. Today while the sun shines nourish faith that will take you through some of the darker days, the days that are full of trials. For you younger mothers it may be the trials of mudprints on a freshly cleaned floor, spilled milk, the little one climbing into the bathtub fully clothed, a flat tire on the way to an important ball game, or a child not being included in an activity with other neighborhood children. For mothers with teenagers, trials requiring faith may be the first date of a child, sending a new driver out on the roadways, a teenager not making the team, high-stakes tests, and many other daily trials. We all need a reserve of faith to draw upon when needed.

Our family learned much about faith from our oldest son. While serving as a missionary in Germany about 10 years ago, he became ill. Through his faith he fulfilled his mission and when he returned home was diagnosed with a permanent liver disease, primary sclerosing cholangitis. The day of his diagnosis my husband and I were devastated and inconsolable. Our son, Eric, had prayed and pondered his condition and came to us and said, "You two need to pull yourselves together and lean on my faith. I have had a talk with Heavenly Father and I don't know how, but I do know that I am going to be all right."

Eric has continued to live his life with that same faith, and often we have had to continue to lean on his faith. On December 1, 2004, in his third year of medical school in Arizona, he underwent a living liver transplant. Our younger son Kyle, also full of faith, was the donor. Our family's motto was "Doubt not, fear not, and miracles will come," adapted from Mormon 9:21.

As our two sons prepared for the surgery that morning, they were in a room with a number of other people also being prepared for various surgeries. The room simply had curtains between the patients. Our sons were side by side, and Eric was giving Kyle one final boost of faith in what was to transpire. During the long surgery, I left the waiting room to make a phone call. A lady stopped me and asked me if I was the mother of the two young men undergoing the liver transplant. When I told her that I was, she thanked me for what our sons had done for her and her family and other patients in the room. Her husband was also preparing for surgery and was very nervous. She said their family stopped and listened in on the conversation between our sons, and they were buoyed up and encouraged by the faith of these two young men. Our sons constantly reminded us that the Lord was with us, for we had faith in the scripture in Doctrine and Covenants 68:6 that reads, "Wherefore, be of good cheer, and do not fear, for I the Lord am with you, and will stand by you."

President Gordon B. Hinckley has often quoted the Savior's words to Thomas when He said, "Be not faithless, but believing" (John 20:27).[9] We must all believe that our Heavenly Father knows and loves each one of us. Sometimes when I have been faithless and spent time stewing over something, the words to the hymn "How Firm a Foundation" have given me faith and hope. In part, some of the words are:

> Fear not, I am with thee; oh, be not dismayed,
> For I am thy God and will still give thee aid.
> I'll strengthen thee, help thee, and cause thee to stand,
> Upheld by my righteous, omnipotent hand.
>
> When through the deep waters I call thee to go,
> The rivers of sorrow shall not thee o'erflow,
> For I will be with thee, thy troubles to bless,
> And sanctify to thee thy deepest distress.[10]

The scriptures remind us of many of our prophets who have faced immense trials but couched those trials in resolute faith. An example is the prophet Nephi who experienced trials unlike our modern-day trials. His experiences regaining the brass plates from Laban, being persecuted continually by his brothers, and other hardships in his life remind us that he clung to his faith in his Heavenly Father.

Sheri Dew observes, "The Lord, through our individually tailored mortal tutorials, gives us opportunities to practice, rehearse, refine, and develop our spiritual skills—and in particular, to practice having and exercising faith."[11] Our faith provides a way for us to do things we might otherwise think impossible to accomplish, including enduring our individual trials.

3. Take time to love and serve. Jesus Christ is the perfect example of love and service. He explained that He did not come to earth to be served but to serve and to give His life for us (Matthew 20:28). Paul the apostle remembered Jesus' words: "By love serve one another" (Galatians 5:13). There are many examples of His service and love, but one of my favorites occurred just before His crucifixion when He met with His disciples. After teaching them He took a basin of water and a towel and washed their feet. In those days washing a visitor's feet was a sign of honor and was usually done by a servant. Jesus did it as an example of love and service (John 13:5–15). When we willingly serve others in the spirit of love, we become more Christlike.

Returning to the story of our son's liver transplant, that Christmas of 2004 we witnessed as a family an example of brotherly love, of Christlike giving that we shall never forget. At the Eliason home that Christmas there was no shopping, no lights, no wrapped presents under a tree, but oh, there was a gift exchange unlike any other. Ralph Waldo Emerson said, "The only gift is a portion of thyself."[12] Kyle gave something to Eric that he could not give himself, a healthy liver. He viewed it as a privilege even though it was with great physical sacrifice. Kyle returned to Utah before Eric was released from the hospital. As I took him to the airport and wheeled him in a wheelchair as far as security would allow me, Kyle turned to me and said, "Mom, can you do one thing for me? Will you go back to the hospital and tell Eric how much I love him?"

Take time in your busy, daily life to do quiet acts of service without having to be assigned. Look around you, feel the pulse of your family and neighborhood, listen to the promptings of the Holy Spirit and *act* upon them. When we are our brother's keeper, we are willing to give heart, might, mind, and strength to consecrate on the daily altar of brotherhood.

Lafcadio Hearn, the British writer who became a Japanese citizen, gave a dramatic illustration of love for our neighbors from the Asian culture. Once when a great earthquake shook the country, a farmer working on his hilltop farm saw a tremendous tsunami forming in the distance.

Below him, in the lowlands, hundreds of his neighbors were unaware of the impending disaster. Immediately, this farmer set fire to his precious rice fields, knowing that his neighbors would see the flames and rush to his assistance. All of them did. From that vantage point of safety they watched as the gigantic waves engulfed the area they had just left. Only then did they realize that the farmer had saved their lives—and at what cost?[13]

Amidst the iniquity, the selfishness, the indecency and cruelties of one person to another, there is a streak of decency running through mankind. It is this goodness that the Lord expects from all of us when He reminds us so often in the scriptures—love one another, serve one another.

Like the farmer, the summons of the Spirit will be the defining force of our soul's character throughout our lives. Honoring conscience and obedience is what really matters. Our charge is to tune into the Spirit and be guided to what we need to do to serve, love, and grow.

4. Take time to learn something new each day; work on your education. Counseling his son Helaman, Alma said, "O, remember, my son, and learn wisdom in thy youth" (Alma 37:35). We are also admonished to seek learning by study and by faith (D&C 88:118). The world of knowledge is moving quickly. Decade by decade there is increasing application of science and technology. Compared to 100 years ago there is much more knowledge to record, sift through, store, search out, and hopefully use with discrimination and effectiveness.

Education is at our fingertips. Today, there are about 75,000 scientific and technical periodicals that contain about two million articles each year, written in some twenty-five languages. Daily we should seek and work for the knowledge and learning we each deserve. It may mean that we shut out chaos and confusion for a period of time each day and see if we can harness the wonder of learning. We need to view education and learning as a way to live and not as a way to make a living.

In 1994 as a very middle-aged woman, I began doctoral studies at Brigham Young University. I came because of some spiritual promptings and within days of beginning my program of study found myself excited with the rich learning opportunities. I learned from my cohorts and their diverse cultures and experiences. I learned from professors with broad backgrounds of knowledge. I learned from reading great writers and philosophers. True, the learning was often overwhelming, but I recall many evenings arriving home late after commuting from Provo to Ogden and being ecstatic to share with my husband and family new insights I had learned that day. Learning is exhilarating.

The opportunity for education is all around us—reading good books and literature, searching out meaningful information on the Internet, making a habit of going to the library, joining a book club, attending informative lectures and conferences such as you are doing today. The mind has incredible capacity. The Psalmist once said, "As he thinketh in his heart, so is he" (Psalm 23:7). Our actions are usually played out on the stage of the mind before they emerge as behavior. If we can control our thoughts, we can usually control our behavior, and if we can enlarge and broaden the vision in our minds, we can impact what we are actually able to do. The mind has incredible power. It can conquer challenging notions, seek out what is obscured, reveal that which is masked, and examine what is perplexing; so boundless is its power.

5. Take time to build family connections, traditions, and relationships daily. Time has a way of slipping away, and if your family is like ours, before you know it, the children are grown and leave the nest. When you are in the middle of the child-rearing days, you wonder if they will ever grow up, and before a blink of the eye, they are grown and gone. We must cherish the moments and take time to build rich and meaningful memories.

Frances Fowler recalled a memorable day from her childhood in the 1930s. After a long, hard winter, a fantastic spring day arrived. Fowler and her brother slipped away from their chores to fly kites. In the kitchen her mother and sister became so entranced that they stopped their chores and went outside as well. Her father and other farmers also put aside their work to watch the kites. Many neighbors came outdoors to join the fun.

Fowler described the scene this way: "There never was such a day for flying kites! God doesn't make two such days in a century. . . . What a thrill to run with them, to the right, to the left and see our poor, earth-bound movements reflected minutes later in the majestic sky dance of the kites! We wrote wishes on slips of paper and slipped them over the string.

Slowly, irresistibly, they climbed up until they reached the kites. Surely all such wishes would be granted! . . .

"We never knew where the hours went on that hilltop day. There were no hours, just a golden, breezy Now. I think we were all a little beyond ourselves. Parents forgot their duty and their dignity; children forgot their combativeness and small spites."

Although the kites were flown only for the purpose of the sheer joy of flying them, they did have a long-term meaning and value that could not have been predicted. During World War II, one of the boys who had flown the kites that day, according to Fowler, was in the service and returned home after more than a year as a prisoner of war. When asked about it, he said that when things got bad, he thought about the day the kites were flown.

Similarly, a few years later, Fowler paid a sympathy call on a recently widowed woman who had been present on the day the kites were flown. When she offered her condolences, the woman smiled and said, "Henry had such fun that day. Frances, do you remember the day we flew the kites?"[14]

One of our family traditions was going "caterpillering." It was a simple little activity of collecting Monarch caterpillars and then for several weeks watching the seeming magic of the changes into the Monarch butterfly. For years after we have often recalled the sheer fun and enjoyment of our adventures, which have turned into precious memories.

Sweet memories last. Traditions very often have greater value than we might ever imagine at the time we carry them out.

6. Take time to appreciate each day the blessings of our own particular life and circumstance. We are often quick to focus on what we don't have instead of what we do have.

In the children's book *When I Was Young in the Mountains*, author Cynthia Rylant describes her own life growing up in humble circumstances in the Appalachian Mountains. Her grandparents raised her, and she described the simplicity of her life. For example, one page reads: "When I was young in the mountains, we sat on the porch swing in the evenings, and Grandfather sharpened my pencils with his pocketknife. Grandmother sometimes shelled beans and sometimes braided my hair. The dogs lay around us, and the stars sparkled in the sky. A bobwhite whistled in the forest."

I read this story to my children many times as they were growing up. When they came to me with "Why can't I have this, or "Why can't I do that?" I pointed to the print we had over our kitchen table that was an enlargement of one of the pages from the book. I reminded them of the message of the story so beautifully expressed on the last page. Rylant said, "When I was young in the mountains, I never wanted to go to the ocean, and I never wanted to go to the desert. I never wanted to go anywhere else in the world, for I was in the mountains. And that was always enough."[15] She had so little compared to our children today, but it was enough, she was content with what she had. We need to take time to look around us and appreciate what we do have and the blessings we have as members of the Church.

In summary, may we take time to build our testimonies and our faith, to love and serve, to learn something new, to build family relationships, and to find contentment and joy in who we are and our circumstances. When we spend our time well each day, the sun will shine, we will cast the gospel light into the dark places of this world, and we will make a difference.

May we seek the Spirit to know where it is that we need to cast light today, that we may do the will of the Lord and accomplish the purposes He has for each of us.

NOTES

1. Robert Fulghum, *It Was On Fire When I Lay Down On It* (New York: Villard Books, 1989), 173–75.
2. L. Clark, "Today, While the Sun Shines," *Hymns of The Church of Jesus Christ of Latter-day Saints* (Salt Lake City: The Church of Jesus Christ of Latter-day Saints, 1985), no. 229.
3. Neal A. Maxwell, *A Time to Choose* (Salt Lake City: Deseret Book, 1977), 13.
4. William H. Bennett, "Inertia," *Ensign,* May 1974, 33.
5. Gordon B. Hinckley, *Be Thou an Example* (Salt Lake City: Deseret Book, 1981), 60.

6. Neal A. Maxwell, "Taking Up the Cross," *1976 Devotional Speeches of the Year: Brigham Young University Bicentennial Devotional and Fireside Addresses* (Provo, UT: Brigham Young University Press, 1977), 260.

7. Brigham Young, *Teachings of Presidents of the Church: Brigham Young* (Salt Lake City: The Church of Jesus Christ of Latter-day Saints, 1997), 228–29.

8. Ezra Taft Benson, "The Great Commandment—Love the Lord," *Ensign*, May, 1988, 4.

9. Gordon B. Hinckley, "Be Not Faithless," *Ensign*, April 1989, 2.

10. Attributed to Robert Keen, "How Firm a Foundation," *Hymns*, no. 85.

11. Sheri Dew, *No Doubt About It* (Salt Lake City: Deseret Book, 2001), 134–35.

12. Ralph Waldo Emerson, "Gifts," in *The Oxford Book of American Essays*, ed. Brander Matthews (New York: Oxford University Press, 1914).

13. Lafcadio Hearn, "Gleanings in Budda-Fields," A Living God (Boston: Houghton Mifflin, 1897). Retrieved on-line at http://www.inamuranohi.jp/english.html.

14. Frances Fowler, "The Day We Flew the Kites," *Reader's Digest*, July 1949, 5–7.

15. Cynthia Rylant, *When I Was Young in the Mountains* (New York: E. P. Dutton, 1982), 24, 27.

LOAVES AND LESSONS
FROM GRANDMA

Susan W. Tanner

One of my earliest memories is of sitting on my Grandma Winder's back porch in the early morning sun, eating her hot homemade brown bread dripping with melted butter and honey. For the first thirteen years of my life, before her passing, I lived next door in rural Granger, Utah, to my grandpa and my grandma, Alma Eliza Cannon Winder. Grandma's influence upon me was profound. I felt loved and cherished by her, and I returned that love in my childlike ways.

Later, as I've learned more about her life, I have come to know that this loving act of sharing her bread with me was representative of her constant kindnesses to others. Her goodness came from her natural optimism and her faith in God. This faith helped her endure life's inevitable trials. She epitomized to me a woman who could stand on her feet and go forward by putting her trust and faith in Him.

President Gordon B. Hinckley has told us to stand on our feet and move forward. He has repeatedly admonished us to be the best we can be, to rise to the divinity within us. He has given us counsel by which he has lived, as did my grandma. He said:

Susan W. Tanner is currently serving as the general president of the Young Women. She graduated from Brigham Young University in humanities. Sister Tanner is a former president and counselor in all of the women's auxiliaries, on both the ward and stake levels. She has also been a curriculum writer for the Primary organization. Sister Tanner and her husband, John S. Tanner, have five children and eight grandchildren. Her favorite roles are wife, mother, and homemaker.

"Do not nag yourself with a sense of failure. Get on your knees and ask for the blessings of the Lord; then stand on your feet and do what you are asked to do. Then leave the matter in the hands of the Lord. You will discover that you have accomplished something beyond price."[1]

In a similar vein he also said: "Never lose sight of the great reassuring power of the Atonement of the Savior to lift and save. . . . I have been quoted as saying, 'Do the best you can.' . . . We must get on our knees and plead with the Lord for help and strength and direction. We must then stand on our feet and move forward. I am absolutely confident that heaven will smile upon us. The Lord will hear and answer our prayers if we will commit ourselves, giving our very best to this work."[2]

I think of this counsel as having five simple parts: (1) Don't nag yourself with feelings of failure; (2) Get on your knees and plead with the Lord; (3) Get on your feet and go forward; (4) Trust in the Lord, and (5) You will find you have accomplished something beyond price. This counsel reminds us to have faith in Jesus Christ, following His example as He prayed for strength to know the will of the Father and then do it, accomplishing something beyond price in behalf of each of us.

President Hinckley has lived this way. My grandma did too. She was optimistic despite her trials. She gave no place for self-pity. She "went about doing good" (Acts 10:38), as Jesus Christ did, choosing to forget herself in service to others. She endured to the end with patience and even much good humor. Her determined faith in Jesus Christ and modeling of His goodness not only carried her through her challenges but left for her posterity a legacy beyond price.

Grandma was a naturally happy person. She was positive in her outlook and very social in her love for other people. Yet as a young mother she knew deep sorrow. Tragedy struck twice—first with the death of Barbara, their firstborn child, and then later with the untimely death of another little daughter, Helen Margaret. Grandma tells in intermittent journal entries a few details about the circumstances and her feelings about the deaths of these two little girls. She says about six-year-old Barbara:

"Oh, the whole thing is such a horrible nightmare. On January 30th Mother stayed out here and Babs was very sick, so the next morning we took her in, intending to go right to the hospital, but [the doctor] advised us not to so we stayed at Mother's. . . . The next day we went to the doctor and . . . he was very reassuring. . . . She seemed so much improved. However after dinner she began going delirious and by 5 o'clock was right out of her head. The last word she ever said was 'That's all.' When I think of that night I turn cold, for dear little Babs nearly died. . . . She was taken to the hospital immediately. I went home that night, but five more nights I spent at the hospital. She never regained consciousness and it was pitiful to watch her. Tuesday she nearly died again, but rallied. They got meningitis serum in her and she seemed better. . . . It first helped but Saturday she became worse, and Saturday night she was gone. When she was gone there was no hope, but before I had never given up hope. I just felt at first like I couldn't stand to live without her, but when I saw Ed and the boys I knew I would have to live for them.

"It is now nearly two months after and oh, my heart just aches. I sometimes think I am unequal to the task of going on without her. I am sure I couldn't have stood it if Ed and the kiddies and everyone hadn't been so nice. Oh, but I loved Babs and miss her so. Little would anyone dream from the outside appearances just how lonesome I am for my darling."[3]

There are no specific journal entries about Helen Margaret's death. But other children in the family recall that when she was about two and a half months of age she suddenly became ill and was also hospitalized for a week before she died. As a mother myself, I can imagine the devastation my grandparents must have felt to lose another daughter. Yet in spite of her suffering, Grandma chose to move forward, living for her husband and other children. It was her eternal commitment to her family that moved her forward. She said that she was more empathetic and tried to be kinder with others because of her own trials.

Later in her life, when I lived next to her, she suffered from a blood disease that I never knew anything about. To me, she was simply my loving grandma who read to me, invited me to tea parties, brought homemade soup to me when I was sick, taught me how to laugh at myself, and always had hot, homemade brown bread coming from her oven. She never mentioned the disease, but since then I have read occasional journal entries where she mentions what a sore trial this was—such as this one:

"I am 61 and my skin has been broken out about 7 years. It came on all of a sudden. They don't seem to know just what it is. The eruption leaves in the summer. I am writing this so if any of you children ever have the same thing, develop the philosophy I have tried to develop. 'Things that can't be cured must be endured.' It has been a great trial to me, but I am sure I have been more tolerant of people and tried to be sweeter and kinder because of it."

A year later she wrote, "I still have my skin disease after about 8 years. . . . I used to feel so peppy and now I have felt kind of sick most of the time. . . . Even so, it could be worse and I am thankful I am alive. Dad [my grandpa] has been such a darling, understanding fellow in spite of my blemishes—Bless him—I will always be grateful to him."

Her last entry came a month before she died about eight years later. She said: "My skin trouble has taken a turn for the worse. . . . Lumps have developed on my side and back. They are bad sores . . . but I am grateful to my Heavenly Father for letting me live this long. Dad has been so good, kind and sweet to me."

When I read her journal now as an adult, knowing what I now know about her seventeen-year-long illness, I am astonished at how few times she mentions her debilitating disease. Instead, she focuses on the welfare of her family and friends and expresses joy in life. Only after her death did we learn that Grandma died from what was then a rare blood cancer manifesting itself in skin flare-ups. Only then did we glimpse what the grandma who loved to laugh with us, to have us for tea parties, and to ask us about our "beaux" had so graciously endured.

Here was a woman who didn't dwell on her feelings of inadequacy. Instead, she got on her knees and prayed for strength, then got on her feet and went forward cheerfully serving her family and neighbors, trusting in Heavenly Father, and enduring to the end. She lived by her motto that if something could not be cured, it could and must be endured. Grandma not only endured, she prevailed. She never wallowed in self-pity. Instead, she reached out to others in goodness, in kindness. She was, as King Benjamin taught us we should be, "meek, humble, patient, full of love, willing to submit to all things which the Lord seeth fit to inflict upon [us]" (Mosiah 3:19). All the years I knew her, she was sick, but I never knew it. Her legacy of goodness, patience in suffering, and endurance with a smile is something beyond price for each of her posterity.

How can that legacy live on? Grandma taught us to share—to share both intangible kindnesses of the heart and tangible kindnesses of our hands. Recently, our daughter's family home evening lesson emphasized kindness. She taught how important each member of their little family is. The activity was to each choose a name from a hat for whom they could show special kindnesses during the week. Daddy chose two-year-old Eliza. The first thing he did to show kindness to her was to share part of a package of candy with her, much to her delight. Then he put the rest of the candy on top of the refrigerator and forgot about it. Later in the week Eliza stood by the fridge looking up longingly and said to her mommy, "May I please have some kindnesses?"

Grandma also gave tangible kindnesses. Among Grandma's tangible kindnesses were pots of soup for the sick, dairy products for the neighbors, and hot loaves of bread for anyone in need. She followed what King Benjamin taught: "I would that ye should impart of your substance to the poor, every man according to that which he hath, such as feeding the hungry, clothing the naked, visiting the sick and administering to their relief, both spiritually and temporally, according to their wants" (Mosiah 4:26).

In a sense, Grandma's simple loaves of brown bread were miracle loaves which have miraculously multiplied over the years as we, her daughters and sons, granddaughters and grandsons, have tried symbolically and literally to share bread with others.

Sharing blesses the giver and the receiver. For the giver, the effort may sometimes feel like jogging uphill feels to me. Even the slightest incline requires so much effort. But once I have made that effort and I'm on the downward slope, I say over and over to myself, "Now let the road carry you."

When we are in the midst of a personal challenge, if we can make that huge uphill effort to think of others in need and serve them, then that very act will carry us over our hills of discouragement. And the road can carry us the rest of the way toward renewed purpose and hope. Perhaps in a sense, Grandma's kindnesses to others helped carry her through her own problems.

I remember a day not too long ago when sharing some tangible kindnesses carried me through some personal struggles. After first getting on my knees and praying fervently for answers and strength to deal with my problems, I felt impressed to rise to my feet and make a dozen little loaves of whole wheat bread to take with me to the office. Each time I gave one away, the recipient opened his or her heart and shared some tender feelings. A secretary said, "How did you know it was my birthday; no one else has remembered me." A much-admired General Authority lamented, "Some days I wish I had at least one thing, like making bread, that I could do well." The parents of an open-heart surgery patient confided, "Let us share with you the priesthood miracles involved with this surgery for our daughter." An executive director said, "I will give this to my wife who is sitting each day in the hospital with our daughter who has leukemia." Another leader reminisced, "This brings my mother back to me, because she too made bread." These little experiences touched, taught, strengthened, and carried me along that day.

President Hinckley said: "You want to be happy? Forget yourself and get lost in this great cause, and bend your efforts to helping people. . . . Look to the Lord and live, and work to lift and serve His sons and daughters. You will come to know a happiness like you've never known it before. I don't care how old you are, how young you are. You can lift people and help them. Heaven knows there are so very, very many people in this world who need help. . . . Let's stand a little taller and reach a little higher in the service of others."[4]

The little loaves became miracle loaves for me as much or more than for those with whom I shared them—just like Grandma's loaves. On those summer mornings of my childhood, Grandma gave me more than hot, brown bread dripping with butter and honey. Little did I realize that she was giving me something far more precious and lasting. She was giving an example of service, faith, courage, and endurance that has sustained and nourished my soul over the years. She taught me what it meant to get on your knees every day to ask Heavenly Father to bless you and then to stand on your feet and forget yourself by cheerfully going about doing good. As a result of her daily choice not to nag herself or others with feelings of failure but to stand on her feet and serve, she accomplished something of great price.

Her loaves of kindness have been multiplied through the generations and nourished multitudes, becoming miracle loaves. I know that the day of miracles has not ceased and that Heavenly Father is a God of miracles.

He loves each one of us, and He will bless us through our trials as we exert our faith in Jesus Christ and follow His examples of love, service, and endurance. I know we have a called prophet of God on the earth whose revelatory words strengthen and inspire us and teach us of our Savior.

May each of us participate in our own miracle of the loaves by being "steadfast and immovable, always abounding in good works that Christ, the Lord God Omnipotent, may seal you his, that you may be brought to heaven, that ye may have everlasting life" (Mosiah 5:15).

NOTES

1. Gordon B. Hinckley, "To the Women of the Church," *Ensign*, November 2003, 114.
2. Gordon B. Hinckley, "Standing Strong and Immovable," Worldwide Leadership Training Meeting, January 10, 2004, 21.
3. Journal of Alma Eliza Cannon Winder, in family's possession.
4. Gordon B. Hinckley, in *Church News*, September 9, 1995, 4.

"And I Went on My Way Rejoicing"

Heidi S. Swinton

Just weeks ago my husband and I, our son, and daughter-in-law sat in a waiting room at a local research hospital. We were there for a second opinion. Did our son have cancer? He sat there looking composed, just 23 years old, hearty and we thought healthy, recently married, full of life. And perhaps, cancer?

You don't picture yourself in such a setting any more than you see yourself standing at the grave of a child. Indelibly imprinted in my mind is the day my husband strode into my hospital room and, with all the courage a young father could muster, announced that one of our twin sons, only one day old, had just died.

There have been other such scenes. I recall sitting in waiting rooms so many times as our surviving twin son essentially was taken apart, his leg reconstructed and put back together, doctors trying to combat the effects of a debilitating childhood disease.

I don't like hospitals, but there we were at the hospital, the four of us. We made small talk as we sat amidst some who were bald, all their hair a casualty to treatments. We marveled at the beautiful wood, the stunning architecture, even the comfortable chairs that made us feel more like we

---

Heidi S. Swinton has served as a member of the Relief Society general board. She is a popular author and screenwriter. A wife, mother, and grandmother, she is serving with her husband who is the mission president of the England London South Mission.

were in executive offices with a promotion in the wings rather than sitting, waiting for bad news. For some, such news is a death sentence.

This was not a good time for this to be happening. Our plate already was full of stress. My husband had been called to serve as a mission president, and we were leaving in late June. The challenges of setting our lives aside for three years here to serve the Lord full time there were already weighing us down. And then I caught myself. Trials, by their very nature, are the stuff of our eternal timetable. In our mortality, we have a tendency to put everything in context of date, time, and place, often forgetting that this is the time for men to prepare to meet God (Alma 12:24). That is not lofty expression; it is the very essence of our earthly experience.

In the back of my mind, with this speaking assignment before me, came the words of Elder Henry B. Eyring: "The great test of life is to see whether we will hearken to and obey God's commands in the midst of the storms of life."[1]

This was a storm, a big one. And hearken to God's commands? It didn't seem that this situation was an "either, or." But, oh my, it was. "Trust in the Lord with all thine heart; and lean not unto thine own understanding" (Proverbs 3:5). This was a test of trust. Trust that the Lord loved the four of us, each experiencing a different anguish; all needing to trust him and his promise: "Let not your heart be troubled, neither let it be afraid" (John 14:27).

How do we do that? How do we exercise trust when the mortal reaction might be to shake a fist at the sky and say, "How could you let this happen to me? Right now? Look at what I have done." (As if to lay before the Lord the kingdom we have created and for which we think we deserve thanks instead of being called to serve in another part of the vineyard—where the work is hard, where the work is the work of the heart. That's the hardest work we do.)

Trust requires both action and attitude. It couples what we do with how we do it. How do we sustain in our hearts meekness and humility, love and gratitude, patience and forgiveness when the adversary is pushing us to clench our fists?

Isn't the "great test of life" described by Elder Eyring the willingness to submit our wills to that of the Father? The hardest words we may ever embrace are the words uttered by the Savior: "Not my will, but thine, be done" (Luke 22:42). The Lord does not need to justify to us why we are sitting at the cancer institute, why this setback or that disappointment, this challenge or that trial stands before us. The circumstance is a backdrop; hearkening to God's commands is about the feelings and response of the heart.

Will ours harden? Will we turn towards Him or turn away? Will we sustain and more importantly increase our trust in Him—come what may? Will we hearken with the devotion of a disciple of Christ or simply go through the motions, hoping to scurry back to our old way of doing things, learning little from the divine schoolroom in which we have been placed? Will the Atonement of Jesus Christ become the strength and comfort that we need right now?

Elder Jeffrey R. Holland adds great insight to these questions. He says, "Christ walked the path every mortal is called to walk so that he would know how to succor and strengthen us in our most difficult times. He knows the deepest and most personal burdens we carry. He knows the most public and poignant pains we bear. He descended below all such grief in order that he might lift us above it. There is no anguish or sorrow or sadness in life that he has not suffered in our behalf and borne away upon his own valiant and compassionate shoulders. In so doing he 'giveth power to the faint; and to them that have no might he increaseth strength. . . . [Thus] they that wait upon the Lord shall renew their strength; they shall mount up with wings as eagles; they shall run, and not be weary; and they shall walk, and not faint.'"[2]

Wilford Woodruff taught that lesson in his life. Time and again in his journal we read of the challenges he faced, the composure with which he responded, the trust he exercised in the Lord. He wrote of an assignment to lead fifty-three new converts from Maine to Illinois, a 2,000-mile journey. It was late fall, "such a trial," he explained, "I never before had attempted during my experience as a minister of the gospel." Already for Wilford, it is hard.

He wrote, "My wife Phoebe was attacked on the 23rd of November by a severe headache, which terminated in brain fever, she grew more and more distressed daily. . . . At the same time our child was also very sick." A few days later he wrote, "a trying day to my soul. My wife continued to fail, and about four o'clock in the afternoon appeared to be stricken with death."

Now, he's on the Lord's errand. His experience debunks the myth that as long as we do everything we are supposed to, life will be easy. No, as long as we trust in the Lord, He will make more of us than we can make of ourselves. The Lord was preparing a prophet, though it would be 40 years before he was called to that service.

"The 1st of December, . . . I stopped my team, and it seemed as if she then would breathe her last, lying there in the wagon. . . . I cried to the Lord, praying that she might live. . . . Her spirit revived." He took her to a home where he cared for her for several long days. "December 3rd found my wife very low . . . the day following. . . . She seemed to be sinking gradually, and in the evening the spirit apparently left her body, and she was dead. . . . The spirit and power of God began to rest upon me until, for the first time during her sickness, faith filled my soul, although she lay before me as one dead." He consecrated oil and "bowed down before the Lord . . . laid my hands upon her, and in the name of Jesus Christ I rebuked the power of death." His wife related afterwards that "her spirit left her body, and she saw it lying upon the bed. . . . [A] messenger said to her that she might have her choice—she might go to rest in the spirit world, or, upon one condition, she could have the privilege of returning to her tabernacle and of continuing her labors upon the earth. The condition was that if she felt she could stand by her husband, and with him pass through all the cares, trials, tribulations, and afflictions of life which he would be called upon to pass through for the gospel's sake unto the end, she might return. . . . 'Yes,' she said, 'I will do it.'" Woodruff wrote, "The power of faith rested upon me, and when I administered to her, her spirit reentered her tabernacle. . . .

"On the morning of the 6th of December, the spirit said to me, 'Arise, and continue thy journey,' and through the mercy of God my wife was enabled to arise and dress herself; she walked to the wagon, and we went on our way rejoicing."[3]

"We went on our way rejoicing." That needs to be stamped on the forehead of every one of us. It needs to be the close to a very bad day and of every succession of terrible times. "I went on my way rejoicing" says that

I can see farther, feel love that is eternal, trust the Lord is in charge. This is easy to say, and not easy to do.

Think of the many labors that lay before Wilford Woodruff and his wife. Think of the trust they exhibited. They had promised the Lord they would stand strong. So have we. We have covenanted to take upon us His name—and hence, to act accordingly, to draw upon His strength in the face of any hardship—and to conclude our experience with confidence in the great plan of happiness as did Wilford Woodruff. "We went on our way rejoicing."

We have a tendency to think of the Lord and the Atonement leading up to His death in light of the misery, the awful sufferings which He experienced at the hands of evil men. We dwell on the lashes to His bare skin, the nails that pierced His flesh, the agony of the cross. But, there is great rejoicing. Did not the angel proclaim, "He is not here: for he is risen" (Matthew 28:6)? Indeed, profound cause to go "on our way rejoicing."

Yet, we seem to focus on what's not working, what hurts, what is painful and undeserved. And as we get caught up in that storm, that maelstrom becomes all we can see and feel. I picture Wilford Woodruff sitting at the side of his wife, day after day, waiting on the Lord. Do we do that? Or do we flail about, anger and unsteadiness throwing us out of balance and out of the reach of that hand Peter felt when he jumped over the side of the boat at the call, "Come" (Matthew 14:29).

I love the account in Matthew that teaches us what it means to come unto Him. "But the ship was now in the midst of the sea, tossed with waves: for the wind was contrary. And in the fourth watch of the night Jesus went unto them, walking on the sea. . . . Jesus spake unto them [the disciples], saying, Be of good cheer; it is I; be not afraid.

"And Peter answered him and said, Lord, if it be thou, bid me come unto thee on the water. And [Jesus] said, Come" (Matthew 14:24–29).

What happens next? Peter jumps over the side of the boat and begins to walk on the water. "But when he saw the wind boisterous, he was afraid; and beginning to sink, he cried, saying, Lord save me.

"And immediately Jesus stretched forth his hand" (Matthew 14:30–31).

Peter was out on unfamiliar ground. When we are called by the Lord to come, we usually step onto unfamiliar ground. That's the setting.

Maybe it's illness, death, relocating, a new calling, or a new family member. The list of challenges is endless. But this scripture encourages us to look beyond the swirling water lapping at our feet, to keep focused on the Lord there before us. He is waiting for us. We need to keep walking. When He reaches out, He offers the power only He can give, which is the power to save.

We have to learn that truth again and again. The Good Shepherd calls after us. He knows us; we know His voice. Do we lay aside the things of this world? Think about it. Do we hearken? "Come unto me, all ye that labour and are heavy laden" (Matthew 11:28), He says. Most of us are heavy laden with a host of everyday things. We may not be desperate, but everyday irritations may get the best of us. Things like anger, annoyance, and pain.

Not long ago I was driving from my home to a meeting. I was swirling with frustration and pain. Someone had attacked me—unjustly I thought—and for 45 minutes on the phone had itemized all my failings. I was without defenses; it was so unexpected. We've all been there. I listened; I get eternal credit for not lashing back. I kept telling myself, "Don't get mad." Jacob said it better, "Why should I give way to temptations, that the evil one have place in my heart to destroy my peace and afflict my soul?" (2 Nephi 4:27). I gripped the steering wheel harder and harder. I laid out my case in my mind, I elaborated my defenses, I wept. And I felt my heart harden. I paused and with that break in my inner turmoil, the thought came to me, "The Lord has already paid for what you are feeling. He has paid for the pain, the frustration, the angst. You can choose to carry it and play it out. But He has already atoned for those sins."

I nearly stopped the car in the middle of a very busy road. I had been taught. Jesus had "stretched forth his hand" (Matthew 14:31) to me. For me it was a profound moment. Again Elder Eyring's words, "The great test of life is to see whether we will hearken to and obey God's commands in the midst of the storms of life." Swirling in every storm are the words "Be still and know that I am God" (Psalm 46:10).

We have a heritage of that trust in the Lord: the emigrants of the Willie and Martin handcart companies, tested to their limits on the snow-encrusted hills. "Come," the handcart pioneers heard in 1856. Come across the Atlantic, come to Iowa City, come with the fire of Israel God's burning in your hearts. Come with the grit forged by taking upon you the name of Christ in spite of opposition and derision; come walk on unfamiliar ground. "And if ye do always remember me ye shall have my Spirit to be with you" (3 Nephi 18:7).

Their deprivations and deaths have become the signature of the Mormon Trail. British convert John Jaques wrote, "When [the Lord] calls His Saints to do anything, if they will rely upon Him and do the best they can, He will fit the back to the burden, and make everything bend to the accomplishments of His purposes."[4]

Little did they know what lay ahead. Unfamiliar ground it was. And it was soon covered with snow. "Our old and infirm people began to droop," John Chislett wrote, "and they no sooner lost spirit and courage than death's stamp could be traced upon their features. Life went out as smoothly as a lamp ceases to burn when the oil is gone."[5] Wrote Elizabeth Horrocks Jackson, "I listened to hear if my husband breathed—he lay so still. . . . I put my hand on his body, when to my horror I discovered that my worst fears were confirmed. . . . He was cold and stiff-rigid in the arms of death. . . . I was six or seven thousand miles from my native land, in a wild, rocky, mountain country, in a destitute condition, the ground covered with snow, the waters covered with ice, and I with three fatherless children with scarcely nothing to protect them from the merciless storms."[6]

But the Lord stretched forth His hand. He inspired Brigham Young to muster a rescue that would save the lives of hundreds of faithful emigrants. He was a prophet; he saw beyond the sun in the sky or the success of three recently arrived handcart companies. Soon, the rescuers encountered the same snows, blizzards, bitter winds and ice-choked streams that stranded the Willie and Martin Companies in Wyoming. "Many declared we were angels from heaven," wrote rescuer Daniel Jones when the Martin Company finally was located far back on the trail. "I told [the handcart emigrants] I thought we were better than angels for this occasion, as we were good strong men come to help them into the valley."[7]

The Lord can fix anything, but most often He heals our hearts. When the rescuers arrived, the half-frozen and starving emigrants embraced them and praised the Lord. The scriptures are filled with those whose hearts were hardened by their experiences. What sorrow! The heart feels the hand of the Lord; the heart feels the love of the Lord; the heart feels the goodness of His word and His promises. The heart feels the power of the Atonement. So the question is, how is your heart? Is it rejoicing? How do we take all the burdens crowding our hearts and cast them on the Lord? And then go on our way rejoicing? I asked the Lord that as I drove in the car. *How do I do this?*

"How" is a mortal term. We have to think eternally. We have to trust the Lord. We have to know Him and His strength and power. It comes from experience. It comes from study, earnest and heartfelt poring over the words of the Lord in scripture. It comes from prayer and repentance. It comes from yielding our hearts to God. I so resonate with the words in the hymn, "Come, Thou Fount of Every Blessing." The phrase, "Here's my heart, O, take and seal it; Seal it for thy courts above."[8] We have to bring to mind the words of Alma, "I say unto you, . . . if ye have experienced a change of heart, and if ye have felt to sing the song of redeeming love, I would ask, can ye feel so now?" (Alma 5:26).

That's what Wilford Woodruff and his wife Phoebe understood. They felt to sing the song of redeeming love—they chose "to go on their way rejoicing."

So, let me take you back to the hospital. We saw the doctor and he confirmed our fears. Within days our son was wheeled into surgery and the cancerous tissue was removed. We sat again in the hospital waiting room—waiting. When he was ready to go home, the nurse wheeled him in a chair to our waiting car. Unsteady, he sank into the seat, and we pulled away from this first round of treatment. Let it be said, "We went on our way rejoicing."

He had been given a priesthood blessing that he would be healed. His name had been written on prayer rolls and voiced in petitions to our Father in Heaven by family and dear friends. He had entered this crucible of trial with an obedient heart and a testimony that God lives, that the Savior has taken upon Himself all our pain and suffering and encircles us in the arms of His love. He trusted the Lord with all his heart. These are the strengths we draw upon. These are the reasons for "our rejoicing."

How grateful I am for the gospel of Jesus Christ. I am grateful to know that my Father in Heaven hears my prayers and knows my heart. He loves me. I can feel it. He expects me home when this life is over, and I rejoice in knowing I will be with Him. I love the Lord Jesus Christ. How many times I turn to Him; He is always there. May we trust in Him—come what may—and go forth on our way rejoicing.

NOTES

1. Henry B. Eyring, "Spiritual Preparedness: Start Early and Be Steady," *Ensign,* November 2005, 37.
2. Jeffrey R. Holland, *Christ and the New Covenant: The Messianic Message of the Book of Mormon* (Salt Lake City: Deseret Book, 1997), 223–24.
3. Wilford Woodruff, *Wilford Woodruff, His Life and Labors,* comp. Matthias F. Cowley (Salt Lake City: Deseret Book, 1916), 95, 96, 97–98.
4. Stella Jaques Bell, "Life History and Writings of John Jaques" (n.p.: Ricks College Press, 1978), 75.
5. "Mr. Chislett's Narrative, Part II," in T. B. H. Stenhouse, *The Rocky Mountain Saints: A Full and Complete History of the Mormons* (New York: D. Appleton and Company, 1873), 320–21.
6. Elizabeth Horrocks Jackson Kingsford, *Leaves from the Life of Elizabeth Horrocks Jackson Kingsford* [1908]. Church History Library, Salt Lake City, Utah. See also http://www.lds.org/churchhistory/library/pioneer details.
7. Daniel Jones, *Forty Years Among the Indians* (Salt Lake City: Juvenile Instructor Office, 1890), 62.
8. Robert Robinson, "Come, Thou Fount of Every Blessing," *Hymns of The Church of Jesus Christ of Latter-day Saints* (Salt Lake City: The Church of Jesus Christ of Latter-day Saints, 1948), no. 70.

EXTREME MAKEOVERS

Mary Ellen Edmunds

When I realized my topic was repentance, I thought of starting with a list of the 15 R's, but I couldn't remember them all. . . .

Recognize, Resist, Repay, Recycle, Refuel, Repeat, Roar, Run . . .

Then I thought of using the title of an old movie: *The Good, the Bad, and the Ugly.*

Keep the *good!*

Get rid of the *bad!*

Deal with the *ugly!*

When I was about 15 years old, I was in San Francisco with my parents and a couple of my sisters, and we went to a new John Wayne movie, *The High and the Mighty.* I watched it again a few weeks ago on TV.

It's about a flight which left Hawaii headed for California. After the plane had been in the air quite a while, there were some problems. They had passed the point of no return, so they kept heading for the coast. But they ended up having to dump a bunch of stuff out of the plane to lighten the load.

The movie stayed with me. I think I was trying to figure out what *I* should throw overboard so that I can make it all the way Home. What

---

Mary Ellen Edmunds has served as director of training at the Missionary Training Center in Provo, Utah, and as a member of the Relief Society general board. She has been a faculty member at BYU and has served full-time missions in Asia and Africa. A popular speaker, she is also the author of several books.

226

kinds of experiences in my life would change my mind about what mattered most and what could be tossed?

One of the things I remember best about the movie is that everyone got *real*. There was a dramatic moment when a woman, who was headed to meet a man for the first time with whom she'd been corresponding, took off all her makeup, including her long, fake eyelashes.

What happened to her was like an *extreme makeover* in reverse—she really looked different!

Extreme makeovers have become pretty popular, haven't they? There are contests to lose weight, or there's a home that is remodeled, or someone gets a new hairdo, a lot of dental work, and a fancy wardrobe.

I remember seeing a woman on TV once who'd had so many plastic surgeries on her nose that she could no longer breathe through it!

I Googled the phrase "extreme makeover," and I got half a million hits! They have all kinds of information, including stuff about how to sign up for a transformation, news about the plastic surgeons and cosmetic dentists, and a whole gallery of pictures.

These "before and after" pictures are pretty dramatic. I find it interesting that often the "before" picture shows someone who isn't smiling or standing up straight. They're not at their best. Can they help it if they're having a bad day? That's not a very fair time to take a picture.

I looked at an application for a makeover. Wow! You make a three-minute video and then they ask you to go from head to toe, explaining what you would like changed. "List everything you would like to have altered." The application has questions such as "How will this change your life?" and "Besides altering your appearance, what is your biggest dream?"

What is it people are looking for?

What is it that's missing?

Why do we seem so anxious to make changes?

It's as if we want to be like toothpaste, shampoo, or laundry detergent: New and Improved!

Isn't it fantastic what can be done with just the right clothes and makeup? With the perfect outfit and accessories, the inner beauty can shine forth and bring such joy to the one who's changed. Families, friends, studio audiences, and viewers clap their hands and shout for joy at the amazing changes. "Come on out! Hubba Hubba!"

It would be interesting to have a show called "Where Are They Now?" I would hope that some people who've received a dramatic physical change would have found lasting happiness.

I'd like to try to describe a true "extreme makeover." This transformation is an *inside* job. And it *really* changes lives and helps dreams come true. It definitely causes people to clap their hands and shout for joy. And the joy lasts. *Forever.*

You likely know someone who has experienced this type of makeover. Maybe it's you. I'm persuaded that it's a lot more dramatic than anything you'd ever see in a magazine or on TV.

There are descriptions of such makeovers in the scriptures. In the book of Mosiah in the Book of Mormon, King Benjamin has finished his remarkable message and wants to know if his people have *believed* what he has taught them.

"And they all cried with one voice, saying: Yea, we believe all the words which thou hast spoken unto us; and also, we know of their surety and truth, because of the Spirit of the Lord Omnipotent, which has wrought a mighty change in us, or in our hearts, that we have no more disposition to do evil, but to do good continually" (Mosiah 5:2).

There were two major changes: "no more disposition to do evil" and "to do good continually." No wonder it's called a "mighty change"!

The same thing happened to King Lamoni, his wife, and all those who were converted during Ammon's mission. They were spiritually reborn, and they were forgiven of their sins.

"They did all declare unto the people the selfsame thing—that their hearts had been changed; that they had no more desire to do evil" (Alma 19:33).

Oh, doesn't this kind of a makeover sound incredible!

Have you ever wished you were a car? That you could roll into Jiffy-Abs and be changed instantly? You could get an oil change, your tires rotated, and a brand-new filter. Or go to Midas for a new muffler, and MAACO for a paint job, and POOF! You're better than ever! You could drive through at Checker Auto or Johnson Tire and say, "I need a new heart!" And you get it in ten minutes!

Well, it doesn't work that way, does it? The changes we need to make are more than just a change of outward appearance or even a change of behavior. We need a change of heart!

President Ezra Taft Benson taught this:

"Repentance means more than simply a reformation of behavior. Many men and women in the world demonstrate great willpower and self-discipline in overcoming bad habits and the weaknesses of the flesh. Yet at the same time they give no thought to the Master, sometimes even openly rejecting Him. Such changes of behavior, even if in a positive direction, do not constitute true repentance. . . .

"Repentance involves not just a change of actions, but a change of heart. . . .

"When we have undergone this mighty change, which is brought about only through faith in Jesus Christ and through the operation of the Spirit upon us, it is as though we have become a new person. Thus, the change is likened to a new birth. Thousands of you have experienced this change. You have forsaken lives of sin, sometimes deep and offensive sin, and through applying the blood of Christ in your lives, have become clean. You have no more disposition to return to your old ways. You are in reality a new person. This is what is meant by a change of heart."[1]

In 1991 I met a wonderful woman named Betty, who was just returning to church and gospel activity after having been gone for fifty years. In a letter to me, she explained that she had been "wandering in the wilderness, in absolute misery, for so many, many years." She told me a lot about her life and about her remarkable return.

And then she wrote: "I am aware of that 'other' Betty disappearing and the 'new' Betty emerging." She got it! She really understood what was happening to her!

A few years later we had the privilege of going to the Salt Lake Temple together, and she further described the wonderful changes which had come. She really *did* have a new heart!

Listen again to the description of repentance from the Bible Dictionary. (It's past the "Tropical Guide" in your Bible.)

"The Greek word of which this [repentance] is the translation denotes a change of mind, [as in] a fresh view about God, about oneself, and about the world. Since we are born into conditions of mortality, repentance comes to mean a turning of the heart and will to God, a renunciation of sin to which we are naturally inclined. Without this there can be no progress in the things of the soul's salvation. . . . [We] must be cleansed in order to enter the kingdom of heaven. Repentance is not optional for salvation; it is a commandment of God" (Bible Dictionary, 760–61).

I like that a lot! A change of mind! A "fresh view" about God, ourselves, and the world. Turning our hearts and will to God, and turning our backs on sin. We *all* need to make some changes in our lives from time to time, don't we? Some turning and returning.

At 5:31 A.M. on January 17, 1994, I was getting ready to leave for work, and the light flickered and the refrigerator "hiccupped." I said, "Stop it" out loud and didn't think much more about it.

But when I got to the Missionary Training Center and saw something on TV about it, I realized I had felt (in a very small way) some effects of a huge earthquake that had happened in Northridge, California. Someone was broadcasting in the dark, and I was imagining that they included an announcement that a voice had been heard from heaven:

"O all ye that are spared because ye were more righteous than they, will ye not now return unto me, and repent of your sins, and be converted, that I may heal you?

"Yea, verily I say unto you, if ye will come unto me ye shall have eternal life. Behold, mine arm of mercy is extended towards you, and whosoever will come, him will I receive; and blessed are those who come unto me.

"Behold, I am Jesus Christ, the Son of God" (3 Nephi 9:13–15).

Imagine!

I love the use of the word "turning." I think it's a beautiful way to picture the process of repentance—a process of turning and returning. As Jacob put it, "O, my beloved brethren, turn away from your sins; shake off the chains of him that would bind you fast; come unto that God who is the rock of your salvation" (2 Nephi 9:45).

We turn around and head away from the darkness and towards the Light of the World, the Savior. It's a process of conversion.

President Harold B. Lee taught: "One is converted when he sees with his eyes what he ought to see; when he hears with his ears what he ought to hear; and when he understands with his heart what he ought to understand. And what he ought to see, hear, and understand is truth—eternal truth—and then practice it. That is conversion."[2]

Have you noticed that even those who are pretty good are invited to be better—that conversion becomes a lifelong process? Look at what happened when King Benjamin talked to his people; they were pretty good, but what did he say to them? What did the Savior say to those who had been spared because they were "more righteous" than those who had perished? How do you feel when President Gordon B. Hinckley speaks of wanting to improve his life—to do better and be better?

Without striving to be better when we're already pretty good, we may stop progressing. We may block the process of our heart and stop turning to God, which is so critical to the salvation of our souls.

I have always been moved by the king of the Lamanites as he responds to Aaron's teaching. The Spirit has touched him, and he asks Aaron some important questions.

"What shall I do that I may have this eternal life of which thou hast spoken? Yea, what shall I do that I may be born of God, having this wicked spirit rooted out of my breast, and receive his Spirit, that I may be filled with joy, that I may not be cast off at the last day? Behold, said he, I will give up all that I possess, yea, I will forsake my kingdom, that I may receive this great joy" (Alma 22:15).

He's willing to give up all his possessions, and even his kingdom, to be born of God and receive His Spirit! Aaron teaches him that he needs to pray and repent. So the king kneels down and pours out his soul to God.

"O God, Aaron hath told me that there is a God; and if there is a God, and if thou art God, wilt thou make thyself known unto me, and I will give away all my sins to know thee, and that I may be raised from the dead, and be saved at the last day" (Alma 22:18).

At first he's willing to give up his possessions and kingdoms, but *now* he is ready to give away all his sins! Can we do that? Can we give away *all* our sins to know God and become like He is and have His Spirit?

Listen again to Nephi: "Awake, my soul! No longer droop in sin. Rejoice, O my heart, and give place no more for the enemy of my soul" (2 Nephi 4:28).

Not the enemy of the way you look, your wardrobe, or your popularity, but the enemy of your *soul*!

President Hugh B. Brown talked about the problem with sinning:

"Sin creates inner conflict, causes loss of self-respect, saps moral strength, causes injury to and estranges others, makes men more susceptible to temptation, and in numerous other subtle ways retards, delays, and blocks our journey toward our goal. Its enticements tend to divert us from moral ideals and to obscure our vision of desirable objectives.

"True repentance halts this disintegration and . . . places one's feet on the highway of successful living. With the companionship of [the Holy Ghost], one may release the power which is in the human soul even as men have been able to release the power of the atom. This power, when released and given divine direction and guidance, will lead to immortality and eternal life."[3]

We can be healed through repentance and forgiveness. Once there was a Primary teacher who was telling her class about Samuel the Lamanite. She asked the class, "What's the name of the man who stood on the wall to preach to the people?" One little boy called out, "Humpty Dumpty!"

I know you've heard the little rhyme:

> *Humpty Dumpty sat on the wall,*
> *Humpty Dumpty had a great fall*
> *All the king's horses and all the king's men*
> *Couldn't put Humpty together again.*

(To me it's kind of a funny thing to imagine: *horses* trying to put a broken egg back together.)

The King of Kings, the Prince of Peace (and pieces) knows where *all* the pieces are and where *all* the pieces belong. He can put us back together again! Trust Him! He came to heal the brokenhearted. He came to make *spiritual* healing possible as well as *physical* healing.

Consider some words from a wonderful hymn.

> *In the furnace God may prove thee,*
> *Thence to bring thee forth more bright,*
> *But can never cease to love thee;*
> *Thou art precious in his sight.*

God is with thee, God is with thee;
Thou shalt triumph in his might.[4]

There are many blessings which come with forgiveness, including peace of conscience, peace of soul. Do you remember the way Enos described his feelings? "My guilt was swept away" (Enos 1:6). Guilt and pain can be removed from our hearts!

From the Doctrine and Covenants 58:42: "Behold, he who has repented of his sins, the same is forgiven, and I, the Lord, remember them no more."

President Boyd K. Packer taught, "The Atonement has practical, personal, everyday value; apply it in your life. It can be activated with so simple a beginning as prayer. You will not thereafter be free from trouble and mistakes but can erase the guilt through repentance and be at peace."[5]

Once we experience this peace of conscience, this peace of soul, we have an increased desire to extend this forgiveness to others. Can we forgive those who drive the speed limit when we're in a hurry? Can we forgive those ahead of us in line at the store who have a full shopping cart and a *ton* of coupons? Can we forgive the people sitting behind us with restless, noisy children?

As President Hinckley said, "One cannot be merciful to others without receiving a harvest of mercy in return."[6]

Can you think of *anyone* in the scriptures who sincerely cried for mercy who didn't receive it?

A grandma and grandpa had a room in their home which was the "Precious Room." In that room they kept their treasures. Grandchildren were welcome in their home and could laugh and play inside and out, but not in the Precious Room. One day two little grandsons were playing tag and, without realizing it, they ran into the Precious Room. Grandfather was sitting in his chair reading and heard the crash. He heard Grandmother, almost hysterical.

Then two little boys came into the living room, one of them sobbing.

"What happened?" Grandpa asked.

"I broke the lamp, and Grandma said I have to pay for it."

"How much did she say it is?"

"She said it's $300, and I only get 50 cents a week for my allowance."

Grandfather made out a check to Grandmother for $300 and said to the little boy: "Here, take this to your grandmother and tell her you just met Mr. Mercy."

"With what measure ye mete, it shall be measured to you again" (Matthew 7:2). So measure *generously* and *kindly*—give lots and lots of love and mercy to others!

I'd like to share a few invitations:

Think of one thing you'd like to change—just one—work on it, focus on it, get heavenly help and any other help you need.

If there's any way you can go out in the night to a spot where there are as few city lights as possible, look up into the heavens and ask God, "Do you love me?" And then just listen!

Make the partaking of the sacrament a more meaningful experience in your life.

Elder Melvin J. Ballard spoke of the sacrament and healing in this way: "I am a witness that there is a spirit attending the administration of the sacrament that warms the soul from head to foot; you feel the wounds of the spirit being healed, and the load being lifted. Comfort and happiness come to the soul that is worthy and truly desirous of partaking of this spiritual food."[7]

And one more invitation: Don't give up!

President Gordon B. Hinckley shared an important reminder: "We are far from being a perfect society as we travel along the road to immortality and eternal life. The great work of the Church in furthering this process is to help men and women to move toward the perfection exemplified by the Savior of mankind. We are not likely to reach that goal in a day or a year or a lifetime. But as we strive in this direction, we shall become better men and women, sons and daughters of God."[8]

I ask again:

What is it people are looking for?

What is it that's missing?

Why do we seem so anxious for extreme makeovers?

I share the first three verses of another hymn:

Come unto Jesus, ye heavy laden,
Careworn and fainting, by sin oppressed.
He'll safely guide you unto that haven
Where all who trust him may rest, may rest.

Come unto Jesus; He'll ever heed you,
Though in the darkness you've gone astray.
His love will find you and gently lead you
From darkest night into day, to day.

Come unto Jesus; He'll surely hear you,
If you in meekness plead for his love.
Oh know you not that angels are near you
From brightest mansions above, above?[9]

"Wherefore, my beloved brethren, I know that if ye shall follow the Son, with full purpose of heart, acting no hypocrisy and no deception before God, but with real intent, repenting of your sins, witnessing unto the Father that ye are willing to take upon you the name of Christ, by baptism—. . . behold, then shall ye receive the Holy Ghost; yea, then cometh the baptism of fire and of the Holy Ghost; and then can ye speak with the tongue of angels, and shout praises unto the Holy One of Israel" (2 Nephi 31:13).

NOTES

1. Ezra Taft Benson, "A Mighty Change of Heart," *Ensign*, October 1989, 2, 4.
2. Harold B. Lee, *Stand Ye in Holy Places* (Salt Lake City: Deseret Book, 1974), 92.
3. Hugh B. Brown, quoted in Spencer W. Kimball, *The Miracle of Forgiveness* (Salt Lake City: Bookcraft, 1969), 323–24.
4. Thomas Kelly, "Zion Stands with Hills Surrounded," in *Hymns of The Church of Jesus Christ of Latter-day Saints* (Salt Lake City: The Church of Jesus Christ of Latter-day Saints, 1985), no. 43.
5. Boyd K. Packer, "'The Touch of the Master's Hand,'" *Ensign*, May 2001, 24.
6. Gordon B. Hinckley, "Blessed Are the Merciful," *Ensign*, May 1990, 70.
7. Melvin J. Ballard, *Sermons and Missionary Services*, ed. Bryant S. Hinckley (Salt Lake City: Deseret Book, 1949), 149.

8. Gordon B. Hinckley, "150-Year Drama: A Personal View of Our History,"
    Ensign, April 1980, 14.

9. Orson Pratt Huish, "Come unto Jesus," *Hymns,* no. 117.

TODAY, WHILE THE SUN SHINES . . . OR NOT

Emily Watts

To me, "Today, while the sun shines, work with a will"[1] is a pretty easy concept to embrace. I *can* work with a will when the sun is shining—that's when I feel like doing something. It's today when the sun isn't shining that I have a little trouble with. So I have recast the traditional song (with apologies to the original author) as follows:

> Today, while the kids scream,
> Plaster on a smile.
> Today, with the laundry stacking up in a pile.
> Today, with the deadlines
> Breathing down your neck,
> Bills to be paid, and body gone to heck.
> Today, today, do the best you can.
> Today, today, it's part of the plan.
> Today, today, don't forget to pray
> That heaven will show you the joys of today.

These are the things that I want to think about today, today.

Emily Watts has worked in the editorial department of Deseret Book Company for nearly thirty years. She is the author of several books and audio products. Emily and her husband, Larry, have five children and one grandchild.

Do the Best You Can

Let's start with "Today, today, do the best you can." I think many women have the misconception that "do the *best* you can" means "do the *most* you can." I think that's not necessarily true. I think some days have to be "set-everything-aside-and-go-fly-a-kite" days. I think some days have to be "be-still-and-know" (Psalm 46:10) days. We are prone to panic when we see our lives stretching out before us, revealing everything we imagine we could and should be doing. We assume we haven't done our best because we didn't do it all *today*. No one day can support the full burden of our eternal responsibilities. When we think about doing the best we can, I hope we can get away from the notion that it invariably means doing the most we can.

I also want to explore the notion that doing the best *you* can might mean something different from doing the best someone else can. In that regard, I have been so thrilled with the new direction in the Relief Society enrichment program, which I think acknowledges the fact that women have different talents and different interests. I like the notion that the women who are interested in scrapbooking, for instance, can now get together and enjoy this wonderful hobby together without making the rest of us feel guilty for not doing scrapbooking. I love scrapbooks, and I have several of the supplies that talented women use to create them. I have little eyelets, and brads, and a paper cutter. The things I lack are time and manual dexterity.

For a long time I felt guilty for not being good at scrapbooking. Have you noticed that about every ten years, the thing we feel guilty about not being able to do changes? It used to be that if you couldn't bake bread, you felt kind of guilty; before that, it was if you couldn't sew. Now the guilt producer seems to be if you can't scrapbook and make those cute little cards that are so popular. Somehow, none of those things have shown up yet on any temple recommend interview that I've been in. I'm waiting to see if they turn up there before I start panicking about them.

Meanwhile, a friend I met in Arizona gave me the most marvelous idea. She said: "Let's have an enrichment activity, and we will all come and make one card and a stack of envelopes. Then, when it's time to send the card, you write your message on a sticky note and put it along with the card inside one of the envelopes and send it off. The recipient thus gets not just a cheery remembrance but also a lovely handmade card to pass along to someone else in one of *her* envelopes. The cards could get passed around the ward; they might become heirlooms. You might even get your own card back someday."

I think that is a fabulous idea. I imagine I could contrive to complete one card in the course of an evening, That's my rule for an enrichment activity project: If it can't be done that night, forget it. I have a whole closet full of uncompleted projects; there is no room for more.

On a different note, one of the other little groups in our ward is a book club, and I do usually attend the meetings of that one. I love books, and I love reading the same book as somebody else and then talking about it together. There are lots of women in the ward who say, usually sort of sheepishly, "Oh, I just don't have time to read books." (Some of them are the same ones who are making those beautiful scrapbooks.) Do you know what I think? I think there shouldn't be any guilt in that! Nobody is standing by with a scorecard, saying, "Well, it says here that the book club is worth five celestial points and the scrapbooking group is only worth three celestial points, so if you really want to stack up the points, you'd better get to the book club—and actually you ought to go to both of them." Can you see the danger we might run into if we're not careful? We *can't* do everything that is good to do!

What's really important for us to recognize is that there are different ways that we express and build our love for each other as sisters. Some of us express it with beautiful handmade items, and some of us express it by sharing our thoughts, and both of those ways are valid. We need to not panic that we can't express love in all the ways that somebody else does.

The last thing I want to say about "do the best you can" is that sometimes we need to acknowledge that our best varies from day to day. Sometimes you just have a really good day and you get in there and get a whole lot accomplished, and you think every day ought to be like that.

I was having a day like that at work recently. I had meetings all morning long, and I was going from meeting to meeting, contributing, talking, taking notes, feeling great. The last meeting was a big company-wide meeting involving everybody from all three floors of our corporate headquarters. After that meeting, around 1:00 P.M., I finally escaped to my office for the first break I had had all day. I sat down to regroup, put my head in my hands, and realized, looking down at my feet, that my shoes did not match. They were not only not mates, they were spectacularly unlike each other. I had on a black Mary Jane and a black loafer.

I want to tell you that you can accomplish a lot more if you don't know what you're doing wrong than if you recognize it. My afternoon that day was not nearly as productive as my morning had been. However, that little experience has given me a great opportunity to say every day, when I sit down and try to assess if I did the best I could, "I may not have gotten everything right today, but at least my shoes matched." When you start with such a realistic expectation, everything else seems like a bonus!

Let's face it—all days are not created equal. Sleep patterns and hormonal fluctuations and people's demands and the traffic on the freeway and the line at the grocery store and all kinds of influences can combine to hamper our productivity. Some days just getting out of bed and putting meals on the table and matching shoes on the children's feet (or our own) is truly the best we can do. We can all "try a little harder to be a little better," as President Gordon B. Hinckley urges.[2] But he also invites us to "be a little kinder"[3] and not "nag [ourselves] with thoughts of failure."[4] If today wasn't the best you've ever had, guess what: you get another chance tomorrow!

IT'S PART OF THE PLAN

The second "Today, today" is this: "It's part of the plan." This is both comforting and disconcerting knowledge to me. I have days when I wonder, Did I really vote yes for this? Or was I just going with the crowd—all in favor, manifest by the uplifted hand? Sometimes I'd like to go back to the contract and read the small print and see if I really understood what I was signing up for when I came to mortality.

On those days when you wonder why you voted yes, I would like to suggest this question: Why did you have a second child? When you had the first one, you didn't really know what the future held, but the second time, you knew how hard it was going to be. You knew how miserable it is to be pregnant. You knew why they call it "labor." And you did it anyway. Why did you do that? Because you knew what you wanted. You knew what you were getting. You knew why you wanted children in your home. That's why you put up with all that pain, because you knew where it was going to take you.

I submit that that's why we voted yes. We saw it was going to be hard (although theoretical hardness is not quite the same as practical hardness). We said yes because we knew why we were going to go through those difficult things. We knew what it was for. Sometimes we have to stop and remember that all of our todays are part of that plan. What happens to us today is preparing us to become who we need to be.

I have days when I think, *Did Heavenly Father* plan *for me to have this sorrow in my life?* The other day I met a woman whose nineteen-year-old daughter, she told me, had been missing for eleven days. Was that part of Heavenly Father's plan for her? Did He plan your mother's cancer, or your sister's automobile accident, or your neighbor's house fire?

I don't believe for a minute that that's the way it works. What I believe is that Heavenly Father planned for us to come to mortality, where hard, hard things happen. He knew that some people would exercise their agency in sinful ways. He knew that hurricanes and abuse and wars and addictions and all kinds of difficult, inexplicable things would be a part of the world He sent us to. But He promised that if we were faithful to Him, everything would come out right, through the Atonement of Jesus Christ.

So, no, I don't think He plans specifically for our kids to be rotten to us or for our husband to lose his temper or for depression and disease to strike. I think that the plan was, as He outlined it in Abraham 3:25: "We will prove them herewith, to see if they will do all things whatsoever the Lord their God shall command them," not just when the sun shines, but every day, in every circumstance. That's what makes mortality a test.

Do you remember how agonizing finals week used to be in your college days? My son recently finished his last final, and his pain reminded me of how hard those weeks were. Well, I think we get finals weeks all the time in mortality. We're sailing along, things are going well, we're having no particular problems, and suddenly it's finals week. That's when we get a chance to see if we really understand, if we really believe what we've been studying all along. That's what the plan is.

Don't Forget to Pray

The third thing I want us to consider is "don't forget to pray." I had kind of an interesting experience with this idea one day when my daughter was holding a can of that air-compressed, squeezable cheese you can buy to squirt out onto crackers. We buy that cheese only for long car trips, because it's ridiculously expensive, and it seems like you get about four crackers' worth, but it's a fun comfort food and convenient for the road. So she had this can left over from a trip, and she was reading the print, and suddenly she started to laugh. I said, "What?" and she said, "It says here, 'For best results, remove cap.' Duh!"

I had occasion to remember that seemingly overobvious instruction the next Sunday when we were singing in church, "Ere you left your room this morning, Did you . . . ?"[5] I thought, Duh! For best results . . .

It's not that we don't know it. It's so obvious, it doesn't seem like we should have to be reminded to pray, but we do forget sometimes, don't we? If we want the best result for our day, we need to start by praying.

And one of the things I pray for often is "that heaven will show [me] the joys of today." What I like to do is pray to be able to see things the way Heavenly Father sees them. I think He sees the joys of today, every day. Wouldn't it be great to have that perspective?

I like to say, for example, "Heavenly Father, help me to see my seventeen-year-old son the way you see him today. Because what I see is a kid who never says more than three consecutive words to me, who can down six bucks' worth of Cocoa Puffs in five minutes flat, and whose room looks like a poster for tsunami relief. Help me see what you see."

And He says, "Remember what the three consecutive words were when he walked out the door this morning? 'Love you, Mom.' Remember how last night when you and your husband got home late, he had already walked the dog without even being asked, so you didn't have to? Remember how many times, on Sundays when you've staggered home after three hours of church, he has just gotten saddled up to help collect fast offerings, or to take the sacrament to somebody who was shut in, to share with them the emblems of the Lord's flesh and blood so they could renew their covenants the same as if they'd been able to be in sacrament meeting? That's who I see when I look at your seventeen-year-old son."

Quite a different picture, isn't it? Prayer really can change the night to day!

At work when I'm stressed I post silly signs on my door, sometimes to warn people to leave me alone, and sometimes just to cheer up others who I know are also stressed. A colleague of mine brought me a sign that said, "They told me to count my blessings, and sure enough, I'm missing a few!" I wonder if maybe the reason we miss some of our blessings is that we forgot to pray for heaven to show us the joys of today. We might have missed seeing a blessing not because it wasn't there but because we were looking in the wrong place or with the wrong eyes.

I love the prophet Elisha's response to the servant who was completely overwhelmed by the approaching armies of the enemy. Elisha asked the Lord, "I pray thee, open his eyes, that he may see. And the Lord opened the eyes of the young man; and he saw: and, behold, the mountain was full of horses and chariots of fire" (2 Kings 6:17).

We are often overwhelmed. There's just too much to do. There's always going to be too much to do today, whether the sun shines or not. But when we see what the Lord sees, we realize there are horses and chariots of fire—heavenly help. Heavenly Father can make our time stretch to meet our needs even when we can't possibly imagine how things are going to work out.

On days when you feel discouraged, then, please remember the chorus of our little song:

> Today, today, do the best you can.
> Today, today, it's part of the plan.
> Today, today, don't forget to pray
> That heaven will show you the joys of today.

In closing, I would like to suggest to you that the sun shines every day of our lives, if we spell it "S-O-N." Heavenly Father truly did send "his only begotten Son, that whosoever believeth in him should not perish, but have everlasting life" (John 3:16). That Son shines today and every day, and His promise is this, from John 8:12: "I am the light of the world: he that followeth me shall not walk in darkness, but shall have the light of life." My prayer is that we might always have that light in our lives and recognize the shining of the Son, in all of our todays throughout eternity.

NOTES

1. L. Clark, "Today, While the Sun Shines," *Hymns of The Church of Jesus Christ of Latter-day Saints* (Salt Lake City: The Church of Jesus Christ of Latter-day Saints, 1985), no. 229.

2. Gordon B. Hinckley, "We Have a Work to Do," *Ensign*, May 1995, 87.

3. Gordon B. Hinckley, "Thanks to the Lord for His Blessings," *Ensign*, May 1999, 88.

4. Gordon B. Hinckley, "Rise to the Stature of the Divine within You," *Ensign*, November 1989, 94.

5. Mary A. Pepper Kidder, "Did You Think to Pray?" *Hymns*, no. 140.

BUILDING SISTERHOOD

Diana Halliday

The original title for this chapter was "Mean Girls Grown Up." That's a very profound title isn't it—perhaps even a little shocking? The title was changed to "Building Sisterhood," which is much softer in its presentation. But whatever the title, the reality of needing to make some changes in how we treat each other as women is very real. Can we avoid being catty and competitive and critical? Can we be sisters who build each other up rather than tear down?

All of us have been impacted one way or another by unkindness. It would be great to say that all of us in this room are here because we just need to learn how to teach *others* to be more kind. But I hope we are all willing to think about and learn about how *we* can each be more kind and Christlike. How can *we* build others up and make them feel valuable? How can *we* respond to those who give unkind treatment?

I can tell you that I have heard more stories about "mean girls" in the last five months than I have heard during the previous fifty-four years of my life. I have felt like a "mean girl" story magnet! I'm sure each of you could offer an example that you have experienced or know about. As I've listened to, and thought about, and then prayed about the things I've heard and studied, I've had the Spirit testify to me that this negative

---

Diana Halliday currently serves as first counselor in a stake Relief Society presidency. A gifted musician, she feels blessed to share her testimony through song. She and husband Paul have six children and ten delightful grandchildren—the best part of being this age!

treatment is happening all over the world, and it's keeping sisters from having the loving relationships with each other that Heavenly Father intended for us to have.

Let me share just a couple of examples: As a Laurel advisor a few years ago, I was going with the girls and the other leaders for an overnight trip to a cabin. Each of the advisors was driving a vehicle, and the girls had arrived and were getting in the different vehicles to make the drive. In the backseat of my car were three of the Laurels who happened to be in the class presidency. We were laughing and talking and just waiting to leave.

Another girl from the class got into the front seat of the car. I greeted her and then heard the back doors of my car open as the three girls in the backseat all got out of the car and got into other cars. Did they *say* anything unkind? No. They did not say anything at all. Was their message clear? Definitely! My front-seat Laurel and I ended up the only people in my car, and we drove the hour-and-a-half drive to the cabin by ourselves with her asking me why the others girls did not like her and why they treated her the way they did. It was with a very prayerful heart that I shared with her what I thought she needed to know and how the situation could be made better. It was a pretty tender conversation.

Our time at the cabin was great, and everyone had a fun time. For the ride home the next day, who do you think got into my car? You guessed it! (And not by my invitation!) It was the three girls that got out of my car as well as the Laurel class president. Can you guess what we talked about on the way home?

Example number two is of several women who became friends after they moved to the same apartment complex in a small town in Wyoming at about the same time. They were young married women with small children and were all members of the Church. They did lunch together, went to the park together with their children, did date night with their husbands, and had a lot of fun together.

One of the women was just a little different from the rest. She came from another part of the United States, was a convert to the Church just a few years prior to the move to Wyoming, and wasn't quite as neat and tidy compared to her friends. Gradually, these women began to exclude her from their activities. They didn't call her as often or speak to her in the same friendly way. Soon this little mothers' group had essentially moved her out of their circle.

One night the bishop of the ward called each of these women individually into his office and spoke to them of their excluded friend. He told them of her surprise and hurt feelings at being excluded from their group and that she wondered if she could even keep coming to church. He told them that she wanted to know if this was how the members of the Savior's church treated each other.

As I've read other stories and heard other women's experiences, I have been shocked at how intentional the unkindness and criticism is. Teenage girls E-mail or text-message mean statements to the less "cool" girls in their classes. Young children are left out of games on the playground or not invited to a classmate's birthday party or even excluded from walking home with the other children in the neighborhood. Women are ignored as they walk down the halls in the church or are left to sit by themselves in Sunday School or Relief Society.

Sometimes the unkind acts happen unintentionally. We express our thoughts without even thinking how it will impact those we are talking to or even those who overhear our comments. "You're not as pretty as your sisters, but you'll probably be okay." "Can you believe she is wearing that dress?" "Who cuts *her* hair?" "Aren't you worried that you can never be a choir director like Sister Jones?" "Don't you wish you lived in a family like mine?" "Have you ever been in her house?" "Oh, we'd like to include you in our cooking class, but it's just for the people on our street." Ouch!

So what is it that everyone is looking for in a friend—and as a friend? I know that every one of us in this room wants to be needed and to be included. We all want to be useful, and acknowledged, and loved. This need is as real as the need to breathe. It is no wonder that the Savior tells us in Ephesians 4:32, "And be ye kind to one another, tenderhearted, forgiving one another, even as God for Christ's sake hath forgiven you." Are we thinking each day about what we say, how we say what we say, and the possible effect we are having on others as well as ourselves?

M. Catherine Thomas said, "We are careless and unwary in our associations one with another, not understanding how much the protection of the Spirit depends on whether we treat each other spiritually. . . . Sometimes the veneer of our spirituality is too thin to resist the daily abrasions we experience with each other. We are reactionary, forgetful, and inclined to depart from love and peace and the light of the Spirit."[1] Brigham Young said, "We should live so as to possess that Spirit daily, hourly, and every moment . . . which makes the path of life easy."[2]

In this same vein, M. Catherine Thomas taught, "The very words we speak are spirit and carry a spirit which stirs that same spirit in the person who hears them. Every time we speak we generate spirit. . . . How mindful we want to be to choose our words with care so as to produce continually a higher spiritual influence for ourselves and those around us, thereby avoiding the despair caused by evil influences."[3]

So, can we become women who build up, and accept, and support, and strengthen the sisters in our lives? Of course we can! But we first have to accept and believe of our own self-worth without competing or measuring ourselves to anyone other than the woman we look at in the mirror. Each of us chose to follow the Savior's plan and have been blessed to be on this earth at a most glorious time. We must be the strong, positive women Heavenly Father sent us to earth to be.

There is no other person that can take your place in this life. There can be no other daughter, or sister, or mother, or friend, or visiting teacher, or neighbor that can love and serve and touch another's life like you can. And because of that, building a strong sisterhood in our homes, in our neighborhoods, in our wards and stakes can happen.

When our family moved to Michigan, I wondered what I would do when I had no family closer than 1,800 miles way. I had six children who I wanted to feel accepted. I prayed that they would find new friends and feel safe in their new home and environment. But would I have anyone who would want to be *my* friend? Who could *I* ask for help if I needed it? Would the circles of friendship already formed in Michigan expand to include someone like me?

My questions were answered as I walked into my ward house for church that first Sunday. I was immediately greeted by two women who introduced themselves, asked who I was, where I was from, sat by me in Relief Society, and became my friends—no, my true sisters—from that day to this.

A group of young women who were all seniors in high school are a powerful example of how important being loved unconditionally and not criticized can be. There was a girl in their high school who made an incorrect choice and became pregnant. She continued going to school but in essence became an outcast. She walked the halls alone to class; she ate lunch by herself and was the subject of much gossip at the school. Did she need a friend? Desperately!

These girls who were friends and were well-liked in the high school became very sad at the treatment of their classmate. They couldn't stand how she was being treated! They decided they would be her real friends. They chose to sit with her at lunch, walk with her to class, and include her in their activities outside of school. They recognized, even at their young age, that their friend was important to Heavenly Father and needed to be loved and accepted in spite of a bad choice. Did they make a difference in how their friend felt about herself? Can you imagine how important their love and acceptance was at such a critical time? These girls found the joy that comes when you help someone else feel of worth. They found early in their lives the joy of being sisters.

I want to talk with you about how it feels to be on the receiving end of unkindness for just a minute. I have been hurt at times in my life by those who are my family, those who are my friends, and those who I really do believe love me. At one time I was hurt in a way that actually made me physically ill. For a period of two weeks I couldn't sleep. I couldn't eat. I struggled to understand why I had been treated the way I had. What had I done wrong to deserve such treatment? I turned to Heavenly Father for His help. I prayed. I fasted. I read the scriptures. I went to the temple. In prayer one day I received this message to my mind, "It is not you, and you must forgive them."

I was taught that I had the gift of response and that I needed to respond with love—unconditional love—and that I must forgive them. I chose to follow what I was taught, and the heaviness in my heart was lifted and my spirit came to find peace. We all have the gift of response.

I also want to tell you that I have been on the giving end of hurting someone. I am sure that I have said things many times that I probably didn't even realize offended someone. I'll share one such offense that I *was* blessed to know about.

Not too long ago I had a woman in my ward whom I love very much come to my home. It was Easter time and she brought me a decorative egg. She came to tell me that I had hurt her feelings by something I had said. She said she had struggled with the hurt and wondered why I would say what I had because I had never seemed critical of her before. In thinking about it she said she came to believe that my comment was not intended to be critical or unkind and that I probably had no idea I had hurt her. And then she asked me if I would please forgive *her* for letting her feelings be hurt! Can you imagine how I felt? I will thank her eternally for giving me such a gift.

There is heavenly power in loving and building each other up as sisters. There is heavenly power in paying compliments and acknowledging talents and good works in our sisters. There is heavenly power in giving support when one of our sisters can't carry a burden by herself. There is heavenly power in being a sister to those who are not members of our church—who see and feel our light and want to know where that light in us comes from. We do not become less by giving all of these things to others. Heavenly Father's light in us only grows brighter when we give it away.

Sister Bonnie D. Parkin teaches us that we need to practice holiness. "We must forgive; we must be merciful; we must have charity."[4] We need to be kind in our words and our deeds and our actions—both in our homes and with those around us.

There is no one who can take our place as sisters in this life and as sisters for eternity. We are all sisters participating in the same glorious plan with the same goal of returning to live with our Heavenly Father. I know that each one of us is equally valuable—valuable to our families, to our neighbors, to each other, and most importantly to our Heavenly Father and our Savior, Jesus Christ. In Romans 8:16–17 it reads, "The Spirit itself beareth witness with our spirit, that we are the children of God: and if children, then heirs; heirs of God, and joint-heirs with Christ." May we rejoice in each other, love each other, and treat each other as the eternal sisters and friends that Heavenly Father sent us here to be.

NOTES

1. M. Catherine Thomas, *The Selected Writings of M. Catherine Thomas* (Salt Lake City: Deseret Book, 2000), 231.

2. Brigham Young, in *Journal of Discourses*, 26 vols. (London: Latter-day Saints' Book Depot, 1854–86), 7:238.
3. Thomas, *Selected Writings*, 231.
4. Bonnie D. Parkin, "Not Only to Relieve the Poor, But to Save Souls," Fall 2005 Open House.

INDEX